Henry Green
*and the Writing
of
His Generation*

Henry Green
and the Writing of His Generation

Michael North

University Press of Virginia   *Charlottesville*

THE UNIVERSITY PRESS OF VIRGINIA
Copyright © 1984 by the Rector and Visitors
of the University of Virginia

First published 1984

Library of Congress Cataloging in Publication Data

North, Michael, 1951–
    Henry Green and the writing of his generation.

    Includes index.
    1. Green, Henry, 1905–1974–Criticism and interpretation.   I. Title.
PR6013.R416Z77 1984   823'.912   84–3534
ISBN 0-8139-1028-5

Printed in the United States of America

All genuine poetry is in a sense the formation of private spheres out of a public chaos.

W. H. AUDEN

Contents

Acknowledgments — ix

Introduction: The Generation and Its Fictions — 1

1 The Literature of Debility: *Blindness, Pack My Bag*, and the Thirties Generation — 15

2 "A Thing They Are Doing": *Living* and *Party Going* — 51

3 The Powers of Memory: *Caught, Back,* and the Literature of World War II — 101

4 "This Great Place": *Loving* and *Concluding* — 139

Conclusion: *Nothing, Doting,* and the Fictive Life — 195

Index — 219

ACKNOWLEDGMENTS   *I would like to thank Joseph Cary for introducing me to Henry Green and for providing advice and encouragement during the composition of this work. Other, less immediate, debts declare themselves throughout the notes. I would also like to thank Jim Clinch and Kim Sands for their help in preparing the manuscript.*

Henry Green
and the Writing of His Generation

Introduction
The Generation and Its Fictions

> *My sense of values was to be affected, my emotions falsified, my mind put out of focus, my idea of reality imposed on reality and where they did not tally, reality would be cut to fit.*
>
> Cyril Connolly
> *Enemies of Promise*

THE first of his generation into print and author of the earliest and finest proletarian novel of his period, Henry Green published only one work during the thirties, and that a novel that was in some ways a throwback to an earlier decade. Thus it is not usual to consider him as a member of the generation led by Auden, though he was a lifelong friend of Christopher Isherwood, best man to Evelyn Waugh, roommate to Anthony Powell, schoolmate of George Orwell and Cyril Connolly, literary associate of John Lehmann and Stephen Spender, and host to Auden for a tour of the factory where Green worked in the late twenties. Because of its concentration on the thirties, Samuel Hynes's *The Auden Generation* makes no mention at all of Green. But Green was almost extravagantly admired during his life by the writers Hynes does describe, by Spender, who praised *Living* as a liberation of the novel, and by Auden, who called Green "the best English novelist alive" in the fifties.¹ Despite all this admiration, it is common to assume, as Walter Allen does, that Green is not just different from, but in some basic way opposed to, the main current of literature in his time because he took no part in the political controversies of the decade.²

Green never shared the political radicalism of Spender and Day Lewis, but he did share with them, and with others of the generation, concepts of public and private life more fundamental than politics. Harold Rosenberg maintains that one of the most basic modern attitudes about public life holds it to be inimical to the personal integrity of individuals. Thus one of the most common concepts in modern literature is alienation, a term that, as Rosenberg says, has acquired "at least two meanings that are often unrelated and at times even opposed. It can mean estrangement of a person *from* society or his estrangement from himself *through* society." The second of these definitions, Rosenberg says, has come to be the more common since the Second World War, so that one of the recurrent themes of postwar literature has been the "threat of loss of self through participating in the economic, social and cultural processes of our mass society."³ Rosenberg's two definitions need not contradict one another, however, because both rest on the same assumption, that the private and the public are hermetically sealed compartments, categories defined by their opposition to each other. This idea is, as René Girard says, the legacy of the kind of romanticism that "seeks that which is irreducibly ours in that which opposes us most violently to others. It distinguishes two parts in an individual, that which is superficial and permits agreement

---

[1]Stephen Spender, *The Destructive Element* (London: Jonathan Cape, 1935), p. 237. Auden's comment is quoted in Nigel Dennis, "The Double Life of Henry Green," *Life,* Aug. 4, 1952, p. 85. For assertions that Green and his work are remote from his contemporaries, see Edward Stokes, *The Novels of Henry Green* (London: Hogarth, 1959), pp. 12–13, and Bruce Bassoff, *Toward Loving: The Poetics of the Novel and the Practice of Henry Green* (Columbia: Univ. of South Carolina Press, 1975), p. 3.

[2]Walter Allen, "An Artist of the Thirties," *Folios of New Writing,* 3 (Spring 1941), 145–58.

[3]Harold Rosenberg, *Act and the Actor: Making the Self* (New York: World Publishing, New American Library, 1970), pp. 198 and 201.

with Others and a more essential part in which agreement is impossible."[4]

Modern literature thus commonly expresses a double bind traced by Robert Langbaum as far back as Matthew Arnold's *Empedocles on Etna*. According to Langbaum, Arnold's protagonist "lays aside his magician's robes, because he cannot bear the *public* role that absents him 'from himself.' But he lays aside also his musician's laurel, because he cannot bear the artist's *solitude* that fences him from society."[5] The most politically doctrinaire of the thirties writers, on the other hand, face this choice in an entirely different way, because for them an individual can only become himself through participation in mass society. In his autobiographical novel, *Starting Point*, Day Lewis says, "The individual . . . may deny the reality outside him," that is, the reality of social misery and political change, but to do so is to "do violence to his nature," to "allow himself to be made barren."[6] To ignore the social questions posed by the misery of others is to cripple oneself, to commit suicide in a way, as Edward Upward insists in *Journey to the Border*: "His decision to join the worker's movement would lead to difficulties. But he would at least have come down to earth, out of the cloud of his cowardly fantasies; would have begun to live."[7] The basic idea behind such works is expressed in *The Destructive Element*, published in 1935, in which Spender describes his belief "that the political movements of the time have a greater moral significance than the life of the individual, and, indeed, the chief peculiarity of the individual is that his acts are morally unrelated to the political movement."[8]

Spender's mistrust of the individual is politically motivated, but it appears over and over in the apolitical settings of the abundant autobiographies of the period. The one thing

---

[4] René Girard, *Deceit, Desire, and the Novel* (Baltimore: Johns Hopkins Univ. Press, 1965), p. 212.

[5] Robert Langbaum, *The Mysteries of Identity* (New York: Oxford Univ. Press, 1977), p. 77.

[6] C. Day Lewis, *Starting Point* (New York: Harper, 1937), p. 307.

[7] Edward Upward, *The Railway Accident and Other Stories* (London: Heinemann, 1969), p. 208.

[8] Spender, *The Destructive Element*, p. 206.

all these works have in common is suspicion, mistrust, or fear felt by the writer for himself. Cyril Connolly gives the briefest description of the autobiographies of the decade when he says in *Enemies of Promise,* "I have always disliked myself at any given moment; the total of such moments is my life." Connolly's autobiography is therefore a search for "the causes of that sloth by which I have been disabled . . . the sin whose guilt is at my door . . . those errors of judgement against which the validity of my criticism must be measured."[9] The whole plan of *Enemies of Promise,* in fact, is to show how the fragile genius of a writer is ringed with powerful threats, each of which is strong enough alone to destroy him, and the most insidious of which is often himself. In "The Leaning Tower," Virginia Woolf explains the popularity of autobiography in the thirties by suggesting that it becomes a favored form in times of instability, when political or economic insecurity drive writers back to their own personalities as the only constant.[10] But the self is the least stable point for Connolly, as it is for Isherwood, whose autobiography, *Lions and Shadows,* is devoted to defining the "Truly Weak Man," and as it is for Upward in *Journey to the Border,* where self-hatred is resolved only when the self is given up completely to the Communist party.

The autobiographies therefore offer a definition of behavior, especially the behavior of the generation itself, in which it is not expressive but purely artificial. Hynes remarks, "I am struck, as I read in the histories and memoirs of the 'thirties, by how often . . . actions that men performed were symbolic, and *self-consciously* symbolic acts."[11] This taste for the symbolic gesture in politics expresses itself in private life as a preference for roles, for bits of behavior sanctioned already by habit or convention. Thus it is a common insight of the autobiographies that one's friends behave more like actors

---

[9]Cyril Connolly, *Enemies of Promise* (London, 1938; rpt. New York: Macmillan, 1948), pp. 143 and 260.

[10]Virginia Woolf, *The Moment and Other Essays* (London: Hogarth, 1947), p. 120.

[11]Samuel Hynes, *The Auden Generation* (New York: Viking, 1977), p. 70.

than like actual people. Spender says of Connolly, "He was the spectator of his own life, as though it was lived fiction." Isherwood says of Spender, "He inhabited a world of self-created and absorbing drama, into which each new acquaintance was conscripted to play a part." Anthony Powell accuses Orwell of having consciously created a "genre picture" of himself.[12] A common confession of the autobiographies is that of playacting, such as Spender's admission that at public school "I aped my own exhibitionism, effeminacy, rootlessness, and lack of discipline."[13] Perhaps Upward most neatly expresses the sense of self-defeat that accompanies this aping of oneself: "My instantaneous caricature of my own impression spoilt my chances of discovering what it really was."[14]

The idea that the writer is essentially an actor is, of course, a common one in modern literature, expressed most succinctly in Pound's title for his collected short poems, *Personae*. But there is some difference between the mask assumed by Yeats or Pound and the roles of the thirties writers. Langbaum indicates the general nature of this difference in castigating Erving Goffman's purely sociological explanation of role-playing: "All Goffman's examples are the stuff of comedy . . . for his characters have no psychological depth, no residue of a self that might feel falsified by such masks, that might through rebellion or neurosis foul up the scene's requirements. . . . There is apparently no true self to be betrayed." Langbaum sees Goffman's view as partial because it makes roles into merely acquired forms, whereas most modern writers see them as both "inwardly motivated" and "socially conditioned."[15] That is, the mask may be a means of self-presentation or self-creation, as well as self-negation. Significantly, the particular example given by Goffman in

---

[12]Stephen Spender, *The Thirties and After* (New York: Random House, 1978), p. 215; Christopher Isherwood, *Lions and Shadows* (London, 1937; rpt. New York: New Directions, 1977), p. 224; Anthony Powell, *Infants of the Spring* (New York: Holt, Rinehart and Winston, 1976), p. 103.
[13]Stephen Spender, *World within World* (New York: Harcourt, Brace, 1951), p. 30.
[14]Upward, p. 7.
[15]Langbaum, pp. 12 and 13.

this context comes from Orwell, and Langbaum is correct in distinguishing it from the kind of large abstraction of self practiced, for example, by Yeats. But Goffman is not incorrect in his selection from Orwell. The generation to which Orwell belongs is likely to see its roles as determined by social pressure and to deny that there is any sacrifice in adopting a role, simply because there really is no true self to be compromised.

At least a partial explanation for this difference in the generation's ideas about the self can be found in the shared experiences that, beyond the simple coincidence of age, separate the thirties generation from those before and after. In *The Generation of 1914* Robert Wohl discusses both the generation that fought and the one that just missed serving in the First World War, and he locates the second generation's strong sense of being a separate group in that missed experience. As he says, "The generational idea feeds on a sense of discontinuity and disconnection from the past."[16] Certainly, the writers who matured in the thirties suffered this sense of disconnection in a different way from others who lived through the war. Their very sense of being a group apart comes from the distinction between themselves and those just a bit older who were able to fight. This sense begins, as will be made clear in a subsequent chapter, during the war itself, but the unwanted distinction is most dramatically felt at Oxford and Cambridge in the twenties. Memoir after memoir reports the ways in which the undergraduates of 1923 or 1924 were made to feel like a diminished race. Anthony Powell speaks of a "chasm" between the generations, Day Lewis of the "guilt or inferiority" of his class in comparison to the seniors of his year. Evelyn Waugh says, "We were often reproachfully reminded, particularly by the college servants, of how impoverished and subdued we were in comparison with those great men."[17] The generational idea feeds

---

[16]Robert Wohl, *The Generation of 1914* (Cambridge: Harvard Univ. Press, 1979), p. 39.

[17]Powell, *Infants of the Spring*, pp. 109–10; C. Day Lewis, *The Buried Day* (London: Chatto and Windus, 1965), p. 158; Evelyn Waugh, *A Little Learning* (Boston: Little, Brown, 1964), p. 170.

here not just on a perception of discontinuity with the past but on a sense of failure, of being smaller and less dashing than previous generations.

Wohl notes in the corresponding French generation a similar sense of diminishment, a similar autobiographical introspection and a literary attempt to blame passivity and ineffectuality on the war, as Jean Prévost does in Dix-Huitième Année.[18] Whether a single experience, even such an all-encompassing one as the war, can account for the literary stance of an entire generation is difficult to say, but the important fact is that the generation itself felt as though the war had in some way preempted them. It is, in any case, one of the differences that cause this group to feel a loss of self more radical than and even different in kind from that of earlier modern writers. Other shared experiences seem to have the same effect, chief among them attendance at public school. A number of books have been devoted to the effect of public school education on its students, including studies by John Reed, Jonathan Gathorne-Hardy, and Martin Green.[19] But Cyril Connolly still provides the classic brief account in his Theory of Permanent Adolescence: "It is the theory that the experiences undergone by boys at the great public schools, their glories and disappointments, are so intense as to dominate their lives and to arrest their development. From these it results that the greater part of the ruling class remains adolescent, school-minded, self-conscious, cowardly, sentimental, and in the last analysis homosexual."[20]

The "school-mindedness" of the writers of the generation is one of their most obvious characteristics, marking Auden's poetry from the beginning to the end of his career, Isherwood's stories and novels, Day Lewis's poetry, and Connolly's criticism. This is another way in which the group sees itself as a group, with a secret slang, a set of nicknames, and

[18]Wohl, pp. 30–32.
[19]John R. Reed, *Old School Ties: The Public Schools in British Literature* (Syracuse, N.Y.: Syracuse Univ. Press, 1964); Jonathan Gathorne-Hardy, *The Old School Tie: The Phenomenon of the English Public School* (New York: Viking, 1977); Martin Green, *Children of the Sun: A Narrative of "Decadence" in England after 1918* (New York: Basic Books, 1976).
[20]Connolly, *Enemies of Promise*, p. 253.

an adversarial role toward the outside world best expressed in Isherwood's Mortmere saga. Connolly's explanation for this school-mindedness is, if anything, too generous, because it blames the intensity of public school life for its lasting impact. Rather more important in other accounts is the basic falsehood of life in a cloistered setting, a falsehood expressed by the students in elaborate playacting. Nearly every account in Graham Greene's compilation *The Old School,* published in 1934, mentions the way each student becomes an "earnest little propagandist for his own vices and virtues." The masters tend to choose and exaggerate certain characteristics in themselves "the way that 'ham' actors play their parts," while the boys caricature themselves and the masters, "holding up our caricatures like talismans to ward off the human complexity of the masters . . . to evade as yet the burden of adult life." Elizabeth Bowen blames "restricted possessions, a uniform dictated down to the last detail and a self-imposed but rigid emotional snobbishness shutting the more direct means of self-expression away. Foibles, mannerisms, we therefore exaggerated most diligently."[21] The habitual playacting of the generation thus might begin in public school routine, which Spender describes as if it were a play: "Gradually he learned his cues, his exits and entrances, an an actor learns his part."[22]

Martin Green locates some of this fictionalization in the public school curriculum, especially in the practice of copying poetic forms, which produces, he says, brilliant parodists who are somewhat unsure of the boundary between parody and creation.[23] Gathorne-Hardy suggests a more plausible, because more basic, explanation in the isolation of the school from outside life. Following Erving Goffman, Gathorne-Hardy calls the public school a "Total Society," one that tries to reproduce in a cloistered setting all the institutions, rules,

---

[21]Graham Greene, ed., *The Old School* (London: Jonathan Cape, 1934). The first comment is from Spender's contribution, "Day Boy," p. 91, the second from Anthony Powell's, "The Wat'ry Glade," p. 151. Elizabeth Bowen's comment appears in "The Mulberry Tree," p. 47. The third statement is from Day Lewis's *Buried Day,* pp. 115–16.
[22]Stephen Spender, *The Backward Son* (London: Hogarth, 1940), p. 61.
[23]Martin Green, *Children of the Sun,* pp. 120–21.

and rewards of society at large. Enclosure means that "passions, emotions, aggressions, needs which can normally be dissipated or satisfied in a thousand different ways can only be expressed in terms of, by means of, that little shut off world."[24] The student is forced to develop a school personality just as the school has developed its own versions of outside life. In this analysis, personality becomes contingent on social structure, on roles that are as rigid and independent of actuality as those in Orwell's essay "Boys' Weeklies."

Public schools existed for some time without producing a full generation fixated on its public school background, but the generation of the thirties had more reason for self-consciousness than its predecessors. The world of the public school was obviously coming to an end even as they graduated. The reason Graham Greene gives for collecting the accounts in *The Old School* is to give "a true picture" of what will be in a few years "a vanished system." Connolly refers to the public school as "a doomed seminary of humanism," and Green says, "My generation had been through a time of upheaval and had not in their homes or at their public schools known until joining the University a life they could be sure would continue."[25] To graduate from public school with this generation is to become an instant anachronism, prepared for a world that has ceased to exist. J. M. Keynes noticed as early as 1919 a fundamental change in the confidence of the "great capitalist class," and Orwell found it so profound in 1939 that he called it "middle-class unemployment," an unemployment that results not from the loss of jobs but from the loss of roles, prototypes for behavior, and expected rewards.[26]

The most important fact to separate from all such sociological speculation, however, is that the generation itself precedes all others in analyzing its own failures. Isherwood's is the most complete analysis of the impact of the war, stretched

---

[24]Gathorne-Hardy, p. 207.

[25]Greene, ed., *The Old School*, p. 8; Connolly, *Enemies of Promise*, p. ix; Henry Green, *Pack My Bag* (1940; rpt. London: Hogarth, 1952), p. 211.

[26]J. M. Keynes, *The Economic Consequences of the Peace* (New York: Harcourt, Brace and Howe, 1920), p. 237; George Orwell, *Such, Such Were the Joys* (New York: Harcourt, Brace, 1953), p. 183.

out over several books, fictional, semifictional, and openly autobiographical, Connolly's the most detailed attack on the public schools, Orwell's the most crushing dismissal of the entire group as a cul-de-sac in literary and political history. The group provides a definition of itself that cuts across political lines and generic distinctions among poets, essayists, and novelists. Writers include themselves in this group not by political commitment but by a strong sense of the failure and inauthenticity of isolated individuals, and by a belief in public life that sees it less as a political arena than as a reservoir of fictions for the individual to use.

This sense is perhaps most visible in the novelists, providing some of the basic situations of thirties fiction. For the novelists of Green's age the basic political fact is the utter irrelevance of the individual and his complete helplessness in the world of fact. The characters of Waugh, Powell, Isherwood, and Orwell are all at loose ends, and the almost eerie moral neutrality of the first three is a function of being at loose ends, of having nowhere in particular to go. The comic lack of consequences, the ease with which characters such as Captain Grimes and Herr Issyvoo stay afloat, is an index of their very lightness, their nature as extraneous beings. The moral vacuum of *Decline and Fall* or *The Berlin Stories* exists because the characters have no power, and no personality to be false to.

Writers such as Langbaum and Wylie Sypher have shown that such a "loss of self" is a common plight in modern literature, that, as Langbaum says, "English literature has, since Arnold's time, increasingly lamented the loss of vitality and an assured sense of self."[27] For the thirties generation, however, this loss is less likely to be exacerbated than to be alleviated by participation in social fictions. A particularly clear example is a conversation in Anthony Powell's *A Question of Upbringing* between Nick Jenkins and a Mme Dubuisson. Jenkins delivers a heartfelt farewell speech to Mme Dubuisson, thinking her to be someone else, but "the curious thing

[27]Langbaum, p. 53.

was that its effect had been to provide some genuine form of emotional release. It was almost as if Madame Dubuisson had, indeed, been the focus of my interest at La Grendiére. I began to feel quite warmly toward her, largely on the strength of the sentiments I had, as it were, automatically expressed."[28] Here the surface of conventional life comes, by pure habit, to acquire the genuine and sincere quality formerly reserved for moments of pure revelation. As Graham Greene so often shows in his own novels: "Conventions were far more rooted than morality . . . it was far easier to allow oneself to be murdered than to break up a social gathering."[29]

This sense of the contingency of personality on social context does not, however, lead to a longlasting faith in the objective truth of public expressions. Except for Upward, none of the members of the generation remained committed Communists for long, perhaps because they were too apt to see the personal infection in almost every public act, the power of fantasy and illusion behind seemingly objective movements of history. Thus Cyril Connolly can say, "What illness performs for the individual, war accomplishes for the masses."[30] The boxing match toward the end of Isherwood's *Berlin Stories,* which is more of a dual shadow boxing match, represents in public form the desire to believe that makes his characters both naive and thoroughly phony. Sally Bowles's schemes, Mr. Norris's swindles, Bernhard Landauer's "experiments" are so transparently artificial as to be pathetic, and yet the characters all see themselves as worldly, urbane, and cynical. The mingled childishness and cynicism of such fictions account as well for the curious atmosphere of Berlin, of deep commitments to political movements altered in a day, of private scores settled in ideological terms, of swindlers and

---

[28] Anthony Powell, *A Question of Upbringing* (London: Heinemann, 1951), p. 165.

[29] Graham Greene, *Ministry of Fear* (London, 1943; rpt. New York: Penguin, 1973), p. 71.

[30] Cyril Connolly, *The Unquiet Grave* (1945; rpt. New York: Viking Compass, 1957), p. 127.

aesthetes like Mr. Norris speaking in heartfelt tones about "the Party."

The peculiar genius of such fiction lies in the way it shows the fluid boundary between public materials and the most intimate parts of the self. One of the masters of this kind of fiction is Henry Green. Green's novels are based on the belief that the self is not a truth to be expressed but an expression itself, a fiction. The actions of a typical Green character are not eloquent of the true personality within but are often borrowed or invented for the moment. Thus there is no necessary opposition between the self and the outside world in his work, no feeling of falsification or unfaithfulness created by conformity to rules and rituals. If personality is not a transcendent value, however, the public world is even less so. Public acts are not necessarily impersonal and objective as they often are in novels that emphasize the truth of personality, nor are they presented as somehow more truthful than private acts. They are, rather, fictions as well and respond more to the desires of individuals than to objective forces in economics or politics.

This definition of the role of fiction in everyday life is one under which Green's work and that of his contemporaries can be unified. For Green, as for many other members of the thirties generation, self-extinction is the beginning of literature, not because the self does not matter, nor because it should be sacrificed to impersonal standards of art, but because individuals can achieve by failure what they are too weak to seize by success. Illness and ennui, which an Arnold or an Eliot might lament, become the basis of a victory over facts because it seems the self can attain fulfillment only by abandoning its pretense of vitality and independence in favor of fictional representations. For the same reason, the entrapment so common in Green's novels sets the characters free in a fictional version of their world. Failure, illness, loss of freedom, all the conditions the generation finds so peculiar to its historical place, are not finally to be lamented but exploited, turned to use in the creative acts of ordinary living. No author, it can safely be assumed, will be content to parade his defects without at least suggesting some compensating virtue, even if it is only the candor of Rousseau. And autobiography would hardly have been such a popular form during the thirties had the failures so abundantly revealed been other than a precondition for a more devious kind of success. Green is particularly adept at showing how failure can be turned, through fiction, into strength, and how withdrawal and isolation can offer all the benefits of practical power. To read his novels is to see in a number of ordinary situations a bargain members of his generation first work out in their own lives and in the autobiographical works written about those lives. In these is one of the basic keys to the fiction of Henry Green.

The Literature of Debility: BLINDNESS, PACK MY BAG, and the Thirties Generation

Even though I were blind or a legless cripple,
even though I were led astray by my errors,
I would win the war by dint of losing the
battles.

Jean-Paul Sartre,
The Words

I

IN *The Words,* an account of the first ten years of his life, Jean-Paul Sartre describes the self-made myth that transformed even illness or error into evidence of his future greatness: "Perhaps I would lose an arm, a leg, both eyes. But all that mattered was the way things happened; my misfortunes would be only tests, means for writing a book. I learned to put up with trouble and sickness, I regarded them as the first fruits of my triumphal death, as rungs on the ladder that was leading me to my glorious end. . . . Modest and insufferable, I saw my defeats as conditions for my posthumous victory."[1]

---

[1] Jean-Paul Sartre, *The Words,* tr. Bernard Frechtman (1964; rpt. Greenwich, Conn.: Fawcett, 1966), pp. 146–47.

Defeat is turned into victory, illness into health, because the ten-year-old Sartre has come to think of his life as an artwork, the material for an artistic career, every step of which is turned toward his ultimate apotheosis as a famous writer. The miseries of the child become, in this retrospective before the fact, the steps by which the great man's consciousness is formed.

The Words is an attack on these pretensions, an attempt to strip away the specious grandeur in which the young writer cloaked himself, a kind of antiautobiography that exposes the falsehood of Sartre's boyish pose. It is the purest example of an odd genre in which autobiographical speculation acts as an abrasive against the self, milling it down to the last disappearing kernel of authenticity. The semiautobiographical works of Henry Green, as well as many of those of his contemporaries, belong to this genre. The same exposures are accomplished, the same connection made between writing and falsehood. But literature also acts to transform illness and failure into a kind of power available only to those who willfully abandon the successes of everyday life. The seductive utility of writing is such that it creates around every step of adolescent life an aura derived from its coming transformation into a work of art. Art becomes a means of instant retrospection, in which even the tawdriest defeat is sanctified by its instant placement in a literary past. The particular interest of Green's first novel, *Blindness* (1926), and his partial autobiography, *Pack My Bag* (1940), lies in the explanation they offer for the process, the connection made between it and the experience of Green's generation.

Schematically divided into sections entitled "Caterpillar," "Chrysalis," and "Butterfly" and ending with an ecstatic vision, *Blindness* seems to conform to a common pattern for first novels, where the plot is little more than a preface to the great things promised on the last page. *Blindness* is read as such a novel in most studies of Green, A. Kingsley Weatherhead, in particular, finding in it a pattern of growth whereby the hero "defeats his loneliness in literary expression."[2] This

---

[2] A. Kingsley Weatherhead, *A Reading of Henry Green* (Seattle: Univ. of Washington Press, 1961), p. 20.

kind of novel is such a common opening of a literary career, and expectations of the pattern are so strong, that the point may be lost that Green's hero first *achieves* loneliness in literary expression. The novel begins with John Haye at Noat School, secretary of the Noat Art Society, and self-conscious challenger of the conventional sensibilities of the school. Like Green himself at Eton, Haye deliberately sets himself off from his schoolmates by outrageous behavior. He wears a great coat against the Noat fashion, paints a round straw hat in bright colors to start a controversy, and forms all his conduct "with an eye to theatrical effect."[3] Haye always keeps at least one eye on himself and provokes the outrage of his schoolmates as the surest way of engrossing their attention as well. Yet he has no desire to shine in the conventional way and suffers from an undiagnosable disease that allows him to skip cricket, which he hates, in order to read by himself.

Even before the accident that ends Haye's career at Noat, writing, blindness, and social ostracism are brought together in a mysterious but seemingly necessary combination. As a result of Haye's war with the school at large, it becomes " 'the thing to do' now to throw stones at me as I sit at my window." One of the offenses that bring this on is Haye's private, almost antisocial act of keeping the diary that forms the first part of the novel: "The House rather alarmed and faintly contemptuous to hear I keep this; they have given me up, I think and hope." Though these attacks lead to no real injury, they are followed by mysterious eye trouble: "I had thrown myself down to stop a ball and I saw waving specks in my eyes for two minutes afterward" (p. 7).

Insularity, writing, and eyesight are thus circumstantially brought together even before the accident that blinds Haye and removes him from Noat. This accident, which seems to recapitulate the attacks of his schoolmates, is related in the letter that ends the first section of the book: "A small boy was sitting on the fence by the line and threw a big stone at the train. John must have been looking through the window

[3]Henry Green, *Blindness* (London, 1926; rpt. New York: Viking, 1978), p. 11. All subsequent references are to this edition and in this chapter will appear in text.

at the time, for the broken glass caught him full, cut great furrows in his face, and both his eyes are blind for good" (p. 29). The accident is appropriate in a way, since it removes Haye completely from the school life he disdains, as if his desire to be left out of the school routine, to be relieved of the odious crowd of small-minded athletic types, had been ironically fulfilled.

The blindness becomes, in fact, a subject for competing martyrdoms in the Haye household. Haye's old nanny uses her grief against the other servants, "crying in the servants' hall . . . banking, minting on the fact that she had known him longer than anyone else there" (p. 45). Haye and his stepmother struggle over who should suffer more. When she offers to help with his writing, Haye thinks, "It would bore her so except for the first few weeks when she would feel a martyr, and that was never a feeling to encourage. And how fine it would be to renounce her help in seeing it through" (p. 38). This kind of self-sacrifice, like that of the two women, is obviously a means of gaining, not relinquishing, power. But Haye really need not sacrifice himself any further; having been injured, he realizes, gives him all the power he needs: "Everyone would be sorry for him, everyone would try to help him, and everyone would be at his beck and call; it was very nice, it was comfortable. And he would take full advantage, after all he deserved it in all conscience" (pp. 45–46).

Though he is willing to accept physical dependency, Haye is disgusted that his intellectual life must also depend on others. The accident has thrown him back "on his own reserves of mental fat," to live out a full life on the remembered impressions and sights of adolescence. This is what John Russell calls a subtheme of the novel, "the apparently invidious comparison between enriched past and blasted present."[4] But the theme is central to Haye's psychological condition since his life has been broken into two discrete parts, one of experience,

---

[4]John Russell, *Henry Green: Nine Novels and an Unpacked Bag* (New Brunswick, N.J.: Rutgers Univ. Press, 1960), p. 59.

the other to be treatment, shaping, and use of that experience. Because Haye is a fledgling writer he regrets his lost life most as the loss of material, of ideas, which will now come through to him read or related by his stepmother or the nanny "as steam rollers go over roads, levelling all sense, razing all imagery to the ground with their stupidity" (p. 46). This is a kind of dependency he cannot enjoy.

The only way around this dependency is to believe that physical blindness is compensated for by intellectual insight, to make deprivation of normal experience a condition of, rather than a stumbling block to, intellectual and artistic independence. This is what most of Green's critics take to be the theme of *Blindness,* what D. W. Brogan, in a contemporary review, calls "this revelation of subtler sense, more penetrating perception, than that of sight."[5] Haye comes to accept his blindness when he develops this theory himself, and most critics miss the psychological defensiveness behind it. Haye says, "I will be a great writer one day, and people will be brought to see the famous blind man who lends people in his books the eyes that he lost" (p. 155), and this seems a naive but harmless ambition. More insidious is the claim that "no one cares and I will be as uncaring as any." The proclaimed sensitivity is undercut by its obvious motive, to defeat the indifference of others with a greater indifference, to become independent of others by ignoring them, and to use his vocation as a means of walling out the remains of real life. It becomes apparent that the accident has completed a process purposefully begun at school, the process of inventing an insular life superior to that of other people and of escaping into a fictional existence.

Haye's attraction to Joan Entwhistle, daughter of an alcoholic vicar removed from his living by Mrs. Haye, has the amoral voraciousness of an artist after material, and her life seems suitable to him precisely because it lacks content. At first his relationship with her appears entirely altruistic: "There

---

[5]D. W. Brogan, untitled review, *New Republic,* Dec. 29, 1926, p. 174.

was so much to find out, and, in a sense, so much to discover for others, for when one was blind one understood differently" (p. 124). But Haye's daydreams about Joan expose the fact that he wants his new way of seeing to be more than just a supplement to normal sight. His descriptions should be so engaging that Joan will willingly give up the view he has lost, allowing his descriptions to replace what she actually sees: "He would teach her the view, and she would be so bored with it as she would so want to go on talking about that" (p. 125). Haye wants a pupil who will be so engrossed in his teaching as to ignore the subject taught. The fact that Joan has lived virtually alone, with no chance to meet or talk to anyone, appeals to Haye, since that means "all June would be stored up" (p. 127). None of her life has been spent, not even on herself, so Haye feels able to create her by giving the blank, stored-up life any meaning he likes.

So Haye appropriates her entire life, changing her name from Joan to June because she is "just like June," the illusory female he creates in anticipation of their first meeting. Though Keith Odom asserts that Haye finally accepts reality and calls her Joan,[6] Haye does, in fact, use the false name more insistently and more frequently whenever they quarrel, and especially when they decide to part. In the final two pages of their relationship he calls her June seventeen times, four times in a final sentence of nine words, as if repeating this name will assert his control over her when she threatens to escape the frame he has designed. Haye consciously forces Joan to become a fictional character acting out a plot of his invention. His motives become obvious when he muses over the things he has to write about, inanimate things which he vitalizes so they might come up to be petted: "Great feline table. And the flowers poked their soft heads so confidingly into your palm, tickling. They must get another dog now that Ruffles was dead that he might have his hands licked. Stroking June, her skin would be so alive. There were days when everything

---

[6]Keith D. Odom, *Henry Green* (Boston: Twayne, 1978), p. 39. Odom is apparently referring to a passage on p. 183 in this edition, in which the name occurs in an interior monologue.

was a toy. . . . He would write about these things" (p. 130). The literary imagination to Haye is something which turns indifferent things into pets or toys, which invests objects or people with life that they might fawn on him.

The fact is that Haye is bored and disappointed with a world that makes no attempts to ingratiate itself with him. "When the sun came out for a moment it used to be a great thing for me, and I have sat here entranced, but when you think that all this doesn't bother itself about one at all, it is a trifle boring" (pp. 152–53). At first, blindness intensifies this feeling, since the world, instead of stopping as it should, "goes on, goes on, and that is rather irritating" (p. 154). But finally blindness comes to seem a gain, since it diminishes the power of reality to affect his impressions. If he feels himself ignored he can, in the absence of any contradictory knowledge, turn every chance touch into an embrace. For the same reason the death of his mother, which occurred shortly after he was born, begins to seem a blessing: "There was no pain in his memory of her; if there had been it would have driven her away. That was why it was so lucky he had never known her; another illusion would have gone. . . . Then it was lucky perhaps that he could not see any more, that the little boy had taken his sight away. For she was nearer than she had ever been before, now that he was blind" (p. 132). These deprivations are actually a gain because they create a vacuum to be filled with pleasant illusions. This is the "greater insight" Haye achieves through his accident, the realization that he is free to invent a new world with none of the irritating indifference of the old.

But blindness is not enough. Barwood still has an independent life of its own revolving around his stepmother, and Joan is too crude and too obtusely herself to fill the role of June. Haye convinces his stepmother he must move to London to write, and his reasoning shows that distance from his material is Haye's major prerequisite as a writer: "Life was only nice in retrospect, and they could look back on the mists that coiled around Barwood and make them into an enchanting memory, with Joan rising through them" (p. 183). Haye's need for change is the need to prettify his present life by putting it in the past, just as he is free to prettify the image of his mother because she is dead, or to prettify Joan until he meets her. Writing and retrospection are identical to Haye because the purpose of his art is to give present events that aura they acquire by becoming the past, the aura of distance and romance, but also the specious aura Sartre defines, when every action becomes part of an inevitable process leading to an artistic end. In moving to London, Haye duplicates the effect of the original accident. On the train he wonders whether the "same boy might sit and throw more stones," but Haye has taken on the role of that boy himself, doubling his blindness by renouncing the only home he has ever seen and moving to a place he has no visual memories of whatever. His insistence that he can write only in London exposes the fact that writing for Haye, at this stage of his life, is blindness, the deliberate removal of things from sight so that they can be made "nice."

It is inevitable then that London should become stifling in its turn, so much more so than Barwood that it brings on the fit that ends the novel proper. Haye finds himself smothered rather than inspired by his new surroundings, and the imagery he uses for his problems shows that he can never be comfortable until he finds some literary way to dominate: "It was only that he was dazed by all these new sensations, he would rise above them soon, when he knew how to interpret them, and then he would have some peace" (p. 199). The imagery of sinking and rising continues until the end of the novel, with Haye determined not to be smothered as much for reasons of pride as anything else. He is determined not to be defeated in front of his friends: "He was not going to let them see him crushed under his blindness, they would despise him for it. He must first make out how he stood with life in general so that he could show them how much better off he was than they. He would start a crusade against people who had eyesight" (p. 203).

Haye continues to try to rise above these sensations until the pressure brings on the final seizure. Like the original blindness, the seizure is an accident beyond Haye's control, but it is one he uses in much the same way. At the moment of unconsciousness he sinks into a "deeper blindness," suggesting that his convalescence will complete a process begun with the original accident. And the letter Haye sends to his friend B. G. after the seizure reads like a fulfillment of his plan for a crusade against people with eyesight. It is suddenly "divine to be in London," where the traffic is no more than "busy vibrations." Haye feels at "the centre of things again," no longer excluded from the life around him. John Russell believes this letter has "a tone charged with humility."[7] But Russell ignores the fact that this is exactly the kind of letter called for by the "crusade," one which shows that Haye has not been crushed. It accepts the life of an invalid with a certain jauntiness: "They tell me I have had some sort of a fit, but it has passed now. Apparently my father was liable to them, so that anyway I have one behind me after this" (p. 207). What makes this acceptance possible is that Haye is finally "going to settle down to writing now," as if he had to be bedridden as well as blind to write. The promise to write is obviously still part of a compensatory process whereby Haye's separation from real life is made to seem an advantage and his inability to join in a virtue. His defeats, like Sartre's, become victories when they can be seen as part of a writer's capital.

From his first efforts at school to his final establishment in London, Haye's need to write is a defensive one. The entomological metaphor of the three subdivision titles should therefore be taken ironically, like the snide title "Picture Postcardism," which is attached to the musings of Joan. John has not emerged from but burrowed further into the cocoon of his fiction. Writing is a means to achieve isolation from a group before which he is afraid to fail. His blindness, like the mysterious illness he suffers from at school, relieves him of the need to compete and at the same time stamps him with a mark of difference he can use to claim superiority. The theory that physical blindness brings spiritual insight is just part of the crusade against people who have eyesight, as his fictionalizations of the lives of others are part of a campaign

[7]Russell, p. 71.

to become the only one to establish the accepted version of events. Blindness and writing are both retreats from a state where facts are common property to one where they belong to him alone. Illness and creativity are associated, not because one disposes a young man toward the other, but because they both involve a withdrawal from actuality in order to gain power over it.

Nothing could be further, it would seem, from the equation between literature and action so commonly applied to the writing of Green's peers. But *Blindness* corresponds very closely in its view of illness and writing to Christopher Isherwood's first novel, *All the Conspirators* (1928), not because of any possible borrowing, but because the two books express an attitude toward the vocation of writing common to the whole generation. As in the early unpublished novel that was to have been called *Lions and Shadows,* Isherwood's hero resolves his fears of failure with a timely bout of rheumatic fever.[8] Unable to support himself as an artist, unable, in fact, to force himself to practice his various arts, and unable to resist the pressures of his mother to begin a conventional life in business, Philip Lindsay early on begins to consider illness as an out: "Suppose he had a nervous breakdown? This would, of course, impress them; but, at the same time, it might be serious. How does one get brain fever?"[9] Lindsay considers brain fever, the most literary of afflictions, but it is his own long-dormant rheumatic fever that settles the plot. Out of sheer desperation Lindsay accepts a job in Kenya, with ulterior motives that are correctly diagnosed by his friend Allen Chalmers: "When I was seven, I used to say: I wish the castor

---

[8]Isherwood, *Lions and Shadows,* p. 56. As a joke at his own expense, Isherwood borrows the title of this unfinished novel for his first volume of autobiography.

[9]Christopher Isherwood, *All the Conspirators* (London, 1928; rpt. New York: New Directions, 1979), p. 71. The most extensive critical discussions of *All the Conspirators* are by Paul Piazza, in *Christopher Isherwood: Myth and Anti-Myth* (New York: Columbia Univ. Press, 1978), pp. 19–31, and by Alan Wilde, *Christopher Isherwood* (New York: Twayne, 1971), pp. 27–36.

oil would make me die. Then Nannie'll be a murderess."[10] Like John Haye at Noat, Lindsay depends on the injustices of others to put himself in the right, and he needs to provoke a breakdown to dramatize the psychic punishment his mother is inflicting. As Eliot says of Edward Chamberlayne in *The Cocktail Party*, "Illness offers him a double advantage: / To escape from himself and get the better of his wife."[11] On the eve of his departure for Africa, Lindsay runs away, becoming overtired and wet, conditions that, as Chalmers has warned him, bring back his rheumatic fever.

The illness turns out to be a highly satisfactory substitute for the trip to Africa, solving all of Lindsay's immediate problems and bringing complete victory over the family in the question of his occupation. His mother becomes pathetically proud of the poems and paintings she once despised, because they are now the only products of an invalid otherwise incapable of effort. It is plain that the only way for Lindsay to win is to give in completely, to give in to the bourgeois idea that art is a proper pastime only for invalids or old women, to dominate his family's prejudices as John Haye dominates his stepmother, by becoming completely helpless. The parallels with John Haye's situation extend to Lindsay's relationship with his sister, Joan, who breaks off her engagement to a gratingly normal young man in order to nurse her brother. Her fate is to be the same as that of the Joan in *Blindness*. "Philip's got so used to being waited on by Joan" that no one else is allowed to do it.[12] She is the one he prefers to paint, the only one who reads aloud properly. She, like Green's character, is slowly turned into a work of art, forced to make the choice between marrying and becoming the subject of her brother's paintings. The extent of the power given Lindsay by his situation as an invalid is made evident by the self-hatred Joan feels as she makes her escape, posting

---

[10]Isherwood, *All the Conspirators*, p. 202.
[11]T. S. Eliot, *The Complete Poems and Plays, 1909–1950* (New York: Harcourt, Brace & World, 1971), p. 345.
[12]Isherwood, *All the Conspirators*, p. 242.

a letter to her fiancé that betrays "on two sides of a piece of notepaper, everybody, everything."[13]

The early stories of Stephen Spender, collected in *The Burning Cactus* (1936), are also concerned with "the backward and nervous sons of rich people" whose artistic pretensions go along with a propensity toward illness.[14] Spender's interest in debility is apparent in the title of the first story he wrote, "The Soldier's Disease," which remains unpublished.[15] "Two Cousins," rewritten from a story of the late twenties, throws a sickly, artistic young man into a household whose very healthiness gives him pain. He feels distinctly inferior to his healthier cousins with their comfortable home life and confesses to them, "I took refuge from the life at home in a series of illnesses: the last illness literally almost left me paralyzed, so that after that I decided not to be ill—one can make such decisions—and I haven't been ill since."[16] This defensive assertion that it is in one's power to be well does not, however, help Spender's other heroes to break the hold of their nervous disabilities. Like Till in "The Burning Cactus," they all feel in moments of crisis "the old defeatist, unrelenting pain form like a phenomenon of the weather," a phenomenon which ruins their friendships but which also gives them "a strange triumph," like the feeling of being unfairly abused.[17]

It is young men like these whom Auden pretends to address in "Address for a Prize Day," published in 1931. Assuming the tone of a hectoring schoolmaster, he harangues those who suffer "more and more from cataract or deafness, leaving behind them diaries full of incomprehensible jottings."[18] But Auden also assumes the voice of such young men in a different section of *The Orators*, "Letter to a Wound," in which he

---

[13]Ibid., p. 254.
[14]Stephen Spender, *The Burning Cactus* (New York: Random House, 1936), p. 215.
[15]Stephen Spender, *Letters to Christopher* (Santa Barbara, Calif.: Black Sparrow Press, 1980), p. 72.
[16]Spender, *The Burning Cactus*, p. 136.
[17]Ibid., p. 182.
[18]W. H. Auden, *The English Auden*, ed. Edward Mendelson (New York: Random House, 1977), p. 62.

speaks as an invalid who has come to love his wound like a precious secret, one that has given him insight and set him off from ordinary people. The speaker of this piece addresses his wound as a lover, a confessor, and a work of art. Auden's interest in the illnesses of his friends is well known, as is the relationship of his diagnostic method to the psychological theories of Homer Lane. But illness occurs as an important metaphor for the artist's life in the works of Auden's contemporaries well before Auden discovered Lane, and the allure of debility and defeat extends to writers never under Auden's or Lane's sway, including Cyril Connolly, whose *Enemies of Promise,* published in 1938, is dedicated to the idea of the "Splendid Failure."[19]

Obviously, "Letter to a Wound" does not inaugurate but sums up in an ironic way a tendency in this group to identify the beginning of a literary career with an accident or illness that brings normal, everyday life to an end. The fact that this group came to be known as the most politically active of literary generations, with the most vigorous of ideas about the power of literature, makes this early identification of literature and defeat rather strange. Such writers are not supposed to share the shrinkings of Tonio Kröger or Proust's Marcel. Furthermore, they differ from the Philoctetes in Edmund Wilson's version of the fable in that they are so supremely conscious of the value of their illnesses, courting them, manipulating them, and milking them for all the advantage they can give. They behave, in fact, not like the writers included in *The Wound and the Bow* but like writers who had recently read it.

The unanimity with which these writers associate literature and debility comes not from collusion or group politics but from a shared experience, one that made falsehood and failure seem to be preconditions of their lives and brought literature and collapse together in a glamorous relation. Isherwood's analysis of his own obsession with failure is well known. In *Lions and Shadows* he charges the whole generation with "a

---

[19]Connolly, *Enemies of Promise,* p. 256.

feeling of shame that we hadn't been old enough to take part in the European war."[20] For Isherwood this shame casts a doubt that in itself brings on failure, a purposeful failure like Philip Lindsay's, which saves him from a greater failure at something truly important. Similar feelings of guilt are expressed by writers as diverse as Green, Orwell, Day Lewis, and Waugh, so Isherwood's authority may be respected when he claims to speak for the entire generation.[21] But in the early works considered here failure is only initially a retreat, and collapse is a prelude to a kind of ironic heroism, a "strange triumph" in which the young artist gets the attention and approval he needs by the backhanded method of illness. Though Isherwood's identification of the war as the experience behind these failures is an important one, it can be used to explain more than Isherwood allows it to.

One of the earliest works of literature to express the guilt Isherwood defines is a poem entitled "To the Young Writers and Artists Killed in the War: 1914–18," by Brian Howard, which appeared in the famous ephemeral *The Eton Candle* while Green, Anthony Powell, Orwell, and Connolly were all Etonians. After much gnashing of teeth at the older generation responsible for the war, Howard exclaims to the fallen artists who died in it, "Oh, we will fight for your ideals—we, who were too young to be murdered with you."[22] The basic desire here is obviously not the desire to fight, or even to avenge the dead writers, but to be martyred like them. The envy which comes through in Howard's poem is that of a person who covets the grievance of another, who longs to be injured so that his outrage, which is now only secondhand, can truly become his own.

---

[20]Isherwood, *Lions and Shadows*, p. 55.

[21]Henry Green, *Pack My Bag*, pp. 82–83; George Orwell, "My Country Right or Left," in *The Collected Essays, Journalism, and Letters of George Orwell* (New York: Harcourt, Brace & World, 1968), I, 536–38; Day Lewis, *The Buried Day*, p. 158; Waugh, *A Little Learning*, p. 170. All subsequent references to *Pack My Bag* are to this edition and in this chapter will appear in text.

[22]The full text of Howard's poem is contained in *Brian Howard: Portrait of a Failure*, ed. Marie-Jacqueline Lancaster (London: Anthony Blond, 1968), p. 579.

This desire to emulate the martyred writers of the First World War is not Howard's alone. As Paul Fussell notices in *The Great War and Modern Memory*, the first published works of Howard's contemporaries appear coincidentally with the wave of war reminiscences that began with C. E. Montague's *Disenchantment* (1922) and culminated in Graves's *Good-bye to All That* (1929). For Fussell, and for Samuel Hynes, who describes the same coincidence, the important similarity between the groups is that both divide the world into two camps, those who were responsible for the war and those who, though opposed to it, did most of the fighting.[23] But neither critic notices the method of identification by which the younger group acquires the right to fight alongside Graves, Sassoon, and Montague against the powers responsible for their martyrdom. These writers are the survivors of a group epitomized by Wilfred Owen, who received the war as both a physical and a spiritual wound and who acquired the moral authority to proclaim their spiritual disillusionment in large part from the physical suffering they endured. The younger group acquires this disillusionment almost by birthright, growing up, as Isherwood and Auden did, on the works of Owen, yet they feel, in the privileged surroundings of Repton or Eton, that such disillusionment is unearned. It is for this reason that the earliest literary games of the generation (the Mortmere saga, invented by Isherwood and Edward Upward, which found published form in Upward's *The Railway Accident*, Auden's *Paid on Both Sides,* and Isherwood's "Gems of Belgian Architecture") are characterized by the search for a nonexistent enemy.[24] For the same reason the novels of Green and Isherwood and the short stories of Spender show the young protagonist acquiring moral authority through physical collapse. Philip Lindsay's rheumatic fever is the war wound he never received, the disaster that excuses his inability to mature and at the same time gives him victory over the older generation and the freedom to become a writer.

[23]Paul Fussell, *The Great War and Modern Memory* (New York: Oxford Univ. Press, 1975), pp. 109–13; Hynes, pp. 50–51.
[24]Fussell describes this aspect of the early work of Isherwood, as Hynes does of Auden's.

The war is not explicitly present in *All the Conspirators* because, as Isherwood confesses in *Lions and Shadows,* the true subject of his early work is suppressed.[25] But in the other works mentioned here the identification of the war with the hero's illness is quite apparent. Spender's protagonists in particular suffer from an isolation that comes from living "not in a July of the 1930s but in July 1914." They assume the role of being the only one to truly understand and suffer from the war, as Werner does in "The Cousins," or, like Till in "The Burning Cactus," date their debility from the war.[26] In *The Orators* the war is presented as a spiritual wound, of which only the fatuous can say, "The wound is healing and we can now look back to the war . . . without such painful memories." And, as John Fuller points out, the illness that gradually takes possession of society in "Journal of an Airman" is described in a form borrowed from Ludendorff's account of the first war, while the airman's own debility is described in phrases from Wilfred Owen's letters.[27]

One of the most sustained and subtle of these parallels occurs in Green's *Blindness.* It first appears in John Haye's diary, even before his accident, when a football upset disturbs his vision with "waving specks" while house prayers are being offered "for those in danger on the sea" (p. 7). The parallel is continued in Mrs. Haye's hopes that her stepson's blindness might cause him to take an interest in the village and in so doing give him "the feeling of a regiment" (p. 56). Haye himself tends to compare his accident and the death of his father, a career military man. At one point he asks, "What was he like?" and simultaneously realizes, "so he was blind, how funny" (p. 37).

Haye's most complex vision of himself in relation to the war is contained in a daydream that follows a collapse in his self-confidence. Realizing that he has become isolated by his own efforts to be glib and clever, he thinks, "And now there was no escape, none. A long way away there might be a

---

[25]Isherwood, *Lions and Shadows,* pp. 56–57.
[26]Spender, *The Burning Cactus,* pp. 146–48 and p. 177.
[27]Auden, *The English Auden,* p. 95; John Fuller, *A Reader's Guide to W. H. Auden* (New York: Farrar, Straus & Giroux, 1970), pp. 67–68.

country of rest, made of ice, green in the depths, an ice that was not cold, a country to rest in. He would lie in the grotto where it was cool and where his head would be clear and light, and where there was nothing in the future, and nothing in the past" (p. 78). Around this gravelike grotto would be "a country of opera-bouffe. And little men in scarlet and orange would come to fight up and down little hills, some carrying flags, others water pistols. There would be no wounded and no dead, but they would be very serious." Haye's vision of himself as the entire death toll of a tiny mock war resembles *Paid on Both Sides,* Auden's charade in which a war is fought out both on a northern landscape and in the psyche of the hero, John Nower. But while Nower struggles against the senseless rituals of a grudge war, Haye has given in and found peace in immobility. His point of view is that of a battlefield casualty, one of Hardy's speakers from the grave perhaps, to whom the war, once so crucial, shrinks into insignificance in comparison to the eternal cold.

Being a casualty transforms isolation into a satisfactory feeling of remoteness. It also gives the authority to become a writer. Haye's model for himself as an artist is the blind piano tuner, who, having been blinded in the war, feels his hands burn at "the injustice of it" (p. 131). In announcing his vocation to Joan, Haye assumes this man's indignation and draws an explicit parallel between himself and those wounded in the war: "You see, June, no one cares enough, about the war and everything. No one really cared about my going blind. . . . And I will write about these things—no one cares and I will be as uncaring as any" (p. 155). The accident sets Haye on one side with the war wounded, over against the uncaring multitude. He speaks as if his blindness had been a contribution, an unappreciated sacrifice offered in war. Blindness, like Lindsay's rheumatic fever, is the war wound he never suffered, which sets him apart from the mob of insensitive and inexperienced civilians, a subject about which to write and a grievance to promote.

These first works of the Auden generation thus resemble nothing so much as Siegfried Sassoon's *Memoirs of a Fox-Hunting Man,* which was published in the same year as *All the Conspirators.* As Paul Fussell has pointed out, Sassoon sees his life as having been severed into two parts by the war. His prewar life, rendered unreal by the tremendous dislocations of the war, exists only as material for a postwar reconsideration, and the postwar life exists only as a long meditation on that material.[28] The spiritual and physical wounds Sassoon suffered divide his life into sealed compartments, material and treatment, so that the last thirty years of his life are spent interpreting the first twenty-five. The lives described in the first works of the Auden generation are similarly severed. Green's and Isherwood's heroes end up in bed, looking back over a life that has ended in actuality and will continue only in fiction. This retrospective air is a feature of the early work of most members of the generation, from Spender, whose heroes seem stuck in 1914, to Cyril Connolly, who sees everything in terms of his schoolboy successes and failures. The air of retrospection is all the more odd in that most of these works consider young writers embarking on a literary career who seem to take as a necessary first step the obliteration of their nonliterary lives.

Yet, as Sartre shows in *The Words,* such instant retrospection has its uses. To bring one's life to an end prematurely is to give it the meaning it lacks, to give even the most trivial episode an aura derived from its relationship to the ultimate collapse. Just as Sassoon's utterly undistinguished life as a country sportsman acquires some dignity from the way it ends with the war, Lindsay's and Haye's meager schoolboy lives acquire a sudden importance from catastrophe. These aimless lives are seen to lead somewhere, and even the tiniest action takes its place as one of the steps to the ultimate demise. Illness is therefore the only solution for these characters, not just because it serves to align them with the war wounded as against their domestic adversaries, but because it is the only way their empty lives can be given shape and coherence. Illness lends to life the shape and coherence of art by giving it a formal, but not a final, end.

[28]Fussell, pp. 90–105.

Failure thus becomes inherently artistic, and one's very inability to meet the demands of life becomes the sign of triumph over them. Haye and Lindsay are war heroes through failing to fight in the war. The Truly Weak Man, as Isherwood says in *Lions and Shadows,* performs feats of bravery and courage that arise out of his very attempt to circumvent the challenges met by the Truly Strong Man. It is virtually impossible to measure the ratio of self-mockery to self-advertisement in Isherwood's theory, but Green seems to judge his hero's myth rather harshly by making it ordinary. He does so by placing it in the mouth of old Mr. Entwhistle, shabby defrocked curate and father of Joan. Old Mr. Entwhistle, removed from his parish by Mrs. Haye because of drunkenness, believes his intellect has improved by isolation: "It had been growing, growing ever since in his hermit existence.... He was even more of a genius because he was recognized in his home, a very rare thing surely" (p. 91). Entwhistle cleverly reverses the normal value judgments of the world, making the fact that he is respected only at home proof of his great genius. Failure is thus the proof of a more significant success: "Then he had lost his way in the world. No, that wasn't true, he had found it—this, this gin was his triumph" (p. 91). The whole cycle of ostracism, failure, and compensation in writing occurs in Entwhistle just as it does in John Haye, for just as Haye's blindness removes him from a group he envies and dislikes and rewards him with an artistic gift, the bottle does so for Entwhistle: "It was the only thing that did his health any good, and one had to be in good spirits if he was to think out the book, the great book that was to link everything into a circle and that would bring him recognition at last" (p. 91). Entwhistle even has his own physical disease, "Cancer, that he had been awaiting so long" (p. 88). Like Haye, Entwhistle takes his disease as a martyrdom, a blow from an uncaring world, which will give him the basis of his literary complaint: "Why could not the doctor do something about it? Oh, for a pulpit to say it from" (p. 92).

Entwhistle's case recapitulates and generalizes Haye's, as isolation and debility become again the prerequisites and the raw material for literary work. Such is the attraction of this stratagem, the comfort of turning all one's failure directly into genius, that it seduces even those like Joan who do no writing themselves. Joan has her own wound and her own kind of masochism. She bears a scar on her face like Haye's from a wound inflicted by her father in a drunken rage. Yet she doesn't complain about this attack, reasoning, "Still it was what a genius would have done" (p. 93). This acceptance of the glamor her father has given to illness makes her an easy mark for Haye. The only conflict which faces her is whether to be an adjunct to her father's myth or to Haye's, so it is not at all surprising that when she is forced out of his scenario she rushes to her father's for comfort: "Oh, you go to London. Father an' I've got the book to write. He'll show you all what a mistake you made" (p. 167). All the books projected in *Blindness* are the products of psychological grudges, all are conceived to "show" someone, to replace a lost pulpit, to be "as uncaring as any." All transfer some struggle from real life to fiction, where only the author will determine who will win.

Like every other bildungsroman, *Blindness* offers a definition of literature. In Green's novel literature is the magic book in which lives are rewritten, where all grudges are settled in the author's favor. Each individual, powerless in the real world, carries such a book, which need never be written. The simple presence of the book casts a spell over life so that every tawdry failure, every lapse, becomes, as in *The Words,* another step toward genius. At the end of *Blindness* John Haye settles down to write, and it becomes obvious that the only proper end of his life is writing, and that the end has, as in scholastic philosophy, defined the nature of the thing itself. Literature is important not so much because it elevates or transforms life as because it gives it an end, in the dual sense of a finale and a purpose. In fact, in this definition life lacks a purpose until it ends. The characters are all like Auden's Ishmael, who proclaims, "My injury *is* me."[29] It is just a step

---

[29]W. H. Auden, *The Enchafèd Flood* (London: Faber and Faber, 1951), p. 97.

from this to the autobiography, of which Green's generation wrote so many examples so early, and it almost goes without saying that those autobiographies should take as their subject, not the life of the author, but the utter failure of the author to achieve anything remotely like a life.

II

It is especially peculiar that the autobiographical urge should have struck so many writers of the same generation at almost exactly the same time. Isherwood's *Lions and Shadows* appeared in 1937, as did Auden's *Letter to Lord Byron,* Part IV of which is an attempt "to get my oar in" before Isherwood.[30] Also published in 1937 were Cecil Day Lewis's autobiographical novel, *Starting Point,* and George Orwell's sociological study with an autobiographical insert, *The Road to Wigan Pier. Enemies of Promise* and Edward Upward's *Journey to the Border* were published in 1938, followed in 1939 by Louis MacNeice's *Autumn Journal.* Green's *Pack My Bag* and Spender's "September Journal" were both written in 1939 but appeared in 1940, as did Spender's autobiographical novel, *The Backward Son.* MacNeice's *The Strings Are False* was begun early in 1940, then abandoned and not published until after his death. And in 1940 as well, Orwell produced his comment on the whole generation in the retrospective essay "Inside the Whale," which was followed by a personal account in "My Country Right or Left." These last essays are examples of the tendency of autobiography to force its way into other, seemingly incompatible genres, into criticism as it does in *Enemies of Promise* and MacNeice's *Modern Poetry,* published in 1938, into sociology as it does in *The Road to Wigan Pier,* and even into travel literature, in the chapter of school reminiscences with which Graham Greene began *The Lawless Roads* in 1939.

According to Samuel Hynes, the autobiographies of this generation attempt to provide for each writer a mythical self, a self like the ones described in James Olney's *Metaphors of Self,* formed by the controlling metaphor of the writer's most

---

[30] Auden, *The English Auden,* p. 190.

important work.[31] But these writers seem less to be inventing a mythical self or shaping a real one with some chosen metaphor than to be displaying a gap where a personality should exist. The personality described by the autobiographies is paralyzed and excluded from events, and the predominant emotion is a sense of passive foreboding. Connolly begins *Enemies of Promise* by describing the compromises the coming war forces on intellectual idealists such as himself, until they "cannot be said to remain spiritually alive." MacNeice begins *The Strings Are False* "tense, anxious, muddled, expecting the moon, guilty of the war, so full and so empty of myself." Green begins *Pack My Bag* with the conviction that "it would be asking much to pretend one had a chance to live" (p. 5). Almost every autobiographer takes the course Orwell describes in "Inside the Whale" as the response of the "ordinary individual" to the overwhelming events of the late thirties: "So far from endeavoring to influence the future, he simply lies down and lets things happen to him."[32]

The autobiographical works written in this mood cannot be attempts to produce an honest account of the self or even to provide a metaphor for it because that self has ceased to exist. Rather, they are attempts to account for the paralysis, the irrelevance, the feeling of premature death that is common to them all. They are stories of the loss of a self, each one, as Harold Rosenberg says of *The Words,* "a negative autobiography, a natural history of the not-selves that crystallized in the time span of the living person and displaced him."[33] But they are more than this. Each autobiography becomes the book that, as in the case of the Entwhistles, will sum up and justify the empty life contained in it. The generation produces autobiographies with such indecent haste because, as for Haye and Lindsay, the book gives the life its only shape and purpose. The odd character assassination that each author

---

[31]Hynes, p. 322.
[32]Connolly, *Enemies of Promise,* p. 5; Louis MacNeice, *The Strings Are False* (New York: Oxford Univ. Press, 1966), p. 18; Orwell, *Collected Essays, Journalism, and Letters,* I, 500.
[33]Rosenberg, p. 126.

performs on himself succeeds just as Philip Lindsay's self-induced collapse does, turning failure and weakness into "material," reducing the mistakes of life to a moral neutrality, useful only insofar as they can be described. As it becomes material for a stylistic success, failure ceases to matter, becomes in fact a kind of felix culpa, the very absence of worldly success offering the writer his best chance for literary accomplishment. So the autobiographer is successful when he can paint his own unworthiness, and these autobiographies become a subclass of the genre, in which a style is accomplished by the annihilation of its subject.

Autobiographies appear with such frequency in the late thirties and early forties because that period of helpless anxiety recalls one of the key experiences of the past of the generation. The feeling of guilty helplessness created by the onset of the second war resembles the feeling Haye and Lindsay have about the first, and many of the autobiographies make this comparison into an important structural principle. Orwell's "My Country Right or Left" discusses the coming war almost entirely in terms of his schoolboy reaction to the First World War. "Inside the Whale" also turns toward the First World War in its search for a proper response to the Second. The identification of the two periods is one of the themes of *Lions and Shadows,* as Isherwood looks compulsively forward to another war as the Test he is bound to fail.[34] The peculiar sense of unreality retained from childhood failure to participate in the war is best described by Green, who felt "as though I had missed something through being too young to fight, that I had not come home on leave from the front. I felt I had to make up for lost time which I had not had time to lose" (p. 196). Being perpetually behind or out of step, with no way to catch up or compensate, gradually saps Green's faith in his own reality, as if he were living under false pretences. The second war with its threat of death therefore comes as a retribution, a simple exposure of his falsehood: "The war

---

[34] See Orwell, *Collected Essays, Journalism, and Letters,* I, 535–40 and 523–25. For Isherwood on the First World War see *Lions and Shadows,* pp. 3, 54–55, 203, and passim.

well won for us it appears we forgot those who had lost their lives and that we sat back like victors who had themselves successfully borne arms. It seems in a way as though we have been falsified by the turn events have taken" (p. 209).

This sense of repetition and retribution naturally recalls the whole atmosphere of the first war, colored by the public school life Green's contemporaries led in 1914. The years leading up to the second war come to seem somehow like a return to school, so that another basic principle of the autobiographies is the correspondence between a society dreading and yet gearing up for war and a public school student body. Auden's comparison of public school life and fascism is well known, and it is enough of a commonplace for Green to have echoed it in *Pack My Bag*. But Green also notices how even the democracies come to resemble regimented public schools as they prepare for the coming war. Green sees this war bringing happiness only to those who miss their old school: "It may be they have not enough routine to pass the time as they are now and that a time schedule, as for private soldiers in the army, is what they want, what they miss, and what in a war they will get" (p. 48). But Green himself feels the coming war as acutely as a schoolboy ending a long vacation: "The last few months of peace in Britain was to go back to being a little boy again, however old you are. It was so to speak those last few days of term, but no holidays promised, and the knowledge that having failed in everything, willy-nilly next week would find you in a poorer, harsher academy."[35] This summarizes the mood of all the autobiographies, which return to the past not out of nostalgia but as if the author had failed adulthood and had been sent back to endure in a new war the experience of a public school in the first, until he can truly graduate. The passivity, the terror, the conviction of falsehood and insignificance, are all schoolboy reactions, appropriate enough for the days between Munich and the Blitz but giving the impression in these autobiographies of lives doubling back toward adolescence.

[35] Henry Green, "Firefighting," *Texas Quarterly*, 3 (Winter 1960), 119.

The arc described in a work like *Pack My Bag* or *Lions and Shadows* thus approaches a circle. Life has not reached completion, nor does it progress in a given direction. Instead it burrows further and further into the place from which it began. But as in the early novels of the generation, the self-enforced convalescence that results becomes an odd, inverted kind of heroism, and a stance that comes from one's simple inability to meet the emotional challenge of the new war is transformed until it comes to seem the only stance possible for an honest man. The best expression of this transformation can be found in a review of Julian Green's *Personal Record*, written by George Orwell as the war began:

> *The feeling of futility and impermanence, of hanging about in a draughty room and waiting for the guns to begin to shoot, which has haunted many of us during the past seven years, is present everywhere, and it grows stronger as the diary moves towards 1939. Perhaps even the possession of this feeling depends upon being a certain age (Julian Green is not quite forty), young enough to expect something from life and old enough to remember "before the war". . . . But what is attractive in this diary is its complete impenitence, its refusal to move with the times. It is the diary of a civilised man who realizes that barbarism is bound to triumph, but who is unable to stop being civilised. A new world is coming to birth, a world in which there will be no room for him. He has too much vision to fight against it; on the other hand, he makes no pretence of liking it. . . . It [his reaction] has the charm of the ineffectual, which is so out-of-date as to wear an air of novelty.*[36]

Orwell defines his generation by their very incapacity to face the coming war, their sense of passive dread of a change they are powerless to prevent, and yet he is himself characteristic of the generation to which he belongs in elevating that passivity and failure to a virtue with "the charm of the

---

[36]Orwell, *Collected Essays, Journalism, and Letters*, II, 21.

ineffectual." In "Inside the Whale" Orwell savages the fashionably leftist writers such as MacNeice, Connolly, and Spender and contrasts their programmatic works unfavorably with those of Eliot and Forster written during earlier international crises. Forster said in 1941, "To me, the best chance for future society lies through apathy, uninventiveness and inertia," and this is precisely what Orwell prescribes in "Inside the Whale": "a gesture of helplessness, even of frivolity."[37] But what Orwell has not noticed is that Forster has long been the hero of writers like Isherwood and that even the writers he attacks have been converting to Forster's faith in frivolity. MacNeice, who comes in for heavy blows in "Inside the Whale," ends *The Strings Are False* with accounts of visits to Jack Yeats, a surrealist painter named George MacCann, and a Mr. Popper, whose etymological theories emphasize the letter *P*. These cranks and hobbyists and isolated painters become for MacNeice civilization's only hope: "Like Jack Yeats going on painting and George MacCann reciting stories of drunks and vagrants, Mr. Popper riding his hobby made me feel that perhaps after all the Dark Ages might miss us." This is exactly what Forster says in a review of Orwell: "There, in the useless, lies our scrap of salvation." For the writers of the younger generation, Forster's example transforms the ineffectuality, the uselessness, and the paralysis that characterize the autobiographies into the virtues of the liberal man. Detachment and uninvolvement take the place of commitment as the only possible response to fascism, and a kind of muddled English liberalism replaces communism as the antidote to Hitler. Auden can so confidently admit that "poetry makes nothing happen" because he believes, as he says in a dedication to Forster, that "the inner life shall pay."[38]

[37] Forster's comment is quoted in Robert Hewison, *Under Siege: Literary Life in London, 1939–1945* (New York: Oxford Univ. Press, 1977), p. 177; Orwell's is in *Collected Essays, Journalism, and Letters*, I, 524.

[38] MacNeice's statement appears in *The Strings Are False*, p. 215, Forster's in *Two Cheers for Democracy* (New York: Harcourt, Brace, 1951), p. 61, and Auden's dedication at the beginning of "In Time of War" in *The English Auden*, p. 249. For a discussion of the influence of Forster on the generation, see Hynes, pp. 301–3.

Passivity and uninvolvement become aesthetic virtues as well as political ones. Connolly and Spender, especially, argue for withdrawal, maintaining as Connolly does in "The Ivory Shelter" that "the best modern war literature is pacifist and escapist, and either ignores the war, or condemns it, with the lapse of time." Spender's "The New Realism," published like "The Ivory Shelter" in 1939, is a painful attempt to admit to error without actually recanting and to describe his own "split position" as a writer who has attempted to throw off his "bourgeois environment" but failed. But this political failure is not necessarily an aesthetic liability, and Spender comes around to the idea that the "divided position" of bourgeois writers is "precisely the thing in their historic situation which makes them interesting and valuable." Thus the failure of Spender's political hopes is almost a happy one, since the literature of division, of mixed motives, and of longing is more interesting than that of revolutionary success.[39]

The transaction Spender accepts—trading political ambitions for a greater humanistic sensitivity—is openly espoused by Isherwood and Connolly in their autobiographies. Spender simply makes a virtue of necessity, since the outbreak of war renders his influence nil and destroys the hopes that were the inspiration of his political work. Isherwood makes an issue of his own ineffectuality long before the war, anticipating the crisis that Spender confronts in 1939, taking his failure as a foregone conclusion, and working out his compensations accordingly. His stratagem is the theory of the Truly Weak Man, the man who is so certain of his failure that "with immense daring, with an infinitely greater expenditure of nervous energy, money, time, physical and mental resources, he prefers to make the huge northern circuit, the laborious, terrible, north-west passage, avoiding life." Of course, by taking such a hard way around what a normal man might have confronted directly, the Truly Weak Man proves himself as if he had actually passed the Test itself. His avoidance of

[39]Cyril Connolly, "The Ivory Shelter," *New Statesman and Nation,* Oct. 7, 1939, pp. 482–83; Stephen Spender, *The New Realism* (London: Hogarth, 1939), pp. 19 and 21.

real life becomes a means of conquering it, so that, by simple inversion, weakness denotes strength and failure becomes success. In *Lions and Shadows* Isherwood applies this theory to a much younger self and is at least partially ironic in the application. But the theory can be seen in action even in the mature work Isherwood was producing at the same time as *Lions and Shadows,* in the works eventually collected as *The Berlin Stories.* The utter passivity of Herr Issyvoo, his unwillingness to displease or offend anyone, his simple inability to say no, involves him in the monumental schemes of Mr. Norris and Sally Bowles. The very fact that he is so "bland and anonymous," to use Connolly's description, involves him in escapades and, incidentally, kindnesses, that a more substantial person would have avoided.[40]

Connolly would seem to have reversed this equation, since the basic aphorism of *Enemies of Promise* is "promise is guilt—promise is the capacity for letting people down." Throughout "A Georgian Boyhood" Connolly becomes more retrospectively craven the more his success as a schoolboy increases, as every accomplishment becomes the prelude to a more resounding disappointment. But, as he admits in the preface to the 1948 edition, the style of "A Georgian Boyhood" is meant to be a successful solution to the literary problems outlined in the rest of the book. It is meant to combine the colloquial and mandarin styles Connolly describes, and "should be felt evolving as it goes along."[41] That is, the style is meant to mature as a person does, as the subject of an autobiography should, and "A Georgian Boyhood" is meant to be, as almost all of Connolly's books are, a confession of failure contained within its own stylistic refutation. Like Isherwood, Connolly advances to certain failure, but the twists and turns he describes while getting there become a style, and that style, as Connolly observes triumphantly in the 1948 preface, survives the ten years it seemed no book could survive.

---

[40]Isherwood, *Lions and Shadows,* p. 164; Connolly, *Enemies of Promise,* p. 74.
[41]Connolly, *Enemies of Promise,* pp. 260 and viii.

Literature, therefore, comes to stand, both politically and aesthetically, for uninvolvement, privacy, weakness, for the wound that removes the writer from real life. The literature defined in the autobiographies is based on the uncertain position the writers find themselves in at the end of the thirties, and on the need to find some virtue in a position they cannot alter. It is the literature of defeat, but defeat transformed to become spiritually cleansing and significant. As Raymond Williams says of the group in his study *George Orwell,* they were led to realize "other lives but especially other beliefs, other attitudes, other moods—through their own shifting negations."[42] Their willingness to admit failure, to accept and parade their own nullity far beyond the state of "negative capability" leads to successes like *The Berlin Stories,* in which it seems that the personality of the author has been sacrificed in the guise of Herr Issyvoo to gain him the talent of describing others. This is precisely the bargain made in the autobiographies. Like Mr. Entwhistle and John Haye, the autobiographer bargains away success in life, accepting failure, passivity, uninvolvement, in return for the power to describe these things. The art of Connolly and Isherwood is the art of self-effacement, but true self-effacement in literature is a logical impossibility. Christopher may be low, craven, weepy, but Isherwood has all the power of the perceptions that see these things. The peculiar genius of professional autobiographers like Isherwood and Connolly (even Spender now refers to himself as an autobiographer) is that they make the bargain of Haye and Lindsay work: they accept the obliteration of self, welcome it even, in order to be able to take failure as the theme of triumphant literature.

To do so, however, it is not necessary to be a professional writer. This is where Green expands and generalizes the experience of his generation by showing the extent to which everyday life is a fictional reconstruction, an act of displacement by which failure becomes a successful story of failure. Failure and its displacement are at the center of the theory of

---

[42]Raymond Williams, *George Orwell* (New York: Viking, 1971), p. 91.

fiction given in *Pack My Bag,* especially when it defines fiction as an everyday habit as well as a mode of art. Part of Green's awareness of these fictions certainly comes from his own public school background. A crucial kind of experience occurs twice in *Pack My Bag,* once quite simply, when Green's elder brother dies and Green is put in a room alone where he "cried because I thought I had to cry" (p. 80). The second time, an accident involving his parents sets up a much more complicated sequence of false emotions. Green feels no grief, only a sense of shock, when his headmaster reads out a telegram indicating the accident may have been fatal. "Instead, and I fear this is horrible, I began to dramatize the shock I knew I had had into what I thought it ought to feel like" (p. 145). In every encounter with a schoolmate or master Green creates the emotion he thinks the situation and audience demand. The climax comes when, walking into chapel, he feels the entire school waiting to observe his reaction: "Then throughout the service I let myself go, willed myself to imagine the parents writhing in agony, pulled faces, showed all the agitation I could" (p. 148). Green ends the account by comparing himself to a hunted animal: "I felt, and it is hard to explain, as though the feelings I thought I ought to have were hunting me. I was as much alone as any hunted fox. Only as my feelings turned and doubled in their tracks to the loud blasts of news each cable brought, as conscience the huntsman cast my feelings forward and then back until the fox I was was caught, bowled over at last into genuine surrender, there was something desperate in the noise, the howling at my heels" (p. 152).

Green's reaction here is exactly like that reported by Spender's hero in *The Backward Son,* who feels tremendous guilt when he realizes on the death of his mother that "grief is one of those conditions which may have little to do with what people are actually feeling, but are invented for them by others, when certain circumstances arise."[43] What might

[43]Spender, *The Backward Son,* p. 250.

in another context be a perfectly natural adolescent feeling—guilt at one's inability to take death seriously—brings in the public school context a deep conviction of falsehood, of victimization by a false self. This is so because of the dizzying contrast between the real world of one's parents and the artificial one of the school, and because of the realization, enacted in these scenes, that the artificial world is more powerful, in a practical sense more true, than the real one.

This sense of victimization and failure is only a prelude, however, to a discovery of the possibilities of the world of fictional emotions into which Green is inducted by his public school experience. One of the basic convictions of *Pack My Bag* is that the imagined version of a failed action is somehow more potent than success. Green's failure to kiss a receptive maid, for example, produces a memory much stronger than that of an accomplished kiss: "This kiss which was not exchanged has lasted on where others given or received would have escaped the memory. Indeed it has grown, for better or for worse this incident now at this moment looms quite large" (p. 91). The mind is free to work its art on failure, but it is circumscribed by the actual circumstances of success. Certainty, accomplishment, success, are ends, but "questions unresolved stay in the mind" (p. 35). Green unwittingly applies in a new way Valéry's famous distinction between poetry and "utilitarian language," language that, "when it has served its purpose, evaporates almost as soon as it is heard."[44] Any utterance, any action, can approach the status of poetry if its utilitarian purpose is thwarted. The useless, the misunderstood, the mistaken, achieve a literary power and endure precisely because failure prevents them from dissolving in the completion of a task.

Language, therefore, has its greatest interest for Green when it misleads. He is fascinated by what George Steiner calls "alternity": "the counter-factual propositions, images, shapes

---

[44]Paul Valéry, *The Art of Poetry,* tr. Denise Folliot (New York: Pantheon, 1958), p. 72.

of will and evasion with which we build the changing, largely fictional milieu of our somatic and our social existence."[45] Like Steiner, Green sees man as achieving humanity through lies and as having his most authentic community in deception: "Surely shyness is the saving grace in all relationships, the not speaking out, not sharing confidences, the avoidance of intimacy in important things which makes living, if you can find friends to play it that way, of so much greater interest even if it does involve a lot of lying" (p. 126). Confidences, shared truths, are never revealing, but a person is expressed and characterized by the lies he chooses. Green speaks of people "islanded by their exchanges, lying no doubt but always with half-truths like truffles just under the surface for one or the other to turn up to find the inkling of what human beings treasure, rather than what they think they know of themselves" (p. 128). The specious revelations of "intimacy," offered in the mistaken assumption that one knows something about oneself, are useless, but the lie is pure gold, the thing itself, because it, paradoxically, shows the liar naked, revealing himself by the falsehoods he chooses.

This explains Green's very strong interest in arbitrary conventions, rules, and taboos that make a subject interesting by withholding it. His novels are characterized by a kind of communication which takes place at a distance and which appears on the surface to be a failure of communication. But Green's characters only begin to live when failure and isolation overcome them, and their social lives begin to thrive only when lies are necessary. As Steiner insists, there is something fundamentally human in the need to say "the thing which is not," to evade and deny what is.[46] Thus whatever impedes real life, roughens it, or abrades the smooth flow of social intercourse sets free a humane alternative, a fictive life of immense creative possibilities.

[45]George Steiner, *After Babel* (New York: Oxford Univ. Press, 1975), p. 222.
[46]Ibid., p. 223.

Therefore, communication is likely to thrive in Green's works when accomplished across a distance. Green describes himself engaging in this kind of communication across a distance in an anecdote about a girl in a French home where he boarded to brush up his French. Their relations are embarrassingly awkward until a routine is established: "We had long talks the subject of which was prearranged . . . as we were to be here six weeks together, we should talk for a fortnight as though we were engaged, for another two weeks as though we had just been married, and for the time that was left as though we had been married for ages" (p. 189). The whole household soon joins the fiction, within which the two adolescents achieve a much greater intimacy than they could have without it.

The social transactions that interest Green all have a certain formality, a rigidity, and a fictive quality that seem to limit their usefulness as communication. But it is exactly this surface failure, this carefully sustained distance, that is their value. For example, the factory workers among whom Green worked after leaving Oxford have a mode of conversation as artificial as his own with the French girl. "At least once in every week we discussed where a certain Stony Lane had been, which, soon after the war, had been obliterated in a clearance scheme in the district." Green calls this discussion "a regular turn" with its own rules and an almost ritualistic repetition. The discussion is also highly abstract, since the lane no longer exists, and therefore the discussion can continue forever, with no intrusion from real life. This talk is to Green "more like that of intellectuals than the half-baked talk about novels people who fancy themselves put over" (p. 239). It is a kind of stylized, prearranged discussion that displaces idle gossip and keeps the workers from prying into one another's lives. For though the group was intensely interested in the affairs of people far away, there was an "almost cryptic dismissal of a fellow worker's personal affairs" (p. 240). This distance from one another, this protection of their own lives by the smokescreen of formal talk, preserves the individual dignity of each worker: "They may say they agree but they never listen, and this is one reason why they express themselves with an unheard of clarity" (p. 241). It is distance that allows social life to continue, a kind of stiffness in formal conversation that makes it the sustaining act of a group, and a studious, assumed deafness to others that keeps the individual fresh within himself.

Only in this way is it possible to understand Green's most categorical pronouncement about writing. It comes as he is deciding whether to include proper names in his memoir, a question he settles by saying, "Names distract, nicknames are too easy and if leaving both out as it often does makes a book look blind then that to my mind is no disadvantage." The blind look of *Pack My Bag,* its relative lack of interest as gossip, is therefore calculated, Green preserving his distance as the factory workers did. This interest will be replaced, however, by a virtue arising out of the very obliquity of his method. Prose, to Green, "is not quick as poetry but rather a gathering web of insinuations which go further than names however shared can go." In the anecdotes that have been described little meaning is shared, but this lack of surface intimacy allows a web of insinuations to grow. This is what Green means by saying, "Prose should be a long intimacy between strangers with no direct appeal to what both may have known." That is, no overt connection should be sought. Strangers should be allowed to remain strangers, with no attempt at identity made, so the gap can allow intimacy to exist as it does in the anecdotes. Only in this way can prose "slowly appeal to feelings unexpressed" and "in the end draw tears out of the stone" (p. 88). As Green shows in his anecdotes, the unexpressed is fostered by formalities, conventions, rules, and restrictions which seem to thwart communication but which in actuality make the fragile web of insinuations possible.

For this reason Green's characters tell the truth about themselves when they are lying, dramatizing themselves, or acting out conventional behavior. When Green narrates himself, it is usually in a crabwise syntax, a purposely clotted prose designed to impede the easy communication that prevents understanding. Both his prose and the odd evasions of his characters seem idiosyncratic. But as an examination of the autobiographies and the early autobiographical works of his contemporaries shows, both emerge from a personal and historical situation Green shares with a number of other writers. The weakness and insubstantiality of the individual, his virtual lack of existence in the real world, leads in each autobiographical work to a belief in the creative power of failure. Weakness in the real world opens up infinite possibilities in a fictional one, just as blindness calls into being a completely new existence for John Haye. The autobiographies, together with the early fiction already considered, constitute a substantial body of literary theory in the guise of personal description, a theory that defines literature as the creative evasion of the blockades that thwart and diminish the individual. This theory stands behind each of Green's novels. The basic situation of each novel is obstruction: blindness, fog, air raids, isolation by geography or by age. The social relationships of his characters also seem to be obstructed by misunderstanding, fantasy, prejudice, or delusion. Yet it is such obstructions that transform Green's ordinary, completely unartistic characters into creative geniuses who use their own lives for material.

2

"A Thing They Are Doing": LIVING and PARTY GOING

> *The composition is the thing seen by every one living in the living they are doing, they are the composing of the composition that at the time they are living is the composition of the time in which they are living. It is that that makes living a thing they are doing.*
>
> Gertrude Stein
> *Composition as Explanation*

I

WHEN GREEN took a foundry job at his family's Birmingham works in 1926 and began to write *Living*, he became the first of his generation to turn to "proletarian inspiration." Green's experiment in working and living in Birmingham attracted visits from Auden, Waugh, and Anthony Powell, and the novel that resulted was received by Stephen Spender as an example of a new kind of fiction that would escape the old myopic focus on upper-middle-class life. In the thirties a number of novels took experiences like Green's as their subject, until a recognizable subgenre was established. This subgenre includes conversion narratives like the autobiographical novels of Edward Upward and C. Day Lewis, in which the hero seeks out the worker's movement as a final step in his own development, and novels such as Orwell's *Down and Out in Paris and London,* in which the author abandons his upper-class identity along with his money and his possessions and becomes a worker in mind as well as in body. The real achievement of *Living,* however, is to be found in the differences between it and the popular subgenre to which it seems to belong.[1]

The basic conventions of the subgenre can be seen most clearly in Upward's *Journey to the Border,* his short story "Sunday," and Day Lewis's *Starting Point,* all of which end with the confused and guilty hero finding a new, more purposeful life in the worker's movement. The three works all end with an almost religious moment, as the hero agrees to throw off the false, bourgeois life he has been leading in favor of one that is more real, because it is in tune with history: "Whether their hands were grained with coal dust, marked with occupational scars, or pallid from the stagnant air of offices—it was these hands, Anthony believed, which would guide a new world struggling out of the womb." The event has all the significance of baptism, even for Orwell, who does not equate working-class experience with communism as Upward and Day Lewis do. In *The Road to Wigan Pier* Orwell describes the terrible guilt he felt as a colonial policeman in Burma, the essential falseness of his role and the life that led up to it, and describes the way he entered the society of English tramps to cleanse himself: "Once I had been among them and accepted by them, I should have touched bottom, and . . . part of my guilt would drop from me." These motives, which led to the experiences fictionalized slightly for *Down and Out in Paris and London,* resemble the motives Green identifies in *Pack My Bag* as leading to his foundry work: "I had a sense of guilt

---

[1]Green uses the term *proletarian inspiration* in an interview with Nigel Dennis, cited earlier. He describes Auden's visit to the factory in an interview with David Lambourne, " 'No Thundering Horses': The Novels of Henry Green," *Shenandoah,* 26 (Summer 1975), 70. Waugh describes his visit in his *Diaries,* ed. Michael Davie (Boston: Little, Brown, 1976), p. 317, and Powell describes his in *Messengers of Day* (New York: Holt, Rinehart and Winston, 1978), p. 25. Spender's opinion of *Living* is, as cited above, in *The Destructive Element,* p. 237.

whenever I spoke to someone who did manual work. As was said in those days I had a complex and in the end it drove me to go to work in a factory with my wet podgy hands."[2]

Raymond Williams calls this desire for conversion "negative identification," a process by which the writer alters his life by affiliating himself with a group that seems most unlike him. The fact that the process is so common reflects the peculiarly uncomfortable class position of these writers. As Williams demonstrates in *The Long Revolution,* and as Neal Wood further documents in *Communism and British Intellectuals,* the composition of the left intelligentsia in the thirties was overwhelmingly upper and upper middle class in background, with an even higher concentration of public school graduates and Oxbridgians than the generation preceding them. It is natural in this context for working-class experience to represent everything that is opposed to the upper class, as if the working class were a simple photographic negative of the class in which these writers had been raised. Significantly, real workers and real work are quite absent from *Journey to the Border,* "Sunday," and *Starting Point.* They are implied as the simple opposite of everything in the hero's life, as being substantial and satisfying because the former life is, like the life described in the autobiographies of the last chapter, unsatisfying and hollow. As Charles Madge said in 1937, "There is a general wish among writers to be *unlike* the intellectual, *like* the masses. Much 'proletarian fiction' is the product of this wish." Madge implies that the life of the masses is a polar opposite of that of intellectuals, and his quotation marks admit that most fiction based on this assumption is written by upper-class intellectuals desiring conversion.[3]

---

[2]The first quotation is from Day Lewis's *Starting Point,* p. 318. Orwell's statement is from *The Road to Wigan Pier* (London, 1937; rpt. New York: Harcourt Brace Jovanovich, 1958), p. 150, Green's from *Pack My Bag,* p. 195.

[3]Raymond Williams's term comes from his *George Orwell,* p. 16. Statistics on the class background of left sympathizers can be found in Williams's *The Long Revolution* (London, 1961; rpt. Westport, Conn.: Greenwood Press, 1975), pp. 230–45, and Neal Wood, *Communism and British Intellectuals* (New York: Columbia Univ. Press, 1959), pp. 75–90.

Unfortunately, writers who spent some time with the masses found them to be rather different from what Madge's equation assumes. Proletarian writing by real proletarians was not always the unmediated, realistic work that the intelligentsia desired. Orwell observed in a 1935 review that much proletarian fiction had a prose style "modelled upon *Peg's Paper* ('With a wild cry I sank in a stricken heap' etc.)." His experience in researching *The Road to Wigan Pier* also left Orwell with an impression of working-class life different from that implied in the conversion narratives, and different from the one he admitted he had been seeking himself: "The most dreadful thing about the Brookers is the way they say the same thing over and over again. It gives you the feeling that they are not real people at all, but a kind of ghost forever rehearsing the same futile rigmarole." Orwell found that the working class had its own clichés and falsehoods, and some of the best writing he did in the thirties and forties is dedicated to describing the postcards, pulp magazines, sentiments, and stock jokes that were the reality of working-class experience.[4]

Green, who had lived with a working-class family during his employment in Birmingham, just as Orwell did while researching *Wigan Pier*, gives a description of that life which tallies with Orwell's rather than with anything implied by the conversion narratives. As his description of factory workers in *Pack My Bag* shows, Green found his companions to be more intellectual than the intellectuals themselves, only exercising their pedantry on different subjects.[5] Green shared, as Orwell did, the motive behind the conversion narratives,

---

The idea that workers represent natural or real life is surveyed in *Britain by Mass Observation*, ed. Charles Madge and Tom Harrisson (Harmondsworth: Penguin, 1939), pp. 157–60 and 172–74. Madge's statement appears in "They Speak for Themselves: Mass Observation and Social Narrative," *Life and Letters*, 17 (Autumn 1937), 37.

[4]Orwell's review (of Jack Hilton's *Caliban Shrieks*) can be found in *Collected Essays, Journalism, and Letters*, I, 149. The description of the Brookers appears in *Wigan Pier*, p. 17.

[5]Green's living arrangements are described in Powell's *Messengers of Day*, p. 25. Green's description of the factory workers appears in the previous chapter.

to find a life as different as possible, but he resembles Orwell rather than Upward or Day Lewis in that his experience in the factory was remarkably like his experience of public school. Thus his description of working-class life is not based on negation of upper-class habits but on an evenhanded willingness to find those habits anywhere. Green apparently discovered in the foundry exactly the opposite of what the Leftist writers of the thirties were seeking, yet it is his faithfulness to what he did find that makes *Living* reflect with a more complete honesty the sort of life he had shared with Spender, Day Lewis, Upward, and the rest.

II

Discussions of Green often center on his titles, the single words, usually participles, which, because of their terseness, seem to be both forthright and elusive. *Living*, especially, seems a kind of challenge to criticism. It is a title that might be applied to any novel, and yet it is one Green gives without elaboration, as if it were so specific that no other word would do. And this is quite true, not, as Walter Allen says, because Green thinks his novel discloses life in the raw, but because the expression of life as a present participle is both his method and his theme.[6]

Gertrude Stein, in the passage from *Composition as Explanation* given above, accomplishes by redundancy what Green does by the brevity of his title. Her essay was first given as a talk, sponsored by Green's friend Harold Acton, at Oxford in 1926, while Green was still a student there.[7] Whether her insistent repetition of the word *living* gave Green the title for the book he began the next year is impossible to determine, but the intention behind her tactic is certainly the same as that behind the title. Behind Stein's syntactical tangle is the

[6]See Walter Allen, "An Artist of the Thirties," p. 154, for an opinion stressing the supposedly realistic impact of proletarian contact on *Living*.
[7]Gertrude Stein, *Composition as Explanation* (London: Hogarth, 1926), p. 13. The lecture is described in *The Autobiography of Alice B. Toklas* (1933; rpt. New York: Random House, Vintage, 1960), p. 233, and in Harold Acton's *Memoirs of an Aesthete* (London: Methuen, 1948), p. 162.

desire to show living as "a thing they are doing," as an activity, and not a state. It is the composing of a composition, not just the kind of composition found as a static quality in a painting, or in the chemistry of a compound, but the kind that forms a piece of music or a piece of expository prose like *Composition as Explanation*. Stein's playful redundancy is meant to mimic the reflexive process by which people edit and shape what they are doing while they are doing it. She tries, by the difficulty of her prose, to break up the complacency that considers living a known thing, conducted without effort. The baldness of Green's title has the same effect. In the novel the word *living* appears most frequently as part of the idiomatic phrase "making a living," and this is what Green's characters do in a psychological sense as well as an economic one.[8] For them, as for Stein, living is something made, a composition, a laborious construct that always threatens to come apart.

Green's style, as well as his title, is meant to shock the reader into an awareness of the constructive effort that goes into the commonplace. Almost all the critical attention devoted to *Living* has been concentrated on this style, yet no satisfactory connection has been made between its idiosyncrasies and any literary aim detectable in the novel. These idiosyncrasies include random elimination of definite and indefinite articles, possessive pronouns, and the nonadverbial "there," which seems to indicate a desire for bluntness and brevity, and at the same time frequent inversion, repetition, and purposeful awkwardness in the use of comparatives, which affect the prose in exactly the opposite way. Walter Allen's early opinion that the style is "an admirable medium for the expression of the blackness and din of the foundry" is therefore based on half the style, on habits that produce sentences like "Some had stayed in iron foundry shop in this factory for dinner. They sat round brazier in a circle" (p. 1).[9] It cannot

[8]Henry Green, *Living* (1929; rpt. London: Hogarth, 1953), pp. 14 and 186. All subsequent references are to this edition and in this chapter will appear in text.
[9]Walter Allen, "An Artist of the Thirties," p. 154.

account for sentences like the one Green chooses for his epigraph: "As these birds would go where so where would this child go?" Moreover, as Edward Stokes points out, the idiosyncrasies of style are not restricted to descriptions of the foundry nor to the lives of the workers but extend at times into the London drawing room of the factory owner.[10] Any mimetic explanation breaks down in face of Green's perfectly indiscriminate application of his devices. The alternative offered by Bruce Bassoff, that the elisions are meant to convey "the immediacy of impressions and . . . the particularity of the nouns," is just an extension of Allen's theory to the novel as a whole. As Bassoff himself shows, elision of articles is as apt to make the noun seem to stand for a class as for an individual, and the inescapable redundancy of many of Green's mannerisms can only be explained in Bassoff's analysis by the entirely unrelated idea of "prose cadence." Furthermore, Bassoff complains of "lack of tact" when the mannerisms are used in descriptions of London life, as if only nouns in the Birmingham factory could have immediacy and particularity.[11]

Attempts to find a source for Green's style have similarly failed. Allen and Stokes have suggested Anglo Saxon, to which Stokes has added Hopkins, attributions that run against Green's admission that he left Oxford to avoid Anglo Saxon and his repeated confession of complete indifference to poetry.[12] Giorgio Melchiori has noted the similarity between the style of *Living* and Auden's "telegraphese," especially as it appears in *Paid on Both Sides*.[13] The similarity seems undeniable, but simple dating makes any influence of Auden on Green unlikely. *Living* was written in Birmingham in 1927 and 1928, and therefore only Auden's contributions to *Oxford Poetry* in 1926 and 1927 could have influenced it, and these

[10]Stokes, pp. 198–99.
[11]Bassoff, pp. 55 and 56–57.
[12]Walter Allen, "An Artist of the Thirties," p. 154; Stokes, p. 200. For Green's testimony, see Lambourne's interview in *Shenandoah,* pp. 61 and 70, and Alan Ross, "Green, with Envy: Critical Reflections and an Interview," *London Magazine,* 6 (Apr. 1959), 24.
[13]Giorgio Melchiori, *The Tightrope Walkers: Essays in Mannerism in Modern English Literature* (London: Routledge and Paul, 1956), pp. 91–93.

are not in the terse, elliptical style of *Paid on Both Sides,* which was not published until 1930. But if Green was not influenced by Auden or by Auden's influences, Hopkins and Anglo Saxon, he was very interested in an improbable book that may have helped form Auden's style: C. M. Doughty's *Arabia Deserta.*

Doughty is the poet whose pseudo-Icelandic sagas were to be the assigned reading during Pound's stay with Yeats at Stone Cottage.[14] His travel book, *Arabia Deserta* (1888), is better known than his poems, and Louis MacNeice describes Auden reading it in 1928, during the composition of *Paid on Both Sides.*[15] Green's interest in Doughty has been noted by John Russell, who has compared a number of their syntactical oddities, mentioning Green's article on Doughty, but without looking there for the rationale behind his strange syntax.[16] Doughty once said that his aim in traveling to Arabia was "to rescue English Prose from the slough into which it had fallen,"[17] and Green's conclusion to "Apologia," published in 1941, makes it sound as though his factorywork shared this purpose: "Now that we are at war, is not the advantage for writers, and for those who read them, that they will be forced, by the need they have to fight, to go out into territories, it may well be at home, which they would never otherwise have visited, and that they will be forced, by way of their own selves, towards a style which, by the impact of a life strange to them and by their honest acceptance of this, will be pure as Doughty's was." Elsewhere in the article Green refers to the "constraint of his adventure" as the key to Doughty's style, indicating that the benefit of travel to an entirely strange place is not that it frees the imagination but that it forces the imagination up against restrictions that habit has made disappear. This explains why Green is so concerned

---

[14]Richard Ellmann, *Eminent Domain: Yeats among Wilde, Joyce, Pound, Eliot, and Auden* (New York: Oxford Univ. Press, 1967), pp. 69–70.

[15]MacNeice, *The Strings Are False,* p. 114.

[16]Russell, pp. 44–49.

[17]Doughty's comment is to be found in Wyndham Lewis's *Blasting and Bombardiering* (London: Eyre and Spottiswoode, 1937), p. 14.

to establish that Doughty's mannerisms are not merely habits, and why ease, "an elegance that is too easy" in the writing of T. E. Lawrence, is the chosen enemy of his essay. Doughty's virtue is that he "has no elegance, that is, no ease with which to treat of a universal theme." He does not have the virtue of making the strange seem familiar, or even intelligible. "He is harsh, simple to the point of majesty, and not clear, that is his sentences meander." This is his value for writers like Green with experiences like the years of factorywork to relate, that he provides an example of a writer with the strength to resist the urge to make experience simple and intelligible, instead of crabbed and difficult, as Green found it.[18]

Russell accepts the generalization offered by Walt Taylor about the impact of Arabic on Doughty, "that a primitive language is more concrete than a more civilized language; that a civilized language is addressed more to the reason, and is therefore more abstract."[19] Whatever standing these ideas may have in linguistics or ethnology, they hardly describe Doughty's style, or Green's. The mannerisms they share emphasize the difficulty of language, its abstract quality, and a corresponding difficulty in experience that should never be allowed to settle down into habit. Doughty randomly drops his articles, but he is also fond of the redundant conjunction: "The nomad's fantasy is high, and that is ever clothed in religion." He compresses conventional phrases into constructions like "at four afternoon" but enjoys, like Green, the biblical "who": "and reached it to him, who sat all feeble murmuring thankfulness." Doughty favors inversions that increase the difficulty of communication: "no need was then to carry provision for the way"; "there is no Haj in which some fail not." He sometimes simply scrambles what he has to say: "Their aching is less which are borne lying along in covered litters, although the long stooping camel's gait is never not very uneasy"; "Arabians have not wit to burst iron-plate." Such a style, inverted and cluttered with particles, is

[18] Henry Green, "Apologia," *Folios of New Writing*, 4 (Autumn 1941), 44, 48, 50.
[19] Russell, p. 45.

obviously not excessively concrete, nor does it have any mimetic function. It is meant, as Green observes, to prevent experience from being swallowed too quickly.[20]

Green, in his own practice, pursues the same end. The elimination of articles deprives nouns of their context, since something described as "great shape cut down in black sand in great iron box" (p. 4) is neither particular nor general. It is closely observed, but the reader is not drawn up to it with the definite article nor given a class to place it in by the indefinite. Bernard Bergonzi has recently observed that the elimination of articles in Auden's early work is uncharacteristic, and that his mature poetry is marked by excessive use of the definite article applied to general nouns: "the boring meeting"; "the flat ephemeral pamphlet." Bergonzi concludes, "The definite article points to the recognizable if not to the already known. It recalls an actually or possibly shared experience."[21] It therefore follows, if Bergonzi is correct, that avoidance of the definite article in Auden and Green emphasizes the unknown quality of what is being presented; not its "immediacy," as Bassoff argues, but its remoteness.

The elimination of certain words prevents familiarity, while redundancy and inversion prevent the ease that Green felt was inimical to good prose. The result is passages like this well-known one: "Evening. Was spring. Heavy blue clouds stayed over above. In small back garden of villa small tree was with yellow buds. On table in back room daffodils, faded, were between ferns in a vase" (p. 11). The inversion and the terseness together recall Doughty: "All along by the haj road from hence were, as they tell, of old time villages. . . . no need was then to carry provisions for the way."[22] Both writers seem to present description like a pile of fragments purposely scrambled, with normal links eliminated or turned against the reader so as to emphasize that observation

---

[20]Charles M. Doughty, *Travels in Arabia Deserta* (New York: Random House, 1936), pp. 306, 97, 91, 112, 141, 99, 128.

[21]Bernard Bergonzi, *Reading the Thirties: Texts and Contexts* (Pittsburgh: Univ. of Pittsburgh Press, 1978), pp. 41–42.

[22]Doughty, p. 112.

is not a passive partaking but a rigorous organization of disparate elements. They choose to forgo what Lionel Trilling calls, following Henry James, "the grace of ease," in favor of "the grace of uncertainty or of difficulty," the kind of style that chooses to "violate its own beauty" to retain some of the difficulty of actual perception.[23]

It is in this way that Green's style reflects Gertrude Stein's definition of living as composition, since descriptions do not come to the reader as seamless wholes but with all their jagged edges showing and refusing to mesh. It is thus impressed on the reader that the usual organization of experience is not inherent in it but is the product of an assertion of the observer's will. This is also the implicit message of the most common of Green's mannerisms, the construction "thought in mind," which is both redundant and clipped. This construction occurs about two dozen times without a pronoun, and another two dozen times with one, as well as in variations like "cried in mind" or "saw in images in mind." The redundancy makes it seem as though the character is thinking twice, or somehow forcing thought out of the physical world and back into the mind where it belongs. The mental lives of Green's characters, like his own prose, are laboriously constructed before the reader's eyes. Thinking, like living, is an activity rather than a passive state, and simple consciousness takes a certain effort to maintain. The redundancy of the phrase, like that in *Composition as Explanation,* tries to make plain that living is "a thing they are doing." The normal novelistic transition between physical and mental life is made purposely clumsy to emphasize the effort involved.

This change, from life defined as something experienced to living defined as something done, sets Green against one of the more fundamental assumptions of his period. Richard Sennett, in *The Fall of Public Man,* distinguishes between ages in which behavior is a set of predetermined conventions carefully acted out and ones that emphasize spontaneity. The

---

[23]Lionel Trilling, *The Opposing Self* (New York: Harcourt Brace Jovanovich, 1978), pp. 195–96.

fundamental belief of the second is that behavior is most genuine, most truly expressive, when it is not shaped, when "there is no expressive work to be done, 'just living.' "[24] This is surely one of the most basic of the nonpolitical assumptions behind the vogue of the working class in the thirties, that ordinary labor has an authenticity denied to the intellectual. For Green, on the other hand, living *is* expressive work. His characters live in a state which Barbara Hardy, in her book *Tellers and Listeners,* calls "a reverie composed of the narrative revision and rehearsal of past and future."[25] Even to themselves, even "in mind," they shape, edit, rehearse, and drill themselves in fancied roles, but without displacing any more "authentic" self. Both perceptions and responses are shaped because Green believes the self is also the product of an activity, and not the simple acceptance of a state. Every character in *Living,* from the most saintly to the most reprehensible, workers and owners alike, lives in a privately created version of reality like the one John Haye creates after his blindness. The book that a character like John Haye or Mr. Entwhistle uses to dominate life has disappeared because life and book have become one. The process of fictional transformation is instantaneous. Furthermore, this molding of one's privacy into a fiction is no longer limited to self-conscious, aggrieved characters like Haye and Mr. Entwhistle. It is presented instead as a principle of common living. For Green every individual's most basic work is the work of fiction, and thus the two main subplots of *Living,* the layoffs at the Dupret works and the elopement of Lily Gates with Bert Jones, show how both public and private lives are formed to satisfy the formal requirements of fiction.

The most obvious example of a character acting from a private stage is Mr. Bridges, the factory works manager, who, in his most intensely dramatic moment, is granted the supreme redundancy, "so in his thinking he thought now"

---

[24]Richard Sennett, *The Fall of Public Man* (New York: Knopf, 1977), p. 108.
[25]Barbara Hardy, *Tellers and Listeners: The Narrative Imagination* (London: Athlone Press of the University of London, 1975), p. 4.

(p. 113), as if to doubly underscore the labored nature of his interior life. As Edward Stokes says, Bridges "dramatizes himself into a figure of powerful and noble personality, grievously afflicted and under-valued."[26] Green says, "Mr. Bridges in his thinking and in most of his living was all theatre. Words were exciting to him, they made more words in him and wilder thinking" (p. 112). Words for Bridges are not intelligible sounds but cues he uses to prod himself into one or another of his chosen roles.

There is no deviousness about Bridges, however, except in small ways. He truly believes in his own act: "Suddenly, he was acting, sincere in feeling, but acting and words were out pouring, fine sentiments, fine" (p. 113). Bridges simply happens to be most comfortable when he can look at himself in a stereotyped way. Twice in the novel he refers to himself as "a father and mother" to his workers (pp. 1 and 148). He apparently uses this formula so frequently that the workers in their turn sarcastically refer to him as "Father" (pp. 26, 47). They also call Bridges " 'Tis 'Im" (and occasionally call his wife " 'Tis 'Er"), and Bridges is the character most frequently referred to by his title, which in Green's prose, stripped of articles, makes him seem almost automated: "Works manager and Mr. Dupret's son went through sliding glass doors and works manager said this was the iron foundry" (p. 3). Fine sentiments are emotion for Bridges. His real aspiration is to be the workers' father figure, and the highest compliment he can pay to others is to put them into a dime-store mythology, as he does when old Mr. Dupret, the factory owner, dies: "He made Mr. Dupret into angel beaming from sky, he saw Mrs. Dupret and all their servants weeping in front parlour. He saw slavey bring Mrs. Dupret cup of tea from kitchen, 'from humblest to the highest' he was saying in his thinking" (p. 113). Every experience has its proper greeting-card tag that for Bridges does not falsify experience but truly exhausts its meaning: " 'I don't care who 'ears me,' shouted Bridges clinging on to mantelpiece. 'I'd like to call

[26]Stokes, p. 38.

'em all in and say to 'em, we are like a flock that 'as lost its shepherd with the night coming on' " (p. 126). When his emotions are at their most intense they assume the shape of cliché.

Another actor in the same vein is Dick Dupret, heir to the factory owner. Dupret is callow yet less innocent than Bridges, whom old Mr. Dupret calls "so young for his 60 years" (p. 106). Dupret is more his own audience than Bridges is, as Green makes plain with tags like "He thought, he declaimed to himself" (p. 7). Young Dupret is constantly evaluating and annotating his own comments: "He answered he thought planning the evenings most important part of the day. Immediately, as was his custom, he analysed this and thought very clever what he had said, and correct" (p. 35). The only thing that saves Dupret from utter fatuousness is that he often checks himself and finds a witticism lacking. Like Bridges, he often speaks in quotations, sometimes from Bridges himself, as when he parrots Bridges's "What we want is some go, push" to his mother: "What we want in the place is some go and push." Dupret's ability to acquire these quotations unconsciously is signified by his further comment that "it's what none of them seem to realize" (pp. 1, 36). Thus poor Bridges is to be hounded by his own cliché as it comes back to him filtered through the mind of Dupret. But Dupret also consciously speaks in quotations and hopes for a quoted response. His opening gambit with a girl he admires is to mention "a little place I know of," offering this less as a proposition than as an allusion to be picked up: "Why not take up his quotation 'a little place I wot of' he cried in his mind." Unfortunately, the girl only wonders, "Why speak like a serial" (p. 51). Like Green himself in *Pack My Bag,* who courted most happily in French when the courtship was formally established as fictional, Dupret is most comfortable in quotation marks, since without them his emotions lack pattern and force.

Therefore, Dupret uses words as Bridges does, as flails to work himself up into some emotion, without any attention to meaning. After the social failure described above, "temper began to come up gorgon-headed within him, he flagellated it, words hung across his mind—stupidity, and then—angry, and then—old men." He takes his frustration out on the factory management and repeats, without really understanding it, Bridges's catchword for bankruptcy: "Business will go bankrupt, 'to Siam, Siam' " (p. 63). Thus, for Bridges and Dupret at least, language is completely abstract, words functioning simply as triggers for emotion, as flags like the *Siam* which both men wave back and forth whenever they feel threatened.

Criticism of *Living* that emphasizes its proletarian nature would lead to the expectation that the working class lacks such affectations, but the truth is that Green's workers live in a world that is just as highly wrought, as abstract, requiring as much "expressive work" as that of the owners and managers. Lily Gates, for example, draws her most important mental images from the movies. Early in the novel Green purposely obscures the line between audience and film with a characteristically odd use of a demonstrative adjective: "Later they got in and found seats. Light rain had been falling, so when these two acting on screen walked by summer night . . ." (p. 14). "These two" should refer to Lily and her escort, but instead the phrase abruptly transfers them up to the screen, which is not inappropriate, since the film they see foreshadows Lily's brief elopement with Bert Jones and her shameful return. The odd syntax matches a psychological process that Green describes in *Pack My Bag*: "When anyone with a hangover wept at words of his own he put onto the lips of the girl reproving her drunken lover on the screen."[27] This is what Lily does, reenacting the movie in her mind afterward with dialogue appropriate to herself.

The movies, like literature for Dupret and popular, commercialized sentiment for Bridges, provide Lily with the catchwords and images that give form to her emotions. Walking past a tea shop, she remembers a film advertising tea in which the women working had "hands which did not seem touched by the hard labouring" (p. 128). The "infinite ease

---

[27] Henry Green, *Pack My Bag*, p. 211.

of warmth" becomes a dream to her, an essentially false one because she believes the tropical sun "must be a soft thing, not the cruel beating heat it is" (p. 160). Lily repairs to this fantasyland of warmth, so obviously constructed as a positive image of everything Birmingham lacks, whenever she senses failure, and dulls her senses with the thought of sun as if it were actually beating down on her. But the movies are not simply opium. They provide a set of standard catastrophes and punishments like Bridges's dreaded Siam. After Lily has eloped with Bert Jones, and been abandoned, she continues the plot of the first film seen in the novel and expects the inevitable ostracism of the returned fallen woman. When the neighbors fail in their appointed roles, Lily is "a bit disappointed at first" (p. 247), as if she has been cheated of a punishment she had set her heart on. Here she resembles no one more than Dick Dupret, sunk into despair when his companion won't deliver the expected lines.

Even Craigan, the most admired workman at the foundry and the center of the home he has established for Lily and her father, derives his strength from a mythical home life established first in his mind. Craigan's inflexibility about the rules of his household begins with an abstract definition of the role each member should perform. He says, "None o' the womenfolk go to work from the house I inhabit" (p. 13), as if Lily constituted a class all by herself. The specific rules and prohibitions that Craigan lives by, however, are less important than the habits of thought they reveal. Craigan thinks in terms of roles because he has a picture of home life, based on the rural home he abandoned to come to Birmingham, that is complete in every detail as an image in his mind: "Home was sacred thing to him. Everything, his self-respect was built on home. If he had no home to go back into at evening then he would have to move to another town where none knew him. As it was a shame for the Hebrew women to be barren so in his mind was it desolation not to have people about him in his house, though he had never married" (p. 153). The thought of barrenness is significant because the main reason Craigan can allow no deviations from his image of home is that he has never realized it in his own flesh. Instead of marrying, Craigan has acquired by informal adoption the family of Joe Gates, an act of kindness, but one that at the same time satisfies by artificial means a need never met naturally. Craigan constructs his own family to meet the image in his mind and therefore has a set of fairly rigid roles to which the members must conform. He hopes to perpetuate those roles by marrying Lily off to Jim Dale, their lodger, and looks forward "to living in Dale's house, with Lily his wife, till the end" (p. 173). Craigan's relationship to Lily thus resembles that of the Entwhistles, and his artificial family group is the first in a series of similar groups in Green's novels. Complete nuclear families are virtually nonexistent in the later novels, yet the functions of family are performed by various ad hoc relationships, suggesting that the family, just as much as the individual, is a fiction, product of the creative work of the members rather than a state simply accepted from nature.

Yet there is not a touch of calculation in Craigan's relationship to his family. Craigan is one of Green's most moving characters because he has come to love his adopted family and yet has none of the normal claims of family on them. His need for Lily and the tenuousness of his hold over her combine to reduce him from the strongest individual in the book to the weakest. When Lily elopes with Bert Jones, Craigan is at a loss, and the only effort he seems capable of is an intensification of his usual everyday routine: he puts on his best clothes, opens the front room, and simply sits with *Little Dorrit* in his lap, as if the familiar book were a talisman with the power to force things back into their accustomed track.

Even Craigan, barely lettered, uses the mythical power of the book, his nightly reading, to exert control over a disintegrating life. Attempts of this kind are not limited to individuals in *Living,* and one of the most interesting aspects of the novel is the way it shows how collective life can become dominated by versions of individual fictions. Gossip, for example, is the collective version of the revery in which the individuals compose their lives. By telling one another what has happened, people establish a version of events that is more powerful and, in this sense at least, more true than objective fact. When old Mr. Dupret falls and injures himself two groups take his story up: "At the club, they said, 'Dupret has fallen on his shoulder, that sort of thing is a perpetual menace at our age': at the works they said, 'the gaffer's fallen on 'is shoulder so they say, at 'is time of life you don't get over it so easy as that,' and 2 men quarrelled at dinner hour over his age" (p. 56). Both groups deftly remove the dog mess in which Dupret has slipped as inappropriate to the dignity of the occasion, and both groups find the proper cliché by which to assimilate the accident. Thus Mr. Dupret ceases to be an individual dying ignominiously of a false step and becomes a principle, of personal dread for the club members and of an almost filial solicitude for the workers. Critics who emphasize the supposedly concrete quality of the worker's language in *Living* simply ignore the frequency with which unpleasantly concrete details like the dog mess are removed in order to smooth reality down into the shape of cliché. The workers welcome the cushioning capacity of a good cliché, as Albert Milligan, the factory storekeeper, does in quoting the matron of a hospital: "And she said 'we can't keep them 'ere as God wants to take to himself Mr. Milligan.' I reckon that was a fine woman" (p. 5).

The workers refine and dramatize themselves in the same way. The novel begins with Joe Gates gossiping, obviously relishing the story of himself as much as he did the action he describes, and his version of Craigan's near accident later in the book shows how gossip alters and dresses up events with the artistic touches of fiction: "Ah and when I sees 'im standing there I thought to meself it ain't safe standin' there, now if it went now it would get anyone as was standin' there as 'e was. Then it parted. It dain't miss 'im but by inches" (pp. 40–41). Gossip often does more than simply dress up the truth; it often replaces it altogether. When Bridges posts men at the lavatory door to combat smoking there, Bob Bentley becomes convinced, for some reason, that the female factory inspector will find this obscene. When the guard is removed, Bentley triumphantly observes, "As soon as ever I saw a man put on there I said that's a thing a woman won't stand. I 'ad that factory inspector in me mind's eye. I thought to myself she'd never stand for it. And she didn't" (p. 82). And this version, despite all contradiction, despite the fact that no factory inspector has been seen, runs throughout the book as the accepted explanation, with only the reader aware that it is quite false. In the same way, Tupe's false version of Craigan's near accident, in which the molder is made to look like an incompetent malingerer, replaces the truth in the minds of the factory management.

Tupe is the spirit of such gossip, the archetypal apple-polisher who provides everyone with the story they most want to hear. His persuasive power is based on the principle of sensing and then reinforcing the self-image of his listener. Thus he helps Gates to see himself as traduced and exploited at home, supports Bridges in his role as chief victim of the factory, tells spurious secrets to the factoryworkers to make the management seem devious and cruel, and through it all sincerely believes in the truth of what he is saying: "This he meant and he was sincere in this for he saw many free drinks in money Joe would get from that old man" (p. 211). Tupe has no independent existence. He depends like a parasite on the myth of the moment, on the current of gossip, on the role provided by his interlocutor. Yet if there were no such myths, if his listeners had no surreptitious image of events and of themselves, Tupe would have no power.

It is a general principle in the factory, and not just a scheme of Tupe's, to provide individuals with fictionalized roles that precede and finally displace what the victim thinks is his or her true personality. This has already been observed in the way the workers turn Bridges into an abstraction, a comic "father." Craigan's tendency to think of people in terms of their job is general, even Gates feeling a loss of caste in his association with Tupe, not because Tupe is reprehensible in himself, but because Gates "was a step above a labourer" (p. 155). Tarver, the factory's chief designer, betrays the same habit of thought in his continual use of titles such as "Colonel" and "Squire" even when they are not appropriate. This is one of the ways groups arrange themselves, imposing roles to limit the surprises an individual can introduce. René Girard identifies this "eliminative function" in the small social circles in Proust, their ability simply to annihilate facts that cannot be assimilated into their version of the world.[28] In *Living* this function can be observed in the way that gossip sits as a censor over events and in the roles, both self-imposed and group-imposed, that become identical to the individual they contain. This is another of the continuing themes of Green's fiction which are announced in *Living,* the symbiosis between an individual and his social role, the immense convenience that a role provides as a governing fiction both for the individual and the group he is a member of.

These governing fictions, at the factory and in Craigan's home, are not maintained so much by autocratic rule as by unavoidable conditions of human communication. As Eudora Welty says, "The characters would like well enough to speak to each other but most of them are like us, not good at it. But they can create. To create is after all easier than to communicate."[29] Gossip replaces actuality and roles dominate individuals because these seem to make communication, and communion, easier, less hazardous. For the same reason, conversation becomes almost ritualistic. Green's characters rarely listen to one another because the purpose of conversation for them is not to convey information but to act out a dramatic image of themselves and to extract from their interlocutor the concession of an expected response. Bridges is the most adamant of such conversationalists, as the aftermath of a particularly thwarted exchange with Tarver shows:

> *Bridges said Tarver not to be gay with him, he was general manager, people could think they were fine, fine, but he was general manager, was no one disputed that,*

[28]Girard, pp. 198–99.
[29]Eudora Welty, "Henry Green: A Novelist of the Imagination," *Texas Quarterly,* 4 (Autumn 1961), 249.

> *and what he said was what went through in this firm. Mr. Tarver said what he had meant was he hadn't heard. Bridges went on not listening that he'd soon see who stuck himself up against him, whatever friends that one had in London office, he had his friends he'd see who was general manager, while Tarver speaking at same time said what he'd meant saying was pardon me, I could not hear you, girls in office make such noise giggling. Later Mr. Tarver was saying "Yes sir" and Father said "my boy" often then.* [p. 47]

Just as important as the initial misunderstanding and Bridges's tantrum are the code-word concessions both men use to smooth over the dispute. The kind of conversation that succeeds is obviously that which uses a few syllables for their incantatory quality, like the kind of noises made to quiet a frightened horse. These soothing code words, conveying no real meaning but paying homage to each man's role, signify repentance from Tarver and paternal pardon from Bridges and are the means they use to slip their relationship back onto the rails it has jumped.

Such exchanges occur throughout *Living,* with talk acting as a kind of smokescreen behind which people arrange their relationships. Even the question of whether to talk can become a struggle of two wills, as when young Dupret announces, "No, we're going to talk now. The point is this, when I say we're going to talk we're going to talk, from now on." When Bridges retorts, triumphantly, "Well you ain't going to make me talk" (p. 180), the role of talk as a struggle for power is made plain. Successful, satisfying talk tends to use words as meaningless counters, simple noises, the "things senseless as whistling birds" (p. 163) that Bert Jones says to Lily, the things they say to one another, "murmuring and not hearing what they murmured" (pp. 75–76). On one hand, then, talk is a contest, on the other something like a song, but in neither case does anyone listen to anyone else. Disharmony comes when two monologues confront each other, harmony when two voices have agreed, momentarily, to say nothing at all.

All of Green's characters fail to listen, the mimicry of some being the easiest, least thoughtful kind of response. Craigan's refusal to listen, on the other hand, represents integrity, because it is accompanied by a refusal to talk. He alone attempts to resist the process of gossip and word-trading by which the characters make themselves comfortable within the fictive consciousness of a group. As Green reports in *Pack My Bag*, he found in the Birmingham factory a kind of reserved silence that he admired more than clear speech. He found it in a factory girl who refused to respond to his conventional pleasantries: "I had not been speaking to the girl in her language whatever that may have been and she kept her attitude by not replying. . . . She was content . . . just to disagree without saying so, perhaps even to despite, but in any case she was self-confident enough to let it go and thus, if only by silence . . . to make herself real." Green contrasts this to the "gabble" of his school, and calls it "a kind of passionate self-confidence, . . . not joining in while still being a part . . . one of the happiest conditions within the reach of man."[30]

In *Living* only Craigan has the integrity not to listen and the self-confidence not to speak. The earphones through which he listens to German radio signify his isolation even from the talk at home. And in a number of instances his reticence is pointedly contrasted with the weak garrulity of Joe Gates. When Mrs. Eames comes from next door to release a bird trapped between windows, Gates attempts to be convivial by telling a dirty story, then tries to justify himself by pretending the insult is intentional, while Craigan gives the simple compliment: "They had to thank Mrs. Eames for what three men could not do" (p. 20). When Craigan is nearly killed by a defective cable, it is Gates who turns the accident into a drama, developing it into a story complete with dire foreshadowings, suspense, and fateful coincidence, while Craigan simply washes his hands. Craigan's verdict on Gates in general is "you talk more'n is natural in a man" (p. 33).

[30]Henry Green, *Pack My Bag*, pp. 232–33.

His reticence is the cause of a certain prejudice against Craigan in the foundry. By not trading in the chit-chat of the group he seems to be proudly setting himself apart, and nothing shows the purely social function of conversation more than this mistrust of Craigan's silence. Tupe begins a campaign against Craigan for no other reason than his refusal to talk: "He said to young man he was with was no man so deceitful as man he could see walking on other side of road if he looked. No man like it for deceit. And didn't he think a deal of himself for never saying much when that was easy as picking a tart up in this street. 'I could hold my gob for a day and a year if I so wanted' he said" (p. 52). In Tupe's mind the only reason for silence is cunning. To him silence seems a mask, but what Green shows through Tupe's own practice is that speech is the most effective mask, and the most candid man is the most silent. This is the source of both the strength and the weakness of the one story Craigan tells, the account of her Aunt Ellie's elopement which he tells to Lily. Not a particularly long story, it still astonishes Lily like a flood of words from another man: "So much talk from him frightened her" (p. 94). He tells the story without much emphasis or application, yet it leaves Lily in tears. However, his tact in not applying the story directly to her case allows Bert Jones to deflect its meaning. Lily says the message was "not what you might like put into words," but Jones scoffs, "D'you mean to tell me 'e can frighten you into trembles just by talking about something else to you?" (p. 104). Lily is close enough to Craigan to sense his unspoken warning, but Bert is not, and his victory is signified when Lily agrees to join him in incomprehension.

The truth is that Craigan is fighting a losing battle on all sides. When he loses his self-confidence along with his job and Lily, the change is expressed by a sudden desire to talk: "Always Mr. Craigan had prided himself on not lengthily talking. 'Many a man 'as lost everything by it,' he was fond of saying. But more and more now he felt a need to talk and seeing this in himself he said in mind that he was getting old"

(p. 181). Craigan can remain silent only as long as he feels self-sufficient. But his experience with the factory and with Lily both show that his own personal tradition of home life cannot be kept separate from the inner fantasies of others. Two dramas converge on Craigan as Green's way of showing how the personal fictions of a single individual can reach out to dominate the world of fact and determine reality, even for as proudly isolated a figure as Craigan.

The strongest single power impinging on the factory-workers is not economic need or political oppression but fantasy, and the basic struggle is over whose fictional self-image will impress its character on the collective life of the factory. Bridges's conception of himself as a benevolent and unappreciated father has already been described, as has the factory's ironic, mocking willingness to play the family. But Bridges's homely metaphor conflicts with the new spirit young Dupret intends to bring to things, a new spirit that is obviously formed out of Dupret's need to perform a different role in relation to the works.

Dupret's desire for "go, push," his nervous energy, his impatience with everything old, is part of a compensatory role he has fashioned for himself out of his disappointment at losing Hannah Glossop to a young man who seems to have more natural verve. Ironically, Dupret rejects the kind of solution that appeals to his workers: "One might go to foreign countries but what was in these but nausea of traveling, hotels, trains, languages you did not know, Americans?" (p. 171). His romanticism is exactly the opposite of Herbert Tomson's, always dreaming of Australia, or Lily's. Dupret romanticizes the life of work they are dying to escape: "Besides it was work he wanted. . . . He would take Walters and Archer and they would spend a week or two there. They would have a grand clear out . . . an early spring cleaning. Work, that was it, he would work" (p. 171). Dupret cries for work as Hannah Glossop does herself, remembering how she "had enjoyed enormously General Strike when she had carried plates from one hut to another all day" (p. 117). Both of them construct a fantasyland of work where to work means to take yourself in hand, to gain control, to give direction to a stream of incoherent experiences, not as it is for the real workers, to lose power and personal control.

This is the genesis of the layoff of older workers which throws Craigan out of a job. Dupret is feverish for action, and his subordinates Tarver and Archer accommodate him: "But Mr. Dupret said constantly in his mind, 'I must work, work.' After Miss Glossop it was most necessary for him to do something tangible violently, and in this Mr. Archer, and Tarver also, egged him on" (p. 197). They do so because Dupret's fantasy meshes with ones of their own. Tarver is himself frantic for go and push, feverish with the feeling that he is a young man cruelly kept down. Archer, his superior, simply falls in: "This was the opportunity. . . . young Mr. Dupret would be wanting to do something, to assert himself. Now he would work in with young Mr. Dupret, now young Mr. Dupret could splash about, would want to" (p. 56). Bridges is pushed aside because his only advocate in upper management, Walters, identifies himself so much with the factory he is afraid to oppose Dupret for fear of dismissal, a fear he rationalizes as concern for the business: "As all his life he had worked in this business he saw it as his own creation, and did not care to think of that work undone through Tarver's inexperience" (p. 197). Every actor in this drama thinks of the business as his own creation, and each individual defends his business ideas as he would defend some intimate part of himself. The business becomes for them the book in which they rewrite their lives in larger and happier terms. But Green's basic point is that such habits of thought are not doomed because someone will emerge victorious from the squabble and will be successful in forming reality to fit his psychological needs. The everyday lives of the twelve men who are laid off are altered irrevocably because Dupret wins, because his need for action requires that something, anything, be done.

Such alterations of reality are not, however, exclusive to owners of large factories. The other drama that converges with this one on Craigan and transforms his life, the elopement of Lily Gates, follows the same pattern. Lily's dissatisfaction with life at Craigan's begins with a dream she has of a street full of women and "to each one a child" (p. 109). Her subsequent desire for a child of her own is not a desire for offspring as such but an expression of the need to have something of her own, which is ultimately only the need to feel herself as an independent being, outside the routines of the house: "She cried in her, I, I am I. I am I, why do I do work of this house, unloved work, why but they cannot find other woman to do this work. Why may I not have children . . . Why may I not work for mine? . . . Why is there nothing that lives by me" (p. 109). Lily suffers from the artificial nature of Craigan's household, serving two unrelated men and a father who has surrendered his ties to her, instead of a husband and her own children. She feels the need to make a household that is an extension of herself as the factory is for Walters, Dupret, Bridges, and Tarver.

To realize this independent life, Lily attaches herself to Bert Jones. But Jones is nothing more than a necessary fiction. Lily knows that he has few virtues in himself, but is confident of her own ability to mold him: "She knew him that he was not a dependable worker. . . . but she thought when they were married he would be quieter, it would be the responsibility would make him so" (p. 152). And she does in fact succeed in remaking Jones even before their elopement, not because he becomes quieter or more dependable, but because he senses her fears and is afraid to appear as he really is, telling Lily that he is going to a technical school regularly in the evenings when he has in fact ceased to go.

Lily's conception of the new life she and Jones will lead is so strong it acquires a momentum of its own, altering their relationship as it alters Jones. Thus, even before they run away "nearly all spontaneity had gone of their relations to each other" (p. 175), because they both feel the need to act up to their resolve to leave. Though Lily's desire to leave Birmingham comes from a desire to truly become the "I" she feels is thwarted at Craigan's, that desire itself becomes a role as restrictive as the old one. Green symbolizes her powerlessness before her own fiction in the train ride that takes them from Birmingham to Liverpool. At Derby, Lily sees a girl whose "clothes were so much exactly what she liked that seeing her walking there, it might have been her twin" (p. 219). The twin is being courted on a slag heap by a twin of Bert's, and the scene is so familiar that it dramatizes what they are leaving behind: "But O it was so safe and comfortable what that girl was wearing. Temptation clutched at her. . . . Miss Gates felt she didn't want to walk any place where she hadn't walked before. Or to wear any clothes but what that girl and she liked, and that only where there would be others who liked those clothes." But the train pulls them away from this scene of tempting familiarity and Lily feels trapped inside, where even the "underclothes she was now wearing were strange to her, she had made them for this" (p. 224). The momentum of the train and the clothes that feel so alien symbolize the project that carries Lily forward even after she has changed her mind, as if she were trapped inside a false personality she had created for herself.

The horror of Liverpool, their destination, thus resides chiefly in its unfamiliarity. The impact of the noise and confusion of the city on Lily is reminiscent of the way London disorients John Haye in *Blindness*. Lily certainly becomes the first in a line of characters to mimic Haye in her reaction to unpleasantness: "Well she just wouldn't look anymore if it only made her shivery, she just wouldn't notice anything more. . . . she wouldn't look that's all" (p. 231). Finally, she becomes "blank, blank" (p. 236), so blank she hardly realizes what is happening when Bert, in despair at being unable to find his parents as he had promised, cuts and runs.

Lily's decision not to look is the key to her actions for the rest of the book. Even in the utter defeat of her plans for elopement and a better life, she has replaced her old reality with a self-created fiction and completely reordered the routine of the Craigan household. She transforms Jones's ignominious flight into a much more dramatically satisfying, yet fictional, version of itself: "Then 'e took me to a road where the trams went and I thought we was just going on again but I was crying then and no wonder and there, he said, said she extemporising but she believed now he had said it, which he never had, 'well Lil it's goodbye now he says, I ain't no good, you'd better go 'ome' " (p. 244). Like all the other characters who convince themselves that their fictions are true, Lily replaces unpleasant facts with a creation of her own, making Jones look honest even if he is cowardly. Lily begins, in fact, to live in an entirely fictional world. She resembles John Haye more and more as she settles simultaneously into convalescence and solipsism. The two go together here as they do in *Blindness* because Lily comes to think of herself as a "case," as someone settling down to a life cut off from actuality, as an island: "She thought Mr. Jones leaving her like he had done was more and more right and proper, only she was not now interested in him,—she was sure she would never set eyes on him again. That land round which she steamed was every inch of it her own, her case still enchanted her as she kept watch on it" (p. 255). She succeeds here much more completely than she ever could have with Bert in realizing her first dream, her first cry of identity, "I am I," and does so by the same means that Haye uses, withdrawal from the obstinate facts into a private convalescence. She is both island and circling steamer, the center of her own attention, the single character in her own fictional case study.

 Her elopement has the same effect on Craigan, who also takes to his bed, "enchanted" with the unrealizable image of Aunt Ellie. So superficially unlike John Haye, Craigan is implicitly compared to him in the description of his youth, "where he had to go looking through the lanes to find Lily in her aunt Ellie as they both of them had once been," an image that "enchanted him like noise of bells" (pp. 255–56). The two women with their similar names, with their existence dependent on memory, and the bells that are associated with them make this last description of Craigan reminiscent of John Haye, similarly enchanted by bells on the last page of *Blindness*. The Craigan household breaks up into its components at the end of *Living,* each member withdrawing into his or her chosen enchantment, even Joe Gates becoming "transfixed" at a football match. He and his friend Aaron Connolly "took no notice of the crowd, no notice," alone in their own enthusiasm (p. 266). Green drops Dupret and the factory as soon as Craigan has been fired because that plot line has reached its natural completion, as one personal fantasy has come to dominate a corporate body. In the rest of the novel Green shows how the small-scale corporate life of the Craigan household comes apart under the centripetal force of private fictions, each individual sent off by the momentum of his or her own personal kind of enchantment. Yet the peculiar mood of the end of *Living* comes from the fact that such a disintegration does not seem to make the characters particularly sad. After having struggled to impose a certain fantasy on real life, Craigan and Lily relax in their failure and fall back on what had always been present as a kind of cushion, the fantasy itself. The relative repose they find in convalescence suggests that for them, as for all the characters in *Living* and for Green's characters to come, the issues determining a satisfactory life are less the actual ones of employment, marriage, and health than the insubstantial ones of symbolism, drama, and narrative form. This is what living is, as Green defines it, not a progressive struggle toward authenticity, but a search for a more satisfactory, more final, fiction. The most basic human need is for fictional symmetry, for the kind of closure that can be provided by catastrophe as well as by success, so that failure hardly matters as long as one's life is a story worth telling.

III

When Craigan is laid off from the Dupret factory, his life collapses from the sudden lack of routine, a necessity Green describes by this simile: "Like on a train which goes through night smoothly and at an even pace—so monotony of noise made by the wheels bumping over joints between the rails becomes rhythm—so this monotony of hours grows to be the habit and regulation on which we grow old" (p. 204). Craigan, suddenly bereft of habit and regulation, is compared to a stopped train: "Like as if train had stopped outside a station but now it draws in where he must get out" (p. 205). In *Party Going* his situation becomes general, as an entire city full of people, commuting according to what should be an immutable routine, is stopped dead by fog. Both the partygoers who are the focus of this novel and the huge crowd that surrounds them are stalled in a sudden interregnum between routines. Like John Haye, whose train ride comes to a sudden end with his blindness, the two groups are deprived of their normal momentum, their normal monotony, and Green's interest, as in his first two novels, is focused on their construction of a new routine in the vacuum.

Party Going, which ends with the subscript "London, 1931–1938," is Green's only work to be published in the thirties. Yet it spans the decade, not just chronologically, but in the way it brings the subject matter and the stock imagery of the early thirties into collision with the political realities of 1939. If Green had begun the novel in 1938, it is unlikely that he would have chosen so outmoded a subject as a group of partygoers waiting to board a train, a subject reminiscent of the Railway Club Green belonged to at Oxford in the twenties and of the notoriously fashionable parties Waugh lampoons in *Vile Bodies* (1930). And if the novel had been finished in 1931, it is unlikely to have contained the hints of bombing and of air-raid shelters that make it prophetic of the Blitz. During the long composition, prolonged for whatever reason, Green's characters and his subject aged as the decade did, the ignorant, privileged world left over from the twenties infected with the mood of Munich.[31]

The central situation, trains paralyzed by fog and the train station in chaos, represents Green's transformation of a common metaphor of the thirties. For poets like Spender and Day Lewis in their first flush of revolutionary enthusiasm, the train was a metaphor for automatic, inevitable progress. The classic example of this is Spender's "The Express," in which the

---

[31]The exact details of the composition of *Party Going* are difficult to establish. Green told John Russell that the book required "nine or ten beginnings" ("There It Is," *Kenyon Review,* 26 [Summer 1964], 443). This would seem to imply that the bulk of the book was written toward the end of the 1931–38 period. On the other hand, John Lehmann, who eventually accepted *Party Going* in 1938 for Hogarth Press, believes that it had been lying "in a drawer for some years" and had been refused by several other publishers (*In My Own Time* [Boston: Little, Brown, 1969], p. 222).

train, rather than seeming heavy or mechanical, is instead "light, aerial," expressed more by the clean, geometric rail than the engine itself, and free to traverse "new eras of white happiness." Another example is the fifth poem in *The Magnetic Mountain,* in which Day Lewis identifies radical impatience with the locomotive's incompressible steam: "Let us be off! Our steam / Is deafening the dome." Or there is what Auden calls the "strict beauty of locomotive," the clean, surgical completeness of its method of progress.[32] Bernard Bergonzi identifies these poems and the whole school of pylon poetry with Italian futurism, with the romance of guns, planes, and locomotives publicized by Marinetti.[33] Yet despite a few bullying poems written by Day Lewis and Auden, British "futurism" seems more passive than Italian, as Spender's tenderness with planes and locomotives suggests. Technology in Spender's poems is neither violent nor threatening, but soothing, as in this statement from Auden and Isherwood's *Journey to a War:* "There was nothing we could do either to hinder or assist. Everyday life, so complex and anxious, was soothingly simplified to the narrowness of a single railway track. Our little egotisms, our ambitions, our vanities, were absorbed, identified utterly with the rush of the speeding train."[34] The nearly sexual ecstasy of "The Express" is made possible by a similar identification, with life stripped down to a single, clean trajectory. This sense of gratitude and joy at being propelled without decision or effort appears even at the end of the decade, in David Gascoyne's "Farewell Chorus," written for the new year of 1940, in relief that the long-expected war has finally begun: "And so! the long black pullman is at last departing, now, / After those undermining years of angry waiting and cold tea."[35] Above all, the train means simplification, the soothing simplification of motion,

---

[32]Stephen Spender, *Poems* (London: Faber and Faber, 1933), p. 53; C. Day Lewis, *Collected Poems, 1929–1933* (New York: Random House, 1935), p. 111; Auden, *The English Auden,* p. 38.

[33]Bergonzi, pp. 90–110.

[34]W. H. Auden and Christopher Isherwood, *Journey to a War* (New York: Random House, 1939), p. 128.

[35]David Gascoyne, *Collected Poems* (London: Oxford Univ. Press, 1965), pp. 82–83.

of being in transit, yet with no responsibility for direction or destination. In this sense the train can be compared to the myth of the working class as enunciated by Upward and Day Lewis in the way it offers an assured future and a chance to elude the subjective confusion of the individual. One boards the train in the same way one attaches oneself to the cause of the workers, sitting back to let history do the rest.

When the trains refuse to run in *Party Going,* therefore, the central situation has a particular literary significance. The title, considered as a participle, has an especially sardonic tone, since the group is frozen in the act of going, but cannot actually go. The title is, as Frederick Karl says, a verb manqué, describing but not enacting its action.[36] The train, which is such a symbol of ease and freedom for Spender, is the cause of this paralysis, stopped as it is by the almost comically insubstantial fog. It is as if the thirties symbol of progress were being purposely inverted to be used as a symbol of the helplessness of technology against the simple elements, and by extension, of the wreck of the political hopes associated with technological symbolism. In this Green is simply anticipating a reversal in the symbol by the pylon poets themselves. Louis MacNeice uses the train as a symbol in this way in *Autumn Journal* to represent a false sense of progress suddenly interrupted:

> *We slept in linen, we cooked with wine,*
> > *We paid in cash and took no notice,*
> *Of how the train ran down the line*
> > *Into the sun against the signal.*[37]

What both Green and MacNeice do is to use the symbol of the early thirties to describe the mood of the late thirties, a mood that came to be described by a number of writers in the metaphor of the waiting room rather than that of the

---

[36]Frederick R. Karl, *The Contemporary English Novel* (New York: Farrar, Straus and Cudahy, 1962), p. 184.

[37]Louis MacNeice, *Autumn Journal* (New York: Random House, 1939), p. 34.

train. Cyril Connolly does so in his first "Comment" for *Horizon*: "At the moment civilization is on the operating table and we sit in the waiting room." The mood is the same for Spender, who says in "September Journal," "We live in a kind of vacuum now in which the events on which we are waiting have not yet caught up on us, though our hour is very near." Samuel Hynes maintains that the whole character of the Auden generation changed around 1938, when the momentum of events turned against leftists like Spender, and "passive waiting for disaster" replaced speed as a metaphor.[38]

The central situation of *Party Going* therefore brings together two major metaphorical usages of the decade, stopping the train outside the waiting room that was to symbolize British experience from Munich to the Blitz. *Party Going* is part of a body of literature taking its character from the fear and stasis of the time, a body that also includes the autobiographical works included in the first chapter. Accommodating that mood of helplessness required a certain reversal for writers like Spender, which is accomplished partly by autobiographical reconsideration of their lives, but the subject is a natural one for Green, since a sudden loss of psychological momentum is one of the themes of his first two novels. And since he was never close to the political movements of the thirties, Green's treatment of the crisis is less political than psychological. His use of the train metaphor is obviously not polemical. Instead, he takes it as the common, received metaphor for the confidence that progress engenders and transforms it to show the psychological reactions of a group whose confidence is undermined.

Roberta White has pointed out how Green's basic metaphor differs from the romantic conception of railway stations found in *Howards End*. To Margaret Schlegel the various London stations "are our gates to the glorious and unknown. . . . To Margaret . . . the station of King's Cross

---

[38]Connolly's "Comment" is reprinted in Spender's *The Thirties and After*, p. 65. Spender's statement appears on p. 94. Hynes discusses "passive waiting for disaster" in *The Auden Generation*, p. 335.

has always suggested Infinity."³⁹ Green's station, on the other hand, suggests limitation, all yearnings toward infinity thwarted. The psychological impact of this loss is apparent first in the character of Miss Fellowes, in her bout with the inexplicable dead pigeon, and the troublesome pall she casts over the partygoers herself. The pigeon enters Miss Fellowes's life by striking a balustrade and falling "dead, at her feet."⁴⁰ At the most basic level the dead pigeon stands for the problem all the partygoers encounter, the blank wall that stops their progress. But it also starts a chain reaction of mystification and unease, becoming itself a blank wall that stops all attempts at sensible explanation. Miss Fellowes picks up the dead pigeon on impulse and carries it into the station, "everything unexplained" (p. 7). Her impulse is toward tidiness. Thinking the pigeon must be dirty, she commences to wash it and then wraps it up in paper and string. The physical actions mimic Miss Fellowes's mental habits: "Miss Fellowes did not care, she could dismiss things of that kind from her mind and entirely ignore at will anything unpleasant" (p. 24). Washing and wrapping the pigeon is her way of denaturing an inexplicable detail, of making the outré detail fit. Washing it appears to her as "a pious thing" (p. 25). Her piety is devoted to making sense of things, but the pigeon has a way of attracting to itself other inexplicable details like a drop of mercury incorporating smaller drops: "Any dead animal shocked one in London. . . . She remembered how her father had shot his dog when she was small and how much they had cried. There was that poor boy Cumberland . . . what had he died of so young? One did not seem to expect it when one was cooped up in London and then to fall like that dead at her feet" (p. 25). The syntactical confusion of the last line incorporates the untimely death, her own confusion, and the

---

³⁹Roberta Horton White's analysis appears in her dissertation, "The Imagination of Henry Green," Stanford, 1969, pp. 99–100. The quotation is from *Howards End* (1910; rpt. New York: Random House, Vintage, 1954), p. 12.

⁴⁰Henry Green, *Party Going* (London, 1939; rpt. New York: Viking, 1951), p. 7. All subsequent references are to this edition and in this chapter will appear in text.

pigeon, so that any one of the three could be the subject that falls dead at the end. And Miss Fellowes does fall, becoming inexplicably ill, fighting "storms of darkness which rolled up over her in a series, like tides summoned by a moon" (p. 72).

This illness becomes a central preoccupation of the partygoers, an obstacle to their plans, and a theme of obvious importance to Green, yet he refuses to diagnose it or to make clear the relationship between it and the pigeon. His treatment of the problem presented by Miss Fellowes resembles another of Forster's characters, one who finds travel less indicative of hope and infinity than Margaret Schlegel, Mrs. Moore in *A Passage to India*. Both Miss Fellowes and Mrs. Moore are tangential to the primary action of the respective novels. Both have come to see young relatives safely launched and so might be expected to be preoccupied with beginnings. Yet both become concentrated instead on death and languish as a burden to the young people they were supposed to help. Miss Fellowes's loss of control after finding the dead pigeon resembles Mrs. Moore's loss of heart at the Marabar caves. In both cases a chance brush with something nasty and vile saps the character's will to live. And Green's reticence about Miss Fellowes's exact condition resembles Forster's reticence about the episode in the caves and might stem from the same reluctance to be specific about an episode that is fearsome and disturbing precisely because its exact character remains unknown. To explain the pigeon is to remove its threat, and to be more explicit about Miss Fellowes's illness would be to remove exactly the aspect that makes it so disturbing to the partygoers.

Like Mrs. Moore, Miss Fellowes becomes a dead weight on the party she has come to see off. For her niece, Claire Hignam, and Claire's friend Evelyn Henderson, she becomes a physical block, a burden so long as her illness seems to require their presence. But Miss Fellowes has also acquired by transference the mysteriousness of the dead pigeon, and lies before the party as the kind of outré detail that must be washed and tied with string. As Frank Kermode says, "Once loose in the text, the pigeon seems to alight at random on anything,"⁴¹ and wherever it alights it poses the same sort of epistemological problem: " 'I think that what we are both afraid of,' said Evelyn, 'is that parcel she had and what was inside it' " (p. 211). Miss Fellowes tests the ability of Claire and Evelyn to absorb or ignore the inexplicable just as the pigeon had tested hers. Evelyn follows the same procedure of isolating the inexplicable so as to shunt it aside: "You know I have absolute faith in searching out whatever it is that is really worrying one underneath what seems on the surface to be the matter with anything. . . . And I know in my case it was her having picked that pigeon up somewhere and then seeming so ill. . . . I'm sure that's what's been worrying us, but when you come to think of it, darling, there's nothing in it, is there? . . . Anyway, it is definitely not a thing to worry about" (p. 212). In the same way, Evelyn cleverly removes the physical obstacle by convincing Claire that Miss Fellowes, ill or not, cannot benefit from their attendance. Her job is to help her friend "ignore at will anything unpleasant."

Miss Fellowes presents the same kind of problem for each of the partygoers, and each one solves it in a characteristic way. Max Adey, the rich patron of the group, has Miss Fellowes hustled up the back stairs to a private room, and having spent money on the problem, considers it solved. Julia Wray, seeing Miss Fellowes in her sickbed, hears "the authentic threatening knock of doom she listened for so much when things were not going right" (p. 244). The particular doom Miss Fellowes represents to a young woman like Julia is the collapse of appearance. And Miss Fellowes's face seems aged, ironically, "as if she had been travelling." Yet Julia is able to ignore this, since "it was impossible for anything to upset her now they were really going" (p. 244). Miss Fellowes poses a very peculiar kind of epistemological problem for Robert Hignam. Having been sent to find Max, Robert inexplicably asks for Miss Fellowes, and then, to his own surprise, sees her, just as she is beginning to feel ill. The

⁴¹Frank Kermode, *The Genesis of Secrecy: On the Interpretation of Narrative* (Cambridge: Harvard Univ. Press, 1979), p. 9.

unexpectedness of his own conduct fascinates Robert, who tells this story to everyone who will listen. He feels as if his slip of the tongue has conjured Miss Fellowes up, that, having misspoken, he has altered the order of things and destroyed their coherence. It is the kind of small-scale mental aberration which occurs and is forgotten in a second but which, to Robert's dismay, has become a sick woman they can't get rid of.

Finally, Miss Fellowes becomes associated with the mystery man whom Frank Kermode calls the Hermes figure of the novel.[42] This man first sees Miss Fellowes in the bar where she begins to feel ill, follows the party that takes her up to a room, and then haunts the hallway to the confusion and annoyance of the group. What is particularly disturbing to them is that the man can't be placed. The normal social clues are scrambled and useless where he is concerned. The man's accent changes from Yorkshire to Brummagem to BBC English. His demeanour is alternately blustering and cringing. It is revealing that the most threatening kind of figure to this group is one that has no apparent social context. By remaining free of class definition, he gains power over them, as when Alex Alexander feels constrained to offer him a drink out of fear that he may be the hotel detective.

The pigeon, therefore, starts a chain reaction by which its mystery is passed on, first to Miss Fellowes, then to the man in the hallway, increasing with each step the size of the group it can paralyze. It is by means of the pigeon and its attendant mysteries that the physical obstruction of the fog is identified with the mental obstruction of the inexplicable, and the helplessness of technology against the elements comes to signify the helplessness of the mind against the kind of final uncertainties that paralyze Miss Fellowes and Mrs. Moore. If the train stands in the early thirties for certainty and simplicity, its lack of progress here signifies the impossibility of being certain; like the pigeon and the people in the station, it strikes a blank wall. For this reason, any attempt to fill out the pigeon

---

[42]Ibid., pp. 7–9.

or the mystery man with a specific allegorical meaning, as A. Kingsley Weatherhead has done, is not only doomed but is inimical to Green's purpose. *Party Going* has been called Kafkaesque for its atmosphere of purposeless waiting and for a few lurid, almost expressionist crowd scenes.[43] But it is most Kafkaesque in the simple inexplicability of the pigeon, which appears as the indescribable Odradek does in "Cares of a Family Man" and terrifies because it eludes explanation. Walter Allen compares Upward's *Journey to the Border,* another Kafkaesque novel of the thirties, unfavorably to *Party Going,* for precisely this reason, because *Journey to the Border* "can be paraphrased, it is 'about' something, a moral can be extracted as you can extract no moral from Kafka."[44] The reason that Upward's work can be paraphrased is that it recommends a certain course of action, implies, by its very title, the kind of progress toward a new country celebrated in poems like "The Express." The pigeon is unparaphrasable precisely because Green has no moral, no extractable message, because his train passengers are tied up waiting to cross a border they may never reach.

The resistance of this central symbol to analysis has been one of the obstacles to a critical understanding of the novel as a whole. Another obstacle is the assumption that Green uses only one kind of symbol, that all his birds, for example, must be reducible to one level of meaning.[45] But in *Party Going* in particular Green uses symbols in an entirely different way than his characters do. When questioned in the fifties about his symbolism, Green referred the interviewer to "a book by W. B. Yeats on Blake."[46] All of Yeats's writing on Blake begins with and insists on a basic distinction between two kinds of symbol: one suggestive, indefinable, and visionary, the other simply emblematic: "the one is a revelation,

---

[43]Weatherhead's analysis of the pigeon is on pp. 46–47. He compares the book to Kafka on p. 42. Stokes compares it to Kafka on p. 148.
[44]Walter Allen, "An Artist of the Thirties," p. 156.
[45]See, for example, Odom, p. 65, and Russell, pp. 107–8.
[46]Lambourne, p. 67.

the other an amusement."[47] This distinction is basic to *Party Going* as well, offering a way to differentiate between the truly untranslatable symbol, such as the pigeon, and the mere emblems that Green's characters use as a kind of game or as charms to conjure away the threat of that central symbol. Roberta White has defined the symbols in *Party Going* as totems or tokens, arbitrary, changeable symbols used in an almost mechanical way. Bruce Johnson believes that the symbols are "deliberately made to look somewhat ridiculous" as part of Green's belief that "symbolizing is essentially a childish, comic, often ludicrous process of conferring significance on something that has no business meaning anything of the sort."[48] But Green's central symbol is quite a serious one, and the threat presented by the dead pigeon and then by Miss Fellowes is not comic. The symbols used by his characters in their own lives, however, are bathetic, childish, and are so precisely because the threat from that central mystery is so real. Eudora Welty says, in her article on Green, "Signs, omens, charms and works . . . everything sweet or formidable that we go provided with, all in the end will tell what we tried to provide against."[49] Green's characters choose symbols for themselves, and use one another as symbols, in order to protect themselves against the unknown and to define themselves against unpleasant realities they would like to exclude.

The character in *Party Going* who is most in thrall to her personal symbols is Julia Wray, who seems to be a surviving version of Constance, the heroine of Green's unfinished novel, *Mood*. In his 1959 article on *Mood*, Green calls symbolism "the love for a significant object," and each of the characters seems to have been provided with a personal talisman on the

---

[47]W. B. Yeats, "William Blake and His Illustrations to the *Divine Comedy*," in *Essays and Introductions* (New York: Macmillan, 1961), p. 116. The same distinction is repeated in "Symbolism in Painting," pp. 146–47.

[48]White, p. 128; Bruce Johnson, "Henry Green's Comic Symbolism," *Ball State University Forum*, 6 (Autumn 1965), 32.

[49]Welty, p. 247.

order of a lucky charm. Constance has two toy airplanes, which symbolize her relationship with her friend Celia: "Although she had been alone when that aeroplane came overhead yet she had bought two toy aeroplanes, one loveliness for each of them. . . . And Constance who had looked on the aeroplanes as one and the same and had held neither in preference to the other, had chosen one of the two for her own when Celia married, a secret one." The particular appeal of this kind of personal symbol is that its significance is secret, and therefore hers alone: "Nobody would ever know, she sang as she looked about her in Oxford Street, no one, not one of these, not even mother, nobody would know about those aeroplanes."[50]

Green refers to these airplanes as Constance's "pets," while Julia refers to her trinkets as "mascots." Julia's term seems more appropriate, because in either case the symbol stands for the particular character of a tiny group, distinguishing it from all nonmembers. Julia's mascots are her charms, a top, a toy pistol, and a wooden egg. Utterly trivial in themselves, the charms acquire significance by being kept secret. As a child she had buried the pistol in a bamboo grove where she often played with Robert Hignam, which made the grove a place sacred to her, exciting "because the others did not know" (p. 109). The secret is her way of seizing possession of the bamboo grove even though others play there, a way of making it secretly "hers." The charms become so much a mark of her personality that they become necessary for Julia to feel that she is truly herself. They are her ballast, as in the childhood memory in which the weight of the wooden egg seems to keep her from being blown away (p. 110). Julia's method of flirtation, therefore, is to half-reveal the story of the charms. In a kind of psychological striptease she reveals them one after the other to Max, who does not apparently realize that she is really offering herself. When she teases, "I shan't be

---

[50]Henry Green, "An Unfinished Novel," *London Magazine,* 4 (Apr. 1959), 17.

able to tell you about my top," he thinks, "bother her top" (p. 113).

Max's method is to attack directly, not realizing that Julia habitually thinks in terms of symbols and is more accessible by way of her charms. The charms are just an extreme example of Julia's normal way of thought, which is to take chance occurrences into the realm of symbol where they can be altered and their significance manipulated to her advantage. When she sees three sea gulls on her way to the station, she thinks, "Those gulls were for the sea they were to cross that evening" (p. 19). By the time she and Max have begun to spar, the gulls have become "that promise of the birds which had flown under the arch," a promise that will be fulfilled "if only, as seemed likely, she could see sea-gulls that night on their crossing" (p. 151). Julia carefully chooses only those omens that are likely to be fulfilled, but she also alters the physical nature of the occurrence to heighten its appropriateness to her situation: "And now she remembered those two birds which had flown under the arch she had been on when she had started, and now she forgot they were sea-gulls and thought they had been doves and so was comforted" (p. 161). The three gulls become two doves the better to symbolize herself and Max, flying in tandem. This transformation of reality is childish, and as the very word *charms* implies, it is done to protect Julia against unpleasantness or threat. It is a version of Evelyn Henderson's commonsensical debunking of the unknown, only conducted on the primitive level of magical spells.

Though Julia is the most extreme example, she is not alone, because the whole group tends to symbolize itself by certain charms, the secrets of which define the group by excluding outsiders and therefore protect it. When Frank Kermode chooses *Party Going* as an example to begin *The Genesis of Secrecy,* he concentrates on the Hermetic mystery man and so misses the way that the partygoers as a group live by the verse from Mark that is his basic text: "For those outside everything is in parables, so that they may indeed see but not perceive, and may indeed hear but not understand; lest they should turn again, and be forgiven" (Mark 4:11–12). This is the crux of Kermode's discussion, that parables or riddles are meant to exclude those already on the outside, and this is certainly the function of the personal parables of the partygoers.[51] The group has separated itself from the bulk of those waiting for trains by moving into the hotel, and has been further segregated and protected by steel shutters, but they still feel somehow the ancient need to expel the outsider, and their scapegoat is the obnoxious Angela Crevy. As the newest member of the group she is denied secrets, such as the condition of Miss Fellowes. There seems to be no good reason to make this illness into a mystery, and Robert Hignam compares it to their childhood mystery of the bamboo grove, remembering that "Claire was practically brought up with us, wasn't she, when we were small and when she was sent over to play with us you know we never told her about the bamboos" (p. 61). Thus the exclusion once practiced childishly on Claire is now being turned on Angela.

The primary parable, however, is the story of Embassy Richard, an incredibly trivial social episode that is told and retold mainly to give the various members of the group the opportunity to offer inside information and thus show off their status as insiders. Angela commits an immediate gaffe by calling him "Embassy Dick," a mistake so prodigious that Alex corrects her very gently lest he crush her altogether. This makes Angela feel "out of it, that they were keeping things from her," and it makes her decide to reveal some inside information of her own, about Embassy Richard and a certain Prince Royal, to "go for" Alex, since he has been so tiresome (p. 66). But her need to be accepted is too obvious, and Evelyn dismisses all her offerings of gossip by saying, "She's trying to be one of us" (p. 155).

In a strange way, the "mascot" of the group, the "significant object" by which they all identify themselves, is Max Adey. By popular demand Max's life has been turned into

[51]Kermode, pp. 2–3.

myth, a romance invented by others displacing the facts: "It was generally believed that he had lived with this rich lady, there was hardly anyone who would not have sworn this was the case, and indeed they were on such terms that both were glad to admit they had. As it happened they had on no occasion had anything to do with each other" (p. 89). The odd thing about Max is his cheerful acquiescence in this myth, the way he manfully tries to live up to the stories told about him and acts out the character popularly ascribed to him. It seems, for example, that his refusal to allow anyone else in his party to pay for anything is simply reverence for his own image: " 'Can't have it,' he said cheerfully, as people do when they are living up to their own characters" (p. 189). John Russell says that Max is "living up to an image of himself he has had too much time to construct,"[52] but the truth seems more curious. Max is willfully becoming a figurehead for the group, a person who accepts the caricatured version of himself that appears in gossip and patterns his actions to corroborate that myth.

As such, Max is more than just the economic sponsor of the group, the richest man who pays all the bills. In a symbolic sense he is the group, and members assert their familiarity with his past and his routine as a way of showing that they belong. When Amabel mentions "the sloe gin Max gives out shooting," Julia compares it to port, "to show she had been out with him too" (p. 198). Amabel and Julia collaborate to exclude poor Angela, telling teasing anecdotes of past outings, piquing her curiosity and then refusing to elaborate. Angela tries to thrust herself into the group by claiming to have been on previous trips with Max, but since no one believes her, and since her in-group details all tend, like her rendering of Embassy Richard's name, to be a little off, she ignominiously fails. Max becomes another symbol, like Embassy Richard or the bamboo grove, which brings past intimacy and the enjoyment of secrecy together to constitute a group. This suggests a second significance for the title.

[52]Russell, p. 77.

Instead of designating a party on the Continent to which they are going, it could be using *party* in the sense of "group." Green may be intending to show what constitutes a group, what rules go to make it up, and how it defines itself against those who must remain outside in order to give the party its shape. The group needs such outsiders as Angela Crevy, particularly when it feels itself threatened, when, because of the fog and the inconvenience, the party almost collapses. In the face of the fog, the disappointment, the chants of the crowd below, the specter of Miss Fellowes, they need symbols like Max as protection, as a reassertion of their fundamental identity and their power over events.

The only outsider who can hope to prevail against such a group is one who has an awareness of its methods and who can manipulate them better than the group itself. Only Max Adey's mistress, Amabel, qualifies, who goes from being purposely excluded from the trip to being, as Max assures her, its central figure and reason for existence. Amabel seems to belong, with Max, to a race apart composed of people who are so used to seeing themselves as symbols of the aspirations of those below them that they become those symbols. "Amabel had been sanctified . . . by constant printed references as though it was of general concern what she looked like or how beautiful she might be." As Evelyn decides, she "had grown to be like some beauty spot in Wales" (p. 145). That Amabel appreciates herself in the same way is made plain by the way she gives herself a bath, tracing her name in the steam of the mirror and looking back at herself "through the letters of her name" (p. 171). She is obviously the kind of person who thinks of herself as a name, especially a name in the mouths of others. She even sees her own body as though from outside, as something she might work on and perfect, to make it less herself than a symbol of herself: "When she dried her breasts she wiped them with as much care as she would puppies after she had given them their bath, smiling all the time. But her stomach she wiped unsmiling upwards to make it thin. When she came to dry her legs she hissed like grooms do" (p. 173). Like Max, she has a character to live up to, which in her case is her physical beauty, sanctified by its reputation. She has become, in fact, in the eyes of disgruntled acquaintances like Evelyn, more her reputation than herself.

This awareness of her reputation, and the willingness to use it, is the source of her power. She senses in the group that longing to identify itself with a symbol that makes them tag along after Max, and uses it to her own advantage by converting individuals temporarily to her own worship. She understands that the way to convert is to offer secrets, as she does to the most eager of the group, Angela Crevy: "She began to make secrets which was her way when she did not know how things would turn out. Whispering so those others could not hear, she said how nice it was to see Angela" (p. 138). The simple act of splitting Angela off from the group and of making the others jealous by seeming to confide in her is much more important than the information conveyed here, which is, in fact, of no real significance. Amabel understands the power of appearance, so she concocts the appearance of having a little group of her own. She increases her own prestige by seeming to be exclusive, but is, in fact, exclusive with a number of the partygoers in turn, cutting the party up and making each victim feel like a special group of one until she has converted them piecemeal to her own worship. Even Max is unaware of the multiple contradictions in her story and forgets his original intentions for the trip after she grills him alone.

Amabel can succeed only because certain members of the group, such as Angela and Alex, are willing to abandon their own personalities altogether in order to identify with hers. For the most part the group is made up of willing parasites who have come together at the whim of a man who barely cares whether they exist. Though they seem to be better off than the crowd below, with more creature comforts and freedom of movement, they have less control over their own plans than the lowliest commuter. But this is the essence of the trade made with the figurehead of the group: actual freedom and independence are bartered for the illusion of freedom. Each individual personality sacrifices itself in order to assume vicariously the personality of Max or Amabel. This explains the central position of Embassy Richard and his mysterious letter. The letter is a public expression of regret that Richard cannot attend a function he was never invited to. On the surface a declaration of independence, the letter is Richard's confession of his abject dependence on those who can issue invitations. Like similar letters in Dostoevski and Proust analyzed by René Girard, "this letter is meant to be insulting but in reality it is an anguished appeal."[53] It is like the bland statement of Richard's that ends the novel: "I can go where I was going afterwards" (p. 255). Richard implies that he has absolute freedom over his movements, but this is not true, not only because England is, by his own confession, "too hot to hold me now," but because he is so willing to abandon his own plans to be directed by people like Max. He as much as admits that he has no plans, that he has no real existence unless it is connected to Max or Amabel. This closing statement also casts another ironic light on the title, which seems to imply freedom as well as movement. But as Alex finds out when he tries to break up the group, it is held fast by the personality of Max just as it is by the fog or by the inert body of Miss Fellowes. The only difference is that Max's wealth answers their need to feel that the fog or Miss Fellowes's illness does not actually inhibit them. Green says, of the fashionable conformity of the rich, "They are like household servants in a prince's service, all in his livery" (p. 133). They gladly wear this livery and stay in line because they enjoy the reflected power of the prince.

Girard says in his analysis of Proust, "The snob will fawn and cringe in order to be accepted by people whom he has endowed with an arbitrary prestige."[54] Snobbism is therefore, like the writing of John Haye or the inner drama of Mr.

---

[53]Girard, p. 69.
[54]Ibid., p. 70.

Bridges, a sacrifice in the real world that redounds to one's credit in an imaginary one. The snob receives the fame and adulation he would never claim on his own account by abasing himself before someone he has arbitrarily elevated for praise. In the snob's world nothing is enjoyed for its own sake because nothing has any real value except where it is sanctified by the touch of someone else. All value is symbolic value. This is the essence of the inner tirade of Alex Alexander, which is taken as a sociological rant of the author's by many of Green's critics.[55] Alex blames the deterioration of his set, its falsehood, on inexperienced girls who don't play the game as well as Amabel. They make up a party where "you thought only of how you were doing, of how much it looked to others you were enjoying yourself and worse than that of how much whoever might be with you could give you reasons for enjoying it. Or, in other words, you competed with each other in how well you were doing well and doing well was getting off with the rich man in the party" (p. 196). Therefore, everything is ultimately boring, without intrinsic value, because Max has become what Girard calls a "mediator" through whom reality must be filtered to acquire any significance. The partygoers are all chronic sufferers from what Auden calls "West's disease," the simple inability to form a wish of one's own.[56] *Party Going* does have the same atmosphere of nasty, trivialized sexuality, of contempt, fear, and boredom combined, as West's *Day of the Locust* because the transaction between the partygoers and Max or Amabel is the same as that between the audience and the star. The star relieves the audience for a moment of the burden of choice, but since only symbolism is involved and nothing of real value can be exchanged, the inevitable result is rancor, dissatisfaction, and mutual contempt.

Like *Day of the Locust*, *Party Going* also contains a horrible picture of the crowd, trapped, squeezed, and ready to explode. The connection between the principals and the public at large

---

[55]See, for example, Russell, p. 112, Stokes, p. 150, and Odom, p. 61.
[56]W. H. Auden, *The Dyer's Hand* (New York: Random House, 1962), pp. 238–45.

is not made as schematically in *Party Going* as it is in *Day of the Locust,* but there is a consistency between the charades upstairs and those on the floor of the station. Critics point out that the "fellow feeling" Alex says is lacking upstairs is found below by Thompson, Julia's chauffeur, when he is spontaneously kissed by a girl standing nearby.[57] But Thompson's desire for a kiss does not signify an overflow of humanitarian feeling or even an overflow of lust. It is the product of self-pity at having missed his tea, and his kind of "fellow feeling" is self-pity only slightly generalized: "If he and that girl had been alone together, in between kisses he would have pitied both of them clinging together" (pp. 162–63). In fact, there is very little fellow feeling to be found in the crowd at all. The two most vivid vignettes both have to do with people taunting one another, first the young men who are "putting out their yellow tongues" at an old woman on the other side of a window, and then the two maids who are flirting from an open window with some men below. The separation provided by the windows keeps either scene from reaching a consummation. Since the people cannot touch, their actions resemble pantomimes in which social rituals are acted out without respect to the emotions they might denote. Yet this seems to be exactly the way the participants want it, especially the two maids, whose enjoyment is increased by their distance from fulfillment: "These two screamed now like rats smelling food when they have been starved in empty milk-churns. . . . They redoubled their shrieks, they were famished and had not been so charmed for ages" (p. 178). All over the station, it seems, similar scenes are being enacted, and "only those who were getting off with girls could say they were enjoying themselves" (p. 200). The phrasing here recalls Alex's tirade, indicating that the appearance of enjoying oneself, being able to "say" so, is as important as actual enjoyment to the commuters as well as to the partygoers, and that "getting off" is the real aim of both groups and not "fellow feeling."

[57]See, for example, Russell, pp. 109–13.

The stopped train and the crowded station are therefore not primarily sociological or political comments on the situation of England's upper classes in 1939. Green takes the common metaphors for freedom, confidence, progress, and infinity, and closes the fog around them for psychological and philosophical reasons. His interest is in the psychological condition that results when infinity abruptly ceases to exist as a concept. The coming war, forecast in *Party Going* when the massed conversation of the terminal is compared to waves of airplanes and the people themselves to "targets for a bomb," is the factor that makes infinity an untenable concept. The loss of continuity and the paralysis from which the partygoers suffer become even more widespread when the war begins, and the reaction of the partygoers, their instinctive reach for a symbol, their manipulation of their own lives with the tools of fiction, becomes the characteristic activity of Green's wartime novels.

3

The Powers of Memory: CAUGHT, BACK, and the Literature of World War II

I do not know how to see what is before my eyes; I can only see clearly in retrospect, it is only in my memories that my mind can work.

Rousseau
The Confessions

I

THE SECOND WORLD WAR lacks a literature of its own. The common journalistic cry during the second war was, "Where are the war poets?" And most postwar surveys agree that the later war, unlike the first, failed to become a literary event.[1] Yet Green, who published only two books between 1929 and 1939, wrote five in the next ten years, along with a number of short stories and articles. Though the war itself was generally thought to have dampened literary enthusiasm as an event too large, sprawled out over too much territory and time, to be contained in any book,

---

[1] See, for example, Anthony Burgess, *The Novel Now* (London: Faber and Faber, 1967), p. 49, and P. H. Newby, *The Novel, 1945–1950* (London: Longmans, Green, 1951), pp. 13–14.

Green wrote three novels during the war, after having finished *Pack My Bag* just as the war began. The disposition of these works in time shows that Green found inspiring one of the aspects of the war that supposedly made it intractable in fiction. *Caught* takes place in the Phony War, the period of time between the declaration of war and the Blitz, a period in which the war was remarkable for its lack of impact on civilians. Green devoted a short story, "The Lull," to a similar period in 1943 just before what was called the Little Blitz began. *Back* takes place at the very end of the war and deals with demobilization, while *Loving* is situated in Ireland, where the war exists as a kind of cloud in the distance. Obviously, what fascinates Green is the slack time, the lulls before, between, and after great convulsions, the times in which tension is banked up without any outlet in action, so that it is forced to find an outlet in surrogates for action. The mood of *Party Going* is prolonged into the war, as is shown when Green reuses its major metaphor to describe the firemen in "The Lull": "These men were passing through a period which may be compared with the experience of changing fast trains. A traveller on the crowded platform cannot be said to command his destiny, who stands, agape, waiting for the next express.... The unseen approach keeps him, as it were, suspended, that is no more than breathing."[2] All of Green's war novels take place in the shadow of an "unseen approach," a great movement offstage that somehow suspends all movement at the center.

The war, therefore, provided Green with examples of his favorite situation, the interrupted train ride he had been describing since *Blindness*. In fact, the feeling of interruption was general, and this may be why the Second World War failed to produce the kind of literature that was expected of it. The first effect of the war was the total suspension of prewar life, yet the anticipated hostilities failed for a number of months to materialize. A study of the first year of the war administered by Mass Observation found that boredom was

---

[2]Henry Green, "The Lull," *New Writing and Daylight*, Summer 1943, p. 17.

the chief threat to civilians. It was a threat, rather than a nuisance, because of the psychological reactions it caused: "The war, which had started in an aura of emptiness became a kind of series of collective hallucinations. The rumors were projections of the fears and wishes in the minds of the masses."[3] These fears and wishes were the real literature of the war, the kind of literature that had the greatest influence on Green's fiction, the movement to which that fiction belongs.

Critics such as Bruce Bassoff have concluded that *Caught* does not "express any awareness of the socio-historical dimensions of the war." He believes that "none of the characters make decisions reflecting political or ideological pressure." John Russell agrees with this opinion about the effect of the war, finding most of the characters of *Caught* "oblivious to its devastating import."[4] But both critics miss the fact that the war is threatening precisely because of its lack of impact. Green's characters are never oblivious of the war, least of all when they seem to be doing something totally unrelated to it. As Russell himself says elsewhere, "Their inability to take any really decisive measures is what prompts the antic, fitful behavior of the men and women in this novel who wait to be bombed."[5] *Caught* is about waiting, what Green himself calls "this lull of living," about a period of time in which the common response to the "socio-historical dimensions of the war" was to worry because nothing was happening. The period was called the Phony War, and the real pressure it put on individuals was to suspend their prewar lives and replace them with nothing new. For a few months the whole country was convalescent, liberated, in a sense, as John Haye is by his accident, yet feeling as Green's hero Richard Roe does, that he could "not consider that his life in the station, what little he had, could at any time be real."[6] The fire station in which Roe passes his time is a perfect

[3]Mass Observation, *War Begins at Home,* ed. Tom Harrisson and Charles Madge (London: Chatto and Windus, 1940), p. 69.
[4]Bassoff, p. 141; Russell, p. 143.
[5]Russell, p. 14.
[6]Henry Green, *Caught* (London, 1943; rpt. New York: Viking, 1952), p. 28. All subsequent references are to this edition and in this chapter will appear in text.

microcosm of the country as a whole, since, as Green says, "the whole point of a fireman is that he is endlessly waiting."[7] This must be the reason John Lehmann lists *Caught* along with *The Aerodrome* and *Between the Acts* as one of the three novels that most accurately capture the mood of the war.[8]

This mood, this feeling that real life has come to an end to be replaced by something not yet fully realized, is expressed in a number of war novels by Green's contemporaries. One peculiar expression of it is the way that characters feel themselves turning into figures from the serials. In Waugh's *Put Out More Flags,* Alastair Digby Vane Trumpington, about to volunteer for special service, feels himself "turning a page in his life, as, more than twenty years ago lying on his stomach before the fire, with a bound volume of *Chums,* he used to turn over to the next instalment of the serial." The Third Movement of Anthony Powell's *A Dance to the Music of Time* is full of such conversions: Gwatkin with his "personal myth"; Bithel, reader of *Boy's Own Paper,* who sees himself as the hero of *Coming under Fire*; Nick Jenkins himself, buying a tunic in a costume shop, being outfitted for *The War,* as if it were a play. Waugh and Powell deal with this feeling in a comic way, but to some combatants it was tragic—for William Chappell, for example, who wrote in *Penguin New Writing* that he had been turned into "a symbol as unreal and machine made as that pathetic mythological figure of the last war—Tommy Atkins." In 1944 John Lehmann characterized the general tone of wartime contributions to *Penguin New Writing* by comparing it to the feeling of Kafka's Gregor Samsa: "One had been changed by the war—like the man who found he was an insect one morning in Kafka's horrible and prophetic story—into something completely alien to one's old self."[9]

[7]Henry Green, "Firefighting," p. 117.
[8]Lehmann, *In My Own Time,* pp. 346–48.
[9]Evelyn Waugh, *Put Out More Flags* (Boston: Little, Brown, 1942), p. 279; Anthony Powell, *A Dance to the Music of Time: Third Movement* (Boston: Little, Brown, 1968), p. 70 (*The Valley of Bones*), pp. 14–15 and 3 (*The Soldier's Art*); William Chappell "Words from a Stranger," *Penguin New Writing,* 19 (Oct. 1944), 39; John Lehmann, Foreword, *Penguin New Writing,* 19 (Oct. 1944), 7.

Caught, Back, AND WORLD WAR II

The fire station where most of the action of *Caught* takes place is a forcing house for feelings of this kind. The conditions of duty in the Fire Service suspend normal life. A group of men is forced to be on duty in a house conscripted for the purpose, in unfamiliar surroundings with unfamiliar companions. The firemen are in one way the primary victims of the Phony War, since they have been led to expect massive air raids at the first declaration of war, have been removed from their jobs and homes, yet have nothing to do when the raids fail to materialize. They are close enough to their old lives to visit, but are prevented by the terms of duty from actually taking those lives up again. Thus *Caught* begins with Richard Roe, Green's protagonist, returning for a visit to his home in the country, prevented somehow from seeing any of it, the whole visit marked by "the sadness of not finding" (p. 9). Roe rather strongly resembles Green himself, who gave up his job as an executive with H. Pontifex and Sons to volunteer for the Fire Service. Like Roe, Green led two separate lives during the war, roughing it in London as a fireman, a service that was more dangerous than military service for the first year or so of the war, and commuting to a comfortable country existence while on leave. From this commute may come the basic dialectical principle of the novel: each character is suspended between two contexts, the station and home, each of which drains the other of importance. Roe broods on his home at the station, yet finds it strangely remote when he visits, full of memories of station life, which seem equally unreal. This split is epitomized by Piper, the old man who, while undressing, describes every movement to his absent wife: " 'Well mother,' he cried, 'I think I'll take me boots off now' " (p. 42). It is as if Piper is trying to bridge the gap, to narrate his station life as if it could achieve reality only as a story told to people from his former existence.

The basic principle of Fire Service life as Green sees it is that each man, like the characters of Waugh and Powell, is turned into a caricature that exists only in terms of the public life of the station. Each man becomes a simplified version of himself, purposely distorted and reformed to fit the odd, dimensionless context of the war. This is suggested by the names, by the legal anonymity of Richard Roe, which together with the name of the subofficer Pye forms the Greek word for fire, and by the pseudogeneric names of the rest of the crew, Piper, Shiner, and Chopper. The process is described by Stephen Spender, another Fire Service volunteer, in his autobiography, *World within World*: "Living together in one recreation room for forty-eight hours on end out of every seventy-two, our lives became like a documentary play, in which each of us played a role allotted to him. And yet no one was consciously acting. . . . The station created a character for us, based largely on what we really were."[10] All the drama of *Caught*—the disgrace and suicide of the subofficer Pye, the disintegration of Richard Roe—can be traced to tension between the created personality such as Spender describes and the personality of the prewar period. Both dramas illustrate a situation offering two unacceptable choices: to be "caught" in the vacuum of fire-station life or "adrift" in a remembered world that no longer seems to exist.

Much of the humor of *Caught* comes from the mechanical way some of the characters assume their fire-station roles. Piper, for instance, begins as a useful sounding board for Pye, as an eager student at his lectures, but "once started, nothing would stop Piper and before long he was saying 'That's so,' or 'Of course,' every five minutes, nodding his parched head in agreement, looking sideways" (pp. 21–22). This Bergsonian comedy, based on ludicrously unnecessary repetition, shows how easy it is for certain individuals to be swallowed by their fire-station roles. Piper seems almost eager to be swallowed, as if his prewar existence were an old suit of clothes he had been longing to throw away.

Pye's difficulties come, however, from the uncomfortable mismatch between his prewar personality and his new, authoritative role. He is in the same position as the subofficer Spender describes in *World within World,* a regular fireman suddenly elevated to command by the influx of volunteers. For Spender's Alfie this elevation presented a problem of role,

---

[10]Spender, *World within World,* p. 245.

so that he felt constrained to ask his men, "Not so much of the 'Alfie this' and the 'Alfie that' either. . . . If you must call me something, call me Sub."[11] "Not so much of the Alfie" thereafter became a joke in Spender's substation. Pye has a similar problem in that he would very much like to be considered a father to his men, "knowing about their children, even settling differences between husband and wife" (p. 89), but is a subordinate at heart, with the cringing habits of his prewar position. He always wheedles when an order would be respected, and resorts to familiarity at just the wrong time. Pye has the unfortunate habit of attempting to be familiar in bureaucratic language, getting his two selves inextricably mixed up: "No, when I ask a thing, I mean a question of that nature, what I'm getting at is, is there any way I, the individual responsible for the efficiency, and that means the happiness, of this station, is there any reasonable means by which I can alluviate the little things that count such a lot to everyone, not only men, at times such as the present" (p. 61). Pye is hinting here that he would wink if the station's cooks were to stretch the rules a bit, but his smarmy approach offends them and makes them more punctilious than ever. When Pye is threatened or unhappy, though, he retreats completely into the bureaucratic role, demanding, for example, that the cooks respect the regulation requiring a double line at the end of the month in their account books (p. 153).

Even Richard Roe, the character whose experience of the Fire Service most closely parallels Green's own, the character whose life outside the station is most fully described, caricatures himself. Roe closely resembles the picture Green gives of himself in *Pack My Bag,* but the distance of fiction and the lapse of time seem to have allowed him to see himself with some irony. Roe shares Green's conviction that the war means certain death. But it is made clear in *Caught* that this certainty is part of a melodramatic pose that is itself a reaction to the way the war has made his former life seem unreal: "In his self pity he might have been sighing goodbye to adored

---

[11] Ibid., p. 250.

unreality. All that was real to him then was his death in a matter of days" (p. 28). The most sentimental part of this pose is Roe's repetition of the sickly cliché that he is to rejoin his dead wife: "He kept on saying, falsely, and over and over, that he was to rejoin his wife" (p. 28). Roe also resembles Green in the way he reacts to communal living by assuming an interim personality that is a caricature of his own. The station's system of group reward and ostracism is compared at times to that of a public school, and, like Green at Eton, Roe allows his speech, his actions, and even his emotions to be determined by station routine. He looks on his comrades with "a sort of holy falseness" (p. 43), with a perfectly sincere desire to be one of them that is expressed by a distortion of his own personality. In fact, Roe succeeds so well in assuming the Fire Service mentality that he quite naturally delivers the stock Fire Service lecture on the war to every girl he meets "in full always and at the earliest" (p. 70).

This sort of self-caricature is the only way for Roe to fit in, the only way for the group to accept him, when they "had neither of them come across anyone in the least resembling the other" (p. 66). In this sense the Fire Service is a special version of the kind of group seen in *Living,* with the problem of class added to all the other tensions that group manages by stereotyping its members. The group finally overcomes Roe's strangeness and welcomes him into their routine only when it has replaced his actual life with a false, mythologized version. Piper makes public the fact that Roe's son was once kidnapped by Pye's sister, and at this Roe "became almost popular, that is with as many as heard what grew to be the fable started by the old soldier" (p. 153). It is a fable because the facts are rapidly altered to fit the station's feel for poetic rightness: "It was now the sub officer who had taken Christopher away" (p. 154). This makes the conflict more immediate, as does the common misconception that Roe's sister-in-law, who has come unpleasantly face-to-face with Pye, is in fact Roe's wife. Where Roe's own attempts to become part of the group have generally failed, "the whole story made him someone in their eyes. For the first time he became real to the substation, all this from a tale that had expanded remarkably within the thirty-six hours" (p. 154). The basic irony of Roe's situation is that he can become "real" only by becoming a fable. His plight illustrates a common paradox in Green's work, that the artificial version of an individual, polished by the group to remove extraneous elements, has a greater potency with others than he has himself. *Caught* refines the paradox further, because Roe's own attempts to produce a stylized version of himself acceptable to the crew have failed. The caricature Roe produces himself bears too clearly the marks of his actual desires. Only a version that is completely removed from any emotions of his own is pure enough to satisfy the station. Roe assumes a fictional role like the characters of Waugh and Powell, but one which, like many of the roles in *Living,* is determined for him by the group he joins.

But if each character assumes a kind of persona upon entering the substation, this does not mean that life seems more authentic outside it. The station is in a state of suspended animation, isolated from the outside world both physically and temporally, within its repetitive routine. The characters therefore touch the outside world and their civilian existences primarily through memory and anticipation, alleviating the blankness of the present moment by casting themselves backward and forward in time. Civilian existence is therefore less important in itself than it is as an escape from the station, as a myth into which the characters escape. Without any real power in the present, the characters find the power they need in the past and in the future, until civilian life becomes less a reality they have departed from than a mythical state they are moving toward.

James Hall says of Green's characters, "Their pasts, if any— most have none at all—are backdrops rather than moral evolutions."[12] But Hall must not be thinking of *Caught,* in which the past often seems more immediate than the present and in which the characters pick over their memories in a search for

---

[12]Hall, p. 67.

the key to their "moral evolution." The turn toward the past is, as Green says in *Pack My Bag,* a function of the war: "There must be a threat to one's skin to wake what is left of things remembered into things to die with. The crime is to forget."[13] This emphasis on memory affects the form of *Caught,* which is, as Edward Stokes has shown, the most narratively complex of Green's novels. Instead of proceeding steadily forward, the narrative doubles back or jumps ahead, and two events widely separated in time are often described side by side. Stokes's attempt at a time line shows that the narrative is often inconsistent with itself and that Green's matching of the events of the war to those in the fire station is inexact and at times contradictory.[14] But the scrambled form is obviously meant to mimic the restlessness of the characters' minds, which never remain in the present for long but are always ranging backward and forward, as if to elude the mental constriction of the present crisis.

The most comic example of this is Mary Howells, the char who becomes one of the cooks at the substation. She has a general tendency to be theatrical, which is aggravated when her daughter returns home, having left her husband. Determined to have it out with Ted, her son-in-law, Howells decides to go AWOL and becomes "highly dramatic . . . at having decided on action" (p. 83). In fact, she acts out in anticipation her own version of a wartime melodrama:

> She pictured at the back of her eye the descent she was going to make on this camp the rotten, good-for-nothing, lying 'ound her son-in-law hung out in. . . . From under the first a sentry challenged her. . . . "Who goes there?" he would say. And then she could tell him. "A mother," was all she would reply. Yes, he must know that had a mother of his own. "Pass mother." And the next. "Who goes there?" "A mother like you have of your own." "Pass." "Who goes there?" "A mother," right until she was at the gates where that miserable twister would be

---

[13]Henry Green, *Pack My Bag,* p. 54.
[14]Stokes, pp. 104–14.

waiting, froze with his conscience, wiping his white hands, the ponce. [pp. 83–84]

Howells obviously enjoys this role of avenging mother and the drama of inexorable revenge which she invents. Her actual visit to Ted is, however, quite different. Instead of trudging forward like some implacable Fate, she "could not bring herself to mention Brid" (p. 115). She leaves, in fact, without so much as clucking her tongue at the son-in-law, who was supposed to have dissolved in contrition at her feet. Her failure doesn't matter, though, because her memory transforms the virtually nonexistent meeting to bring it into accordance with the drama she anticipated: " 'I said to 'im, I says,' she went on, imagining every word. 'You're no good to no-one, and I got a daughter, I 'ave, 'oo you took, an' when you'd used what you wanted you sent 'er back,' I says, 'more shame to yer, call yerself a man,' I said. 'E went white, Arthur, even if he didn't say nothink. But I wouldn't spare 'im. . . . Only since I been back I can't but wonder if I done right" (p. 117). This revision of reality outstrips Lily Gates's in the way it dovetails so neatly with Howells's anticipations. Anticipation and memory collaborate to squeeze the present almost out of existence.

The larger importance of Howells's mental tricks comes from their resemblance to Pye's. Pye's first visit to his sister, confined in a mental institution in the country, is analogous to Howells's descent on Ted. In both the vacuity of experience is relieved by fictionalizations before and after the fact. Pye imagines this visit in even greater detail than Howells does hers, down to a humiliating argument with the bus driver who will drop him at the institution. He imagines himself running the same kind of gauntlet of sentry posts, manned in this case by surgeons in smocks. Finally he sees his sister, "on the third floor of the cage, hanging to bars like they do in pictures, dressed all in yellow" (p. 85). In reality, his sister's situation bears little resemblance to this image Pye has taken from pictures, but reality has little force because "it had all been so strange that he was ready next day to reject any version left him of what she may have said" (p. 87). The analogy between Pye and Howells can be extended further because they both have to go "adrift," absent without leave, in order to act out these dramas.

The practical difficulties of going "adrift" only mirror the more serious psychological ones. As Stokes says, *Caught* may be described as "dialectical."[15] Each character lives within a mental dialectic composed of the old, personal life and the present life of the substation. As the experience of Howells and Pye suggests, it is necessary to go "adrift" to touch the personal life at all, since neither Pye's sister nor Howells's son-in-law has any official claim on their time. Personal experience, therefore, becomes itself an unauthorized absence, and since it is unauthorized and extracurricular, it ceases to have any real existence once the individual has reentered the substation. The characters are perpetually in transit between two lives, both physically, as they travel outside the substation, and mentally, as they cast themselves backward and forward from the present moment dominated by fire-station routine. But each context drains the other of influence, each existing as an unreal alternative to the other, so that the existence of the characters is one in which they are always "adrift," always absent from the life that is most vividly present in their imaginations.

This dialectical split is the cause of Pye's downfall. Practically, it is the unauthorized absence of Mary Howells and his own jaunt to the country that cause the first suspicions among his superiors and eventually lead to the loss of his job. Psychologically, Pye becomes more and more remote from the physically constraining substation as he loses control of his own memories. Pye's obsession with his sister and with his own past illustrates the rule Green sets down in *Pack My Bag,* that it is not one's actual past that matters but "what one thinks has gone to make one up."[16] His sister's attempted kidnapping and his possible complicity in her illness become

---
[15]Ibid., p. 111.
[16]Henry Green, *Pack My Bag,* p. 8.

an obsession with Pye that rapidly expands beyond control. What seems to liberate the obsession from all practical restraints is the blackout, the almost total darkness produced in London by civil defense regulations, which, according to Mass Observation, transformed everyday objects into "the unseen forms of indigestion dreams."[17] This darkness oddly illuminated by the moon gives everything an unreal quality, setting Pye's imagination free at the same time as it restricts his movements to the substation. It reminds him of "the first girl he had known," because their liaison had taken place on a moonlit night such as those produced by the blackout (p. 40). This experience is associated with Pye's sister because of a fleeting glimpse he had caught of her sneaking back into the house on the same night, "up from off her own back no doubt" (p. 42). The more Pye mulls this over, the more the odd conjunction is transformed, until, with the prodding of a comically Freudian psychiatrist at the mental institution, Pye decides his sister and the girl were one and the same: "In a surge of blood it was made clear, false, that it might have been his own sister he was with that night. . . . So in the blind moonlight, eyes warped by his need, he must have forced his own sister" (p. 140).

The interjection of the word *false* makes it clear that Pye is deluded, that the idea has been put into his mind by the barely veiled suggestions of the psychiatrist. The idea of incest seems to have attached itself to Pye's guilty defensiveness about his sister's crime, a defensiveness that is based on the feeling that he is not doing enough to help her. It is a pathetic delusion because it is not even original, because, like the dramatized version of the kidnapping, its form is determined by others. False or not, the suspicion of incest becomes both inescapable and unresolvable, like an enigma in Kafka. It cannot be resolved because Pye's past is too remote and his sister too unstable, but it cannot be dismissed because the conditions of the blackout and the lull in the war make Pye defenseless against memory. His radical separation from the

---

[17]Mass Observation, p. 187.

past, caused both by the war and by his own efforts to make himself into the caricature of a subofficer, has made him subject to memories he can no longer control.

Pye is finally finished by an unauthorized sally out into the night "to try once more to find how much he could recognize by this light in the bright river of the street" (p. 162). This final experiment is motivated by a "fit of rememberin' back" (p. 166), and is essentially an attempt to recreate the crucial evening. To settle the question of his guilt, Pye must go "adrift," and while he is out, Trant, his superior, calls, catching Pye in what will be his final indiscretion. This is the irony of the dialectic, that in order to understand his personal life, Pye must take unauthorized leave from his official one. Having become obsessed with his past, Pye loses his position as subofficer and subsequently commits suicide. He is defeated because the dialectic has no available synthesis, because there is no middle ground between being "caught" in the official routine of the fire station and being "adrift" in his own memories. Doubts about his past make success at the station impossible, just as the conditions of his life at the station prevent him from clearing up his doubts about the past.

This is the real point of comparison between Pye and Roe, for the balance of Roe's official and personal life is only slightly less precarious. In his case the two halves of the dialectic similarly devalue each other. *Caught* begins with Roe at home on leave from the fire station, but his physical presence seems somehow to make the scene more remote. The countryside is hidden by rain "in the way a veil will obscure" (p. 8); his son seems to have "a veiled face" (p. 9); the memory of his dead wife is removed behind a "web of love and death" (p. 9). The same thing happens on a second visit, when Roe finds himself unable to add to memories formed when he was younger. The house and its grounds seem remote when physically near because Roe has been deliberately falsifying his home life when trapped at the station. His memories of the house are so vivid and his need of them so strong that the real place can't compete with the "false picture of what his home life had been" (p. 92) that he deliberately concocts when most oppressed by the Fire Service. The most important part of this picture is his wife, who is restored to him several times in the book through force of memory. Roe uses this memory in the same way that John Haye uses the false picture of his dead mother, and it allows Roe to sentimentalize himself, to create the myth that he will soon be joining her. A similar myth is created by the temporary loss of his son, Christopher, with a "similar sensation that he was being false" as he exaggerates the impact of the kidnapping on himself. Loss, like the "ever precious loss" (p. 34) of his wife, brings things closer to Roe because the sentimental versions he has of things in memory are more vivid than reality. Thus the physical proximity of the house is disappointing, remote, since it must compete with the sentimentalized version he creates for himself at the station.

Roe is self-conscious enough to observe this process for himself, and he struggles in the later part of the book against his own fictionalizations of experience. The Blitz, when it finally does arrive, temporarily intensifies Roe's problems instead of alleviating them. He is, like the main character of Green's wartime story "Mr. Jonas," "lifted out of unreality into something temporarily worse."[18] Roe finds that "he could not remember what his home life had been only a day or two before" because the pace is so much faster that "he had no privacy with which to ferment those feelings" (pp. 134–35). But instead of restoring Roe to reality, the lack of time unsettles his memories in a way that makes his home life even more unreal than before. On his last leave Roe is so remote that he forgets that his wife is dead and speaks to his sister-in-law "as though she was her dead sister" (p. 174). Here he resembles Pye in the way that the radical disjunction in his life has disturbed his ability to determine identity.

It seems that the intensity of his firefighting experiences has destroyed the memory of Roe's life at home, but this does not mean that his memories of firefighting are therefore vividly real. In fact, the process of moving back and forth

---

[18]Henry Green, "Mr. Jonas," *Folios of New Writing*, 3 (Spring 1941), 17.

between completely separate spheres of existence, each of which seems to cancel out the experiences of the other, has destroyed Roe's faith in memory and in the reality of his experiences themselves. Thus the Blitz appears in *Caught* only as a story Roe relates to his sister-in-law, a story intercut with parenthetical rejoinders that criticize his version of events: "It had not been like that at all" (pp. 176 and 180). These do not necessarily have to be authorial rejoinders, since Roe himself has long since learned to distrust his own memory and his own capacity for dramatizing and sentimentalizing events. He says himself, "Yet I suppose it was not like that at all really. One changes everything after by going over it" (p. 179). Roe's last long attempt to retain something of the Blitz is therefore the thematic climax of *Caught,* the final devaluation of Roe's wartime experiences that corresponds to the war's devaluation of his peacetime life. Roe's sister-in-law tries to help him around these difficulties by arguing for a purely operational definition of reality: "But the real thing . . . is the picture you carry in your eye afterwards, surely? It can't be what you can't remember, can it?" (p. 179). This clever solution fails to satisfy Roe for two reasons. For one, there is so much that can't be described even at the time it occurs: "There's always something you can't describe, and it's not the blitz alone that's true of" (p. 180). Therefore, much of experience never has a chance to register itself in the memory. But even the experience that does register need not be registered accurately, and, most disturbing of all for Roe, the distorting faculty is not necessarily his own. "The extraordinary thing," he says, "is that one's imagination is so literary. What will go on up there to-night in London, every night, is more like a film. . . . Then afterwards, when you go over it, everything seems unreal . . . as you begin building again to describe to yourself some experience you've had" (p. 174). The difficulty in simply accepting memories as if they were real is that to do so is to accept falsifications that are not even your own, as Pye acquires a complex that has been suggested to him by the clichés of psychoanalysis.

Green enunciates here one of the common themes of British writing about the war: the disconcerting tendency toward instant fictionalization of overwhelming experiences. Stephen Spender found this literary tendency among firefighters in his station, where only the one illiterate "told the truth about his fire-fighting experiences. The others had almost completely substituted descriptions which they read in the newspapers or heard on the wireless for their own impressions." The hero of William Sansom's *Fireman Flower* scorns himself for having "a kind of story book fire" in his memory, "the traditional fire of hearsay."[19] As Paul Fussell has demonstrated in *The Great War and Modern Memory*, this tendency for literary stereotypes to stand between experience and memory becomes more common, rather than less so, in wartime. Fussell says that by such stereotypes "the rememberer is enabled to locate, draw forth, and finally shape into significance an event or a moment which otherwise would merge without meaning into the general undifferentiated stream."[20] The need for such management of experience, according to Fussell, grows in wartime because experience is so unprecedented, inchoate, and overwhelming at the same time. But the problem for Roe is that he is conscious of his own literary procedures, and this self-consciousness puts an extra layer of mistrust between himself and the immediate past. Thus Roe's problem is like Pye's in that his conception of himself seems beyond his control. The problem is also a general one, since the impact of the war has suspended normal life, withholding the activities by which people maintain what they think of as their real personalities and substituting activities and therefore personalities determined from outside. This is the gist of Lehmann's complaint about wartime experience, and of the portrayal of wartime figures as characters from the serials in the novels of Waugh and Powell.

---

[19]Spender, *World within World*, p. 248; William Sansom, *Fireman Flower* (London: Chatto and Windus, 1944), p. 215.
[20]Fussell, p. 30.

Roe's attempt to narrate his experiences to his sister-in-law is therefore an attempt to take possession of his own past, to establish his control over memory by forming it into narrative himself. He is following a pattern common in Green's novels, where characters often communicate, even with themselves, by telling a story. The process of making the past into a story is a way of establishing the self, of taking one last stab at saving it, as Green says in *Pack My Bag*: "And if there are things we seek to share, hunched now on the office stool, facing a slow death in the shelter they have made our basement into, we might as well turn back to when we stumbled home through the dark, our faces still burning with the day's sun and then tell ourselves as the syren goes and frightened we begin to forget, because we do not know if we are going to be killed, how we did once find this or the other before we go to die to take with us like a bar of gold."[21] Thus Roe's life seems to depend on his ability to stabilize the past in his own mind, or on his ability to make others see what he can't see clearly himself. But Roe has lost his grasp, not just on the memory of his wife, whom he confuses with his sister-in-law here, but on himself, becoming confused with the false memories he narrates.

Roe is defeated by the very methods he uses and by the paradox that makes all narrative recapitulations of war suspiciously literary. The essential paradox of *Caught*, and a central one for all of Green's work, is that experience cannot be fully realized in the present, that one cannot simultaneously live and apprehend oneself as living. Therefore, all self-knowledge and ultimately all of what we believe is the self is inevitably literary, as a narrated, shaped account existing after the fact. Any attempt to find a real self by reenactment, either dramatically like Pye or narratively like Roe, simply pushes one more fictional layer between oneself and the experience one is trying to recall. The very tools of self-knowledge create the self they seek.

[21]Henry Green, *Pack My Bag*, pp. 53–54.

The stronger an experience is, therefore, the more likely it is to be fictionalized, replaced by a predetermined version of itself. This is the key to Green's descriptions of the general social impact of the war, especially his description of the sexual climate of the first year of the war. Sex as it appears in *Caught* is less a physical or emotional experience than a method of storing material for a later fictional recreation. Roe sees London as full of women who want to die "in his arms that would so soon . . . be dead" (p. 49). They are "driven to create memories to compare, and thus to compensate for the loss each had suffered" (p. 63). These women participate in an endless round of loss and compensation, where each man, so certain to go and possibly to die, exists already as a memory even before the actual separation. These experiences hardly exist in the present, since they occur only to create memories for the future. The present is already retrospective, and every encounter self-reflexive even as it happens. Sex is less a physical act than a way of participating in a nationwide burst of nostalgia. Though Prudence, the girl who becomes Pye's lover, insists that Pye will not remind her of the pilot who has left for the war, still "the lighting in this room made her think of John on a leaflet night raid, his darling face with much of Bert's look . . . who was staring at her now with just that glare John would have into the dangerous, dangerous night" (p. 119). The odd lighting of the Blitz takes her back into the past as it does Pye, with the difference that she is happy with the past because it intensifies the present, because it is a kind of romantic counterpoint to experiences that cannot be fully realized when they happen. Prudence equates sex and war, and Green seems to stand behind the old equation, but not because of any identification of sex with violence. Rather, sex and war are similar because both seem to erase the present and strengthen the past as the only possible sphere of activity. When Prudence confuses Pye with her absent lover, she is enjoying the same aspect of the war that torments Pye, participating in a fiction without the guilty self-consciousness that leads to his death.

When Roe says of Pye, "It was sex finished him off" (p. 195), he is right in a way that he doesn't suspect, because it is Pye's sexual suspicion of himself that draws him slowly out of the present. In this Pye is an extreme version of Roe himself. Roe's relationship with Hilly, like his accounts of firefighting, is characterized by the word *false,* which is scattered obtrusively throughout Green's descriptions as if to underscore the fictionalizing effect of the war. The insistent repetition of the word links the two contexts because both Roe's storytelling and the affair are attempts to get a grasp on the past, and both fail because of Roe's inability to settle for what must be a false approximation. In fact, the stories that Hilly tells to Roe also have this purpose: "Thus, not caring, neither did she notice if she spoke the truth, she began to tell. She told so as to bring in, most particularly, everything ever so closely back to their two selves" (p. 108). Hilly produces a revisionist account of the past that can be "theirs," a history that culminates in their affair, but Roe's falsehood is based on making the present conform to his own, much different, past: "But at this moment he had another use for Hilly. He began to describe to her, as he had tried with Ilse, the architecture of his life in the old days, married, and with a son" (pp. 92–93). Hilly is an opportunity for Roe to indulge in the "false picture of what his home life had been" (p. 92). Sex is for him, as it is for Prudence, a way to grasp the life he has lost. Roe's confusion of his sister-in-law with his dead wife is one he moves toward throughout the book, since each woman he encounters is really nothing more to him than a chance to participate in his own myth. Thus in *Caught* sex is basically a fictional exercise, one that all the characters indulge in because it seems a way of handling the disruptions of the war.

The subplots concerning the loss of children—the derangement of Mary Howells's daughter Brid, Pye's sister's kidnapping of Christopher Roe—seem to indicate much the same thing. Mary Howells makes an offhand comment to Piper that shows the importance of these subplots to Green's analysis of the psychological effect of the war: "Our parents looked on their children to 'elp at the end. But nowadays it's wars every generation, so it's not as if a woman, rich or poor, can call 'er child 'er own" (p. 116). That this idea may have been the germ of the novel is suggested by a passage in *Living,* in which Lily listens to Mrs. Eames's niece go on about "the likeness to parents in their babies." The niece says, of a former conversation, "I said, 'well you're a wonder you are, there's a child, your own flesh and blood in the manner of speaking, and you can say that, why' I said, 'Mrs. Pye, how can you, the poor little lamb.' "[22] This Mrs. Pye has apparently denied the doctrine of the resemblance of children and parents and is thus figuratively if not actually the parent of the Pyes in *Caught.* Such doubts about children are, as Howells's speech suggests, doubts about the reliability and continuity of experience, doubts that become magnified in wartime when the normal relationship between past, present, and future is deranged. The relationship between parents and children, which relies on a natural progression of events, is destroyed by the war, so that Mary is estranged from Brid and Roe from his son Christopher. The more unstable characters express their anxiety by seizing children—Pye's sister kidnapping Christopher Roe and Pye himself picking a lost boy off the street on his last nighttime jaunt, "thinking of Christopher" (p. 119). And the discontinuity of Roe's experiences is expressed by his inability to speak to, or even to become interested in, his own son, who is actually much closer to him in the memories pored over at the fire station. Thus the novel ends with Roe pushing his son aside, telling the whole family to "leave me alone," as if they made it impossible for him to digest his memories of the great fire, just as the experience of firefighting has made it impossible for him to feel that his home life is real.

The war has the effect of fictionalizing experiences that are not directly connected to it, so that the most private relationships become fictional versions of themselves. Roe's temper, his unhappiness, signifies his unwillingness to settle for

---

[22]Henry Green, *Living,* p. 267.

fictional approximations once he realizes how those approximations separate him from the past he wishes to retrieve. Some critics believe that Roe reaches happiness by integrating himself into the proletarian world of firefighting,[23] but this ignores the fact that the experience is presented as actually unavailable to him. And Roe's last action is to send others away, to demand solitude even from his own family. Anxiety about the accuracy of his fictions makes Roe demand solitude, and also sets him off from nearly all other Green characters, who are generally quite happy with their fictions. Roe is almost the only character in Green's work to suffer from the kind of self-consciousness that undermines an individual's faith in his own authenticity. Though he fictionalizes himself as thoroughly as any other character in Green's work, Roe's very awareness of the process prevents him from enjoying the benefits it usually provides.

Though Roe's anxiety may be unique, his predicament is a typical one. The Phony War is a kind of symbol for all of Green's fiction because it is a powerful historical reality that takes possession of the lives of individuals without offering itself to them in any intelligible, or even in an apprehensible, form. Fictional versions of experience are therefore the only kind available, and what was presented in *Living* as a given is shown in *Caught* to be a reaction to certain historical realities. This must be another reason why the Second World War was a period of such creativity for Green, because it brought about a rediscovery of the basis of his own fiction. *Caught* is the record of this rediscovery and as such suffers somewhat from the same self-consciousness that plagues its main character. It ends unhappily, unlike all of Green's other work, in which the lives of the characters usually continue quite serenely, no matter what obstacles have been encountered. And no other main character in Green's novels comes to such an end as Pye. Green seems concerned to show in *Caught* how people can be destroyed by their fictions, rather than showing as he usually does how fictions can sustain a

---

[23]See, for example, Odom, pp. 81–82, and Bassoff, p. 163.

life. It is for this reason that *Caught* and *Back* can seem to be two halves of a single novel, with Charley Summers in a situation very similar to Roe's, yet liberated by delusions as Roe is caught, and able to find the satisfactory conclusion the earlier novel lacks.

II

Despite the fact that *Loving* intervenes between them, *Caught* and *Back* are more closely related than any other pair of novels by Green except *Nothing* and *Doting*. Though there is little similarity between the personalities of Richard Roe and Charley Summers, their basic problem is the same, how to manage a memory that has been unhinged by war. In fact, the whole of *Back* seems an expansion of a single scene in *Caught,* a flashback in which Roe remembers showing his wife around his parents' rose garden: "The roses, when they came to the rose garden, were full out, climbing along brick walls, some, overpowered by their heavy flowers, in obeisance before brick paths, petals loose here and there on the earth but, on each bush and tree of roses, rose after rose after rose of every shade stared like oxen, and came forward to meet them with a sweet, heavy, luxuriant breath" (p. 64). This memory of the rose garden becomes Charley's memory of his dead lover, Rose, evoked by the roses in the cemetery he visits at the beginning of the novel: "For climbing around and up these trees of mourning, was rose after rose after rose . . . those roses gay and bright which, as still as this dark afternoon, stared at whosoever looked or hung their heads to droop, to grow stained, to die when their turn came."[24] The nostalgia that drags Roe back to the rose garden also afflicts Charley, and the fantasy that dominates *Back* also seems to come from an episode in the earlier novel. For brief periods in *Caught* Roe's wife seems to return, and he actually seems to touch "her white rose petal skin" (p. 33), actually

[24]Henry Green, *Back* (London: Hogarth, 1946), p. 5. Unless noted, all subsequent references are to this edition and in this chapter will appear in text.

grasps "her arm, which was not there, above the elbow" (p. 34). This conjuration of the dead prefigures Charley's demented belief that his Rose is still alive, but Roe resembles him even more specifically in the way that he presses a living being into service as a surrogate for the dead. Not only does Roe, toward the end of *Caught,* forget that his wife is dead, but he begins to speak to Dy, his sister-in-law, "as though she was her dead sister" (p. 174). His conversion of the sister is only part of a general confusion of the two which his son Christopher participates in by calling Dy "mum" and which his mates at the fire station foster by assuming that Dy is his wife. Everything conspires to make Dy fill the empty niche, an effort she seems ready to acquiesce in until the very end, when Roe, exasperated at his inability to explain his life at the fire station, drives both Dy and his son away. Virtually the whole plot of *Back* is prefigured in this episode: Charley's return from the war with a set of experiences he can't seem to communicate; his delusion that Rose's half sister, Nancy Whitmore, is in fact Rose, who has been killed during his absence; the collaboration of the other family members to make Nancy into Rose. But *Back* contains the final completion of the process that Roe's self-consciousness frustrates, when Rose is resurrected in the person of her half sister.

Faulty memory is the common affliction of all the characters in *Back*. Experience seems to leak away almost before the characters notice, as it does for Charley at the cemetery, where he "felt what he had seen until the silence which followed, when he at once forgot" (p. 6). Arthur Middlewitch, like Charley recently returned from active service, complains, "I'm so damned forgetful these days" (p. 26). James Phillips, Rose's husband, feels himself terribly afflicted by her death, "which he was forgetting" (p. 83). But the more significant examples of faulty memory in *Back* are not eliminative, but creative, as they are in *Caught*. The most serious case of faulty memory, excluding Charley's own, is that of Mrs. Grant, Rose's mother, who becomes convinced that Charley is her brother John, who was killed in the First World War. As Mr.

Grant says, "Once you begin to lose the picture of this or the other in your mind's eye, it's hard to determine where things'll stop" (p. 14). It seems that the death of Rose has severed her mother from reality and made her fantasies of the past so strong that the present is unable to compete.

Since this delusion so closely resembles Charley's, both characters pressing a living person into the role left by someone who is dead, it seems important that a medical explanation is offered for her case. The doctor who scuttles in and out of the Grant household has told Grant that this delusion "might be nature's way to protect her by letting her forget" (p. 14). This is a very plausible and commonly accepted explanation for partial amnesia, which regards the mind as a passive receptacle that simply spills out what it lacks the capacity to retain. But Mr. Grant refuses to accept this explanation, saying, "Nature's cruel . . . you can't expect mercy in that quarter" (p. 14). The doctor's theory seems further damaged by the fact that even more trauma, in the form of Mr. Grant's crippling stroke, brings Mrs. Grant out of her delusion. And there is some evidence that her memory lapse is, as A. Kingsley Weatherhead assumes, self-serving and self-generated.[25] She says to Charley late in the book, "You know for a long time after that happened I couldn't bear it, I had to put the whole thing behind me or lose my reason" (p. 173). She thus reproduces the overload theory, but with herself as active manipulator of her own mind, rather than passive recipient of nature's merciful blackout. Even at this point in the novel, however, she will not answer directly when Charley asks her about the past, covering her face with her hand instead to mask a "look of sly cunning" (p. 173). This recalls the way she sits during his first visit, screening "her eyes with a hand as if he were seated opposite nude" (p. 16). The habitual pose seems a physical way to protect what Mr. Grant calls "the picture of this or the other in your mind's eye," a screening of that mental picture from contradictory evidence

---

[25] Weatherhead, p. 97.

in the flesh. Mrs. Grant is, like Nanny Swift in *Loving,* willfully blinding herself to what she doesn't care to see, shielding her delusion from the evidence that might dispel it.

Poor memory is therefore a method of escape that is, here at least, under the control of the individual. Elsewhere in *Back* faulty memory appears as a method of escape not just from overwhelming pain but from the constraints of responsibility to other people. If, as Barbara Hardy says, "memory is a type of fidelity to other people and to our past selves,"[26] then amnesia is a way of eluding others, of denying a responsibility to be the kind of person they expect. *Back* is full of such denials, all of them based on a conveniently disordered memory. Mrs. Grant denies her intimacy with Charley, partially because he reminds her of Rose. Arthur Middlewitch, a slippery and changeable character, escapes Charley's importunate acquaintanceship by misremembering his name. Even Jim Phillips finds his memory of Rose waning as his fidelity to her lapses. Early in the novel he remarks of his son Ridley, "Lord, he reminds me at times of his mother" (p. 85). Yet after he has slept with Dot Pitter, Charley's secretary, Phillips tells Charley, "Anyone would think Ridley must remind me of her, but he doesn't" (p. 128). Though Jim accuses poor Ridley of having a bad memory, his own seems to lapse just when a remembrance of his wife could be troublesome. When Nancy Whitmore, Rose's half sister, has decided to like Charley instead of resenting him, she manages the transition by purposely forgetting her early impressions: "Anyway, it took a bit of forgetting, but I've forgotten now all right" (p. 161). What she has done is to forcibly change Charley's personality by altering her memory, in the same way that Mrs. Grant, Arthur Middlewitch, and Jim Phillips change the person they remember through their own errors. In each case memory lapse represents a denial of some person in the past.

Memory lapses can also represent a lack of fidelity to oneself, a method of escaping responsibility for one's actions. One of the definitions Sir Frederick Bartlett gives for memory

[26]Hardy, p. 78.

in his work *Remembering* is "an individual's way of keeping up an attitude toward the environment which it finds or feels to be adequate and satisfactory."[27] Therefore, a lapse of memory can signal the abandonment of one attitude for another. Mr. Grant, for example, sends Charley to see Nancy Whitmore without any particular instructions of any kind, but later insists that he had asked Charley to keep the source of her address secret: " 'Because I particularly asked you not to say where you got her address,' and Charley thought, you lying bastard" (p. 58). As Mr. Grant says himself, "When you come to consider, there's compensations in not remembering" (p. 34), such as remaining unaware of your own inconsistencies.

The self-serving nature of these amendments of the past points up more than anything that memory is active in Green's novels, not passive, and that memory for Green is an act of creation rather than of retention. Here Green's analysis of memory agrees with that of Bartlett, who concluded from his observations, "The first notion to get rid of is that memory is primarily or literally reduplicative, or reproductive. . . . In fact, if we consider evidence rather than presupposition, remembering appears to be far more decisively an affair of construction rather than one of mere reproduction." In Bartlett's final model, memory is "a constructive justification of attitudes assumed in the present."[28]

Mr. Grant's management of his memory to give himself such a justification is especially significant because it shows how faulty memory is used to maintain the pattern of infidelity that gives *Back* its basic structure. Grant needs to keep his wits about him because he is living a kind of dual existence. Having been unfaithful to his wife at the time of Rose's conception, he is the father of an illegitimate child, Nancy Whitmore, who resembles Rose and is almost exactly the age Rose would be had she lived. This act of unfaithfulness, like

---

[27]Sir Frederick C. Bartlett, *Remembering: A Study in Experimental and Social Psychology* (Cambridge: Cambridge Univ. Press, 1967), p. 203.
[28]Ibid., pp. 204–5 and 208.

the lapses of memory, sets up an alternate reality where people appear in a completely different light. Mr. Grant, for example, becomes a different person when seen from Nancy's point of view, and Mrs. Frazier, Charley's landlady, is transformed into a wicked procuress when seen from Mrs. Grant's, because of her role in Grant's old affair.

It is quite common in *Back* for characters to have two or more distinct personalities, depending on the kind of memories through which they are viewed or the part of the past they themselves wish to subdue. Charley's relationship with Rose, like Mr. Grant's with Nancy's mother, creates a secret Rose, one unknown to her husband. This secret is continued in Ridley, whom Charley believes to be his own son. The question of Ridley's parentage becomes for Charley an obsession with the unreliability of identity, just as the question of his sister's sexual experience does for Pye. He begins to ask seemingly unmotivated questions as Pye does: " 'Talking of resemblances,' Mr. Summers suddenly began, and he was still staring at the fire. 'Children, and their fathers and mothers. Would you say they looked like?' he enquired" (p. 34). His anxiety culminates in the final scene, in which Ridley finally encounters Nancy. Charley puts his finger to his lips, but it is uncertain whose secret identity he wishes to protect, Ridley's or Nancy's, whether he wants to keep Ridley's identity as his son secret from Nancy or Nancy's identity as Rose's half sister secret from Ridley. The two infidelities, Mr. Grant's and his own, cross here in a group that could have as many as four different "identities" depending on whose memories acquire the weight of fact.

Back is full of coincidences like this chance encounter with Ridley, and Green seems to be using this device to show how completely identity depends on attitudes that are altered as memory is altered. Mrs. Frazier, who seems amiable enough at the beginning of the novel, begins to seem shadier and shadier as she turns up in different recollections, especially when she is revealed as the go-between for Mr. Grant and his mistress. Arthur Middlewitch turns up in almost every possible connection, with a different character and past for each acquaintance: as a gay blade when he is with Charley, a meek suppliant with Mr. Grant, a down-at-heels failure with Nancy. The point of Green's coincidences seems to be exactly the opposite of that in nineteenth-century novels, where coincidence usually implies the inevitability of fate and the inescapable consistency of character, as when Jingle reappears all along the route of the Pickwickians, or when Pip's convict returns as a judgment at the end of *Great Expectations*. In each coincidental meeting in *Back* characters recur as completely different people, showing that it is context that determines character. Identity is malleable in *Back*. It is a characterization that others can manipulate by altering their recollection of events.

Charley's own delusion can be seen simply as a specialized version of a mental state common to all the characters in *Back*. As H. P. Lazarus says, "In the real world of his office, his landlady, the Grants, and Nancy, Charley finds that obsessions like his are part of the accepted experience of other people."[29] But the real discovery Charley makes in *Back* is that reality is pliable under such obsessions, that faulty memory and purposeful evasion are not aberrations but the normal means by which reality is constituted, since reality is nothing more than an obsession on which two or more people can agree. Charley's progress through the novel is therefore not from delusion to reality, but from a delusion that is his alone to one he can share, which ceases to be a delusion only because it is connived at by others.

The progress of Charley's delusion that Nancy is Rose betrays its managed character, its basic resemblance to the purposeful delusion of Mrs. Grant. The delusion is not wholly beyond Charley's control, but is, as Cyril Connolly says of one of his own delusions in *The Unquiet Grave*, "the inspiration for which he had long been waiting."[30] Charley's own summary of his love entanglements illustrates the way in which he characteristically sidesteps the present, attacking a

[29]H. P. Lazarus, "Henry Green's Technique," *The Nation*, Nov. 4, 1950, p. 416.
[30]Connolly, *The Unquiet Grave*, p. 126.

problem obliquely by transferring it into a new context: "That time, in the office, when he put his face against hers [Dot Pitter's] because she was crying, had led to his call on Nance, which had caused him to take Dot down to Jim Phillips, which, in its turn had pushed him on here to Nance" (p. 179). This series of maneuvers shows that Charley's characteristic way of dealing with any individual who causes him anxiety is to replace that individual with another, to evade Dot by pursuing Nancy, and to evade Nancy, ultimately, by pursuing Rose, as is shown at the end of his summary when he cries out, "Oh Rose, Rose." Here Green resembles Proust, who suggests, as Barbara Hardy says, "that the imagination cannot work on the materials of the present."[31] Neither Charley's emotions nor his imagination can manage the present, so he sidesteps his problems, replacing the recalcitrant existence of a living person with the malleable memories of a dead one. If Charley's memories of Rose represent his fidelity to a dead woman, they also, more importantly, represent his infidelity to the present, a kind of adultery with his own imagination.

It is important to remember that Charley does not return to England with the delusion that Rose is alive, nor does he have any particularly strong yearnings for her at the beginning of the novel. He surprises himself in a conversation with Mrs. Frazier by feeling "nothing at all at her mention of Rose" (p. 35). After having flinched at each chance mention of any version of her name, he finally realizes in this conversation that "Rose was gone" (p. 36). He becomes so secure he begins to use her name in conversation himself, just to enjoy the sense of freedom he has when he feels no pain. Dot Pitter is the agency that brings Rose back, even more so than Nancy. Green says of Charley's renewed emotions on kissing Dot, "He got much more that he had not remembered" (p. 46). This "much more" is the full existence of Rose, in the person of Nancy. It does not manifest itself until Charley goes to

---

[31]Hardy, p. 56.

see Nancy immediately after work, but the renewed memory of the last time he had kissed a woman is obviously what unsettles him into thinking that Nancy is Rose. It is part of Charley's oblique way of meeting anxiety that he should deal with Dot by visiting Nancy, and his delusion that Nancy is Rose is simply a continuation of this method beyond normal bounds. Rose is resurrected less by a desire to relive the past than by a desire to evade the present, to reconstitute it forcibly in a familiar form. The derangement of Charley's memories is not really a form of fidelity to Rose, but, like the derangements in the memories of the other characters, a form of infidelity to the person he is with.

Dot is therefore more important to *Back*, at least as a catalyst, than has been assumed. As Charley says himself, both of the important steps in his pursuit of Nancy come about because of anxiety over Dot. And it is Dot, and not Rose, who is most significantly betrayed by Charley. Though he denies Rose the three times prescribed in scripture, he cannot really affect the existence of a woman who is dead. His denial of Dot, on the other hand, banishes her from the company and effectively alters her personality in the eyes of the firm. Charley's ability to distort what he sees when some advantage to himself is at stake is made evident by the fact that he really comes to believe that it is Dot's unwillingness and not his own incompetence that is responsible for the mess of their office. More significantly, Charley is liberated from Rose as soon as he eliminates Dot. When she is fired she taunts Charley with his precious Rose, and Charley is able to say once more as he had before he met Dot, "Oh, she was just a tale" (p. 151). He is also able, as soon as Dot is gone, to admit that "Nance was a real person" (p. 155). The way in which his obsession with Rose mounts and diminishes along with his relations with Dot shows that delusion is for Charley simply a way of dealing with the otherwise daunting materials of the present. Rose is a "tale," a fiction he uses to help him over the rough spots of his actual life. As Roe's relations with women are primarily a way to reenact his past, Charley's relations with women necessarily lead back to the past because he can't manage the present, because only the past is really available to his imagination.

But Charley is not the only character in *Back* who is involved with the memory of Rose. Even after he frees himself of his own delusions about Nancy, it is difficult to separate the two women because the social circumstances, the demands of the family group in which Charley and Nancy find themselves, so strongly demand the return of Rose. Bartlett says, in trying to determine the nature of group memory, "When a group is faced with a threat of sudden crisis it often seems to adopt a form of response which runs counter to its recent social history, but is at the same time closely related to a more distant past."[32] Mrs. Grant does this as an individual when she returns mentally to the First World War for her response to the deaths of the Second. Though she snaps out of this delusion when Mr. Grant's illness demands that she be coherent and capable, she participates in another, slightly less delusory, return to the past in response to that crisis. As a result of his stroke, Mr. Grant, according to Nancy, "thinks that I'm Rose" (p. 168). Mrs. Grant, too, finds Nancy "more like the darling I lost than I could imagine. . . . It's as if Rose had come back" (p. 170). The family's practical situation demands a loving daughter, since Mrs. Grant is not capable of caring for Mr. Grant alone, and their psychological situation demands the same thing, as the kind of return to the past that Bartlett describes, which is nothing more than a collective version of the return by which Charley manages his personal crises.

Nancy's willingness to play along with this charade makes her the most intriguing character in the novel. Though she is outwardly indignant at Charley's original assertions that she must be Rose, Nancy soon reveals the fact that the supposed resemblance has always interested her. Resembling her dead half sister seems to be a kind of vocation for her: "I consider, being as I am, the dead spit of another, that I've a responsibility, I'm not like the common run" (p. 71). Being

---

[32]Bartlett, p. 297.

Rose's half sister seems almost a calling for her, with special duties and special rewards. As the narrator reveals, "She was intensely proud of the terrible likeness to her late half sister, and had been ever since she first learned of it" (p. 90). Nancy even manages to think like Rose, so much so that she is indignant when Charley brings Jim Phillips to visit, "Him that's met his wife naked in bed with him. . . . Oh, it's not proper" (p. 88). She says this as if Jim could see her by having seen his wife. When Nancy is invited to the Grants to help nurse her father and begins to refer to Mrs. Grant as "Mother" (p. 164), it is obvious that she has moved into a role she has long coveted. To play Rose in the sickroom is finally to possess the legitimacy she has lacked, both legally and psychologically. The need of the family for a Rose neatly dovetails with Nancy's need to be Rose until the simple physical fact that she is not hardly seems to matter. As in the fire station in *Caught,* yet much more completely, the identity of an individual is determined by the dictates of a group.

As Nancy's relationship to the Grants changes, her relationship to Charley changes in such a way as to bring back the delusion he had shaken, by way of bringing him completely into the family fiction. As noted earlier, Nancy purposely forgets her first impression of Charley when she moves in with the Grants. Her reasons for this become clear when Charley too is assimilated into the family group. Mrs. Grant wants a man in the house now that her husband is so ill, and it falls to Nancy to convince Charley to stay. Playing up to him sexually is "the one way she could make him spend the night" (p. 180), so she allows Charley to think the motive for the invitation is hers. Thus it is the general need that pushes Charley and Nancy together, just as it is the general need that converts Nancy into a surrogate Rose. It is inevitable that the need should bring on a recurrence of Charley's obsession.

Charley is virtually dragged back from sanity by the collusion of the family. Mrs. Grant constantly speaks as if the old days when Charley was courting Rose have returned: "Dear, dear, it does bring it all back. You two sitting in here as bold as brass, just like you were grown up, seeming to dare father and me to come in and disturb you" (p. 172). But the two who bring this scene back are Charley and Nancy, as Nancy herself indicates when she tells Charley to "take me where you used to take her" (p. 175). When they arrive at the tiny, blitzed rose garden where Nancy seems to be converted finally into Rose, it is Nancy who asks, of their kiss, "Was it like that?" (p. 177). Her aim here seems to be to become Rose for him as she has for the Grants. When Charley cries out for Rose while Mr. Grant is dying, Nancy appears, as if in answer. And when Charley agrees to go on the trip she has planned for them, she wheedles by calling him "Charley Barley" (p. 202), the pet name given him by Rose. Therefore, his final collapse into tears, and his final cry for Rose while he is embracing Nancy, is no surprise, least of all for Nancy herself, for whom "it was no more or less, really, than she had expected" (p. 208). It is what Nancy expects because all of her actions and all the actions of the family have been biassed toward blurring her identity until it merges with that of Rose. The obsession Charley conceives on his own and conquers on his own by the middle of the novel is returned to him here by the collaboration of all the other actors in his life.

Thus the final scene of *Back* bears an important resemblance to that of *Caught,* and to similar scenes in all of Green's work. Both *Caught* and *Back* end with one woman melting into another, with the past returning as a living woman assumes the role of one who is dead. The function of these women, it should be clear, is not to help their men by some superior, earthy, feminine realism but to introduce them to the fantasies that will liberate them from the constriction of the present. Dy attempts to do this when she offers her operational definition of reality. She is attempting to free her brother-in-law from his terrible self-consciousness by assuring him that reality is what he imagines it to be, that his recollections exist while the actual past does not. But this method of argument plays to Roe's strength as a discursive individual whose ability to question his own mental formulations is too strong to be overcome. Dy's other method, her silent assumption of the role of Roe's wife, is the one Nancy perfects in *Back*. But Nancy succeeds because Charley is so much more passive than Roe. Charley's characteristic reply to any statement is "There you are" or "There it is," a gesture of acceptance he makes more than a dozen times in the course of the novel. The phrase is another indication of Charley's method of dealing with problems, which is headlong retreat.

Charley achieves by this passivity what John Haye wants but fails to achieve, the transformation of a living woman into a fictional one, one who will act out the role Charley requires. In a way Charley is the person Haye fancies himself to be, the returning war hero complete with wound. And this wound, which is more the passivity that Charley brings back from Germany than the loss of his leg, accomplishes for him what it was supposed to have accomplished for Haye. But what is in *Blindness* a quirkish, adolescent method of dealing with experience is seen in *Caught* and *Back* as the inescapable result of modern history. Charley resembles the returned soldiers of the First World War of whom Walter Benjamin asked, "Was it not noticeable at the end of the war that men had returned from the battlefield grown silent—not richer, but poorer in communicable experience."[33] Charley's numb acceptance of any routine offered to him and the blindly mechanical system he introduces into his office recall Hemingway's Nick Adams in "Big Two-Hearted River," a story in which the bland, automatic observation of routine is itself supposed to convey the fact that Nick has been badly wounded in the war.[34] The only detail he ever divulges about his life in the German prison camp is that he kept a pet mouse there. This should not be taken as some special deficiency in him, because it simply reproduces the inability of any of Green's wartime characters to grasp what is happening to them at the time it is happening. Charley's stay in the prison camp is,

---

[33]Walter Benjamin, *Illuminations,* tr. Harry Zohn (New York: Harcourt, Brace & World, 1968), p. 84.
[34]See Scott Donaldson, *By Force of Will: The Life and Art of Ernest Hemingway* (New York: Viking, 1977), p. 245.

like Roe's stay in the fire station, a phony war, one in which nothing seems to have happened, in which normal life is suspended, individual existence destroyed but nothing intelligible put in its place.

Memory functions for all of Green's wartime characters as a way of managing otherwise amorphous, intractable experiences. It functions according to a definition Benjamin quotes from Valéry: "Recollection is . . . an elemental phenomenon which aims at giving us the time for organizing the reception of stimuli which we initially lacked."[35] Green's characters purposely deflect present experience into the past in order to be able to manage it. Like the lovers in wartime London, whose affairs are already memory, or Roe, whose bifurcated existence makes his false memories of home stronger than any reality, or Charley, whose characteristic way of dealing with the present is to assume that it is in fact the past, Green's characters push experience as fast as they can out of the present in order to make it subject to the fictionalizing process of memory. Memory is creative, as Bartlett says, because it must be, because it is not a method of retrieving the past so much as it is a method of experiencing the present. Thus Charley is able to find collaborators where John Haye is not, and is led gently back into his fiction by the public world of the family, instead of having his fiction destroyed there.

All of the characters of *Back* have moved toward the condition of John Haye, incapacitated in the real world but set free in a world of their own devising. This must be why the war was a period of such great literary activity for Green, why *Back* is, as V. S. Pritchett says, "certainly the only novel to have captured the inner life of war-time England."[36] The past returns and death is defeated because an ordinary family has become Proustian, unable to realize their experiences without the mediation of memory, because the war requires more than ever that their lives be lived through the conscious alterations of fiction.

[35]Benjamin, pp. 163–64.
[36]V. S. Pritchett, "Henry Yorke, Henry Green," *London Magazine,* 14 (June–July 1974), 32.

What the war seems to have taught Green is that the relationship between time and identity has been altered, as Mary Howells hints in *Caught,* by a succession of events too bewildering for the individual to assimilate. The basic constituent of a stable identity is temporal continuity, or at least a certain balance between boredom and surprise. But Green saw the life of his generation freed of its original melody and turned into a process of improvisation on previous improvisations. Since memory becomes less a tool of recall and more a way of meeting and defeating chaos, it can no longer function as a preservative of identity, and the prewar personality that once existed outside the fire station disappears. The dichotomy of *Caught* is solved by a resolution in favor of the ersatz persona of wartime. In a sense this is a description of personality Green has been working toward since *Blindness,* and to attach it to as finite an event as the Second World War is to make it seem too mechanical and automatic a response. But the war did enliven Green's eye for this kind of self-creation, and the remaining two works of the wartime period show how he connected the creative in the individual with the oppressive in society at large.

4

"This Great Place"
LOVING and CONCLUDING

*House and field reflect back to the young heir
a stable image of himself. He touches himself
on his gravel, on the diamond-shaped panes
of his veranda, and makes of their inertia the
deathless substance of his soul.*

Jean-Paul Sartre
The Words

I

IN his introduction to the wartime anthology *Lyra,* Herbert Read says, "It is not war in the ordinary sense which we are enduring, but a world revolution in which all conventions, whether of thought or action, break down and are replaced—not by new conventions, for conventions are of slow growth—but by provisional formulas which are immediately tested under fire." British literature of the early part of the war is largely concerned with this subject, with the dissolution of conventions and the growth of new, provisional ones such as the rituals of Green's fire station or the odd new roles forced on the contributors to *Penguin New Writing.* As the war continued, some writers began to look for new conventions, new orthodoxies, to transcend the provisionality and discontinuity that Lehmann mentions in his 1944 comparison of his contributors to Gregor Samsa. In that same Foreword Lehmann expressed his desire for a "generally accepted myth or system of beliefs . . . a myth whose wholeness would heal the wound between war and peace-time occupation, between the past and the present." The same call for a new myth came from Cyril Connolly in *The Unquiet Grave,* in which he says that "validity of the myth" is basic to literature, and that his time and generation suffer from "decadence of the myth." This was also one of the programs of the Apocalypse, as Henry Treece defined it: "To recreate a forgotten truth, and to erect for public recognition those fundamental myths and ideologies which will germinate naturally."[1]

The desire for continuity and stability is certainly the basis for one myth that did germinate naturally during these years, the myth of the great house. Waugh's *Brideshead Revisited,* for example, satisfied a desire both in its audience and its author to escape from a period of insecurity and insubstantiality into a more satisfying past. As Waugh says in his 1959 preface, "It was a bleak period of present privation and threatening disaster—the period of soya beans and Basic English—and in consequence the book is infused with a kind of gluttony, for food and wine, for the splendours of the recent past." Waugh later became rather sarcastic at the expense of this myth, handing it over to the hated literary imposter Ludovic in *Unconditional Surrender.* What irks Waugh about Ludovic's novel, which is a thinly disguised version of *Brideshead Revisited,* is partly the need to escape, which it so blatantly serves, and partly the fact that everyone else in London had written a similar book: "Had he known it, half a dozen other English writers, averting themselves sickly from privations of war and apprehensions of the social consequences of the peace, were even then severally and secretly, unknown to one another . . . composing or preparing to compose, books which would turn from the drab alleys of the thirties

---

[1]Lehmann, Foreword, p. 7; Connolly, *The Unquiet Grave,* pp. 41 and 56. Read's comment and Treece's are most readily available in Hewison, pp. 114 and 179.

into the odorous gardens of a recent past transformed by disordered memory and imagination."[2]

Waugh's repudiation of his own work may be attributable to annoyance at having stumbled onto a popular trend, one epitomized in these years by the novels of Angela Thirkell. But the secluded house fulfilled the need for myth in other serious writers as well. This is the advantage of the remote Irish country house in Elizabeth Bowen's *The Heat of the Day*, "in that by geographically standing outside war it appeared also to be standing outside the present. The house, non-human, became the hub of . . . imaginary life, of fancies, fantasies only to be so called because circumstances outlawed them from reality."[3] The popularity of the great house novel must have come from the sense the secluded house gave of standing outside of time, of inhabiting a time undisturbed by the dislocations of the war. It therefore satisfied the desire expressed by Lehmann, Connolly, and Treece for conventions that would transcend the temporary ones presently in force at the same time that it provided a symbol of physical security. Novels like *Brideshead Revisited* satisfy the need for myth by describing a mythical place, by indulging the nostalgia for a past insulated from temporal change as it is from physical danger. What all of these writers are expressing is, as Lionel Trilling says of *Mansfield Park,* a "need to find security, to establish, in fixity and enclosure, a refuge from the dangers of openness and chance."[4]

Loving can be seen as an example of the same trend, as one of the novels Waugh mocks in *Unconditional Surrender,* and as an analysis of the basic psychological condition underlying the trend. *Loving* is also the culmination of Green's ideas about how personal life is constituted, containing as its basic assumption the idea that people become themselves only when

---

[2]Evelyn Waugh, *Brideshead Revisited* (1945; rpt. London: Longmans, 1968), p. vii; idem, *Unconditional Surrender* (London: Chapman and Hall, 1961), p. 243.
[3]Elizabeth Bowen, *The Heat of the Day* (New York: Knopf, 1949), p. 52.
[4]Trilling, *The Opposing Self,* p. 185.

they enjoy "fixity and enclosure." One of the basic themes of *Loving* is that conventions such as those demanded by the writers of the time do not necessarily falsify individuals, that, as Trilling says, "the self may be preserved by the negation of its own energies."[5] In this sense all of Green's characters have sought enclosure, all from John Haye on have achieved their freedom by accepting some negation of themselves, either blindness, or servility, or a role determined by others. The roles and routines of the household in *Loving* are the most complete of these enclosures, the final fictions within which the characters find their most perfect freedom. In *Loving* the geography of the house is not just a metaphor for the self, it *is* the self, and all of the characters' most intimate concerns are tied directly to it.

Loving is set "in Eire where there is no blackout."[6] Thus Green defines his setting at the very outset by its difference from England. But physical remoteness is only one effect of the setting. Kinalty Castle is a kind of double enclave like the Irish house in *The Heat of the Day,* outside of time because of its distance from the war. Unlike the two novels that bracket it, *Loving* shows absolutely no interest in memory and none in the passage of time. As Edward Stokes points out, "There is only one brief flashback in the whole novel."[7] Stokes's outline of *Loving* shows that the events of the book are entirely restricted to a two-month period and are always presented as they happen, never from another vantage point in time. *Loving* is therefore the direct antithesis of *Caught,* which veers wildly back and forth in time and in which the present hardly exists between the two huge expanses of past and future. But this is not to say that *Loving* exists in an identifiably real present, that it seems more quotidian than *Caught.* On the contrary, it is explicitly set outside time by the first line, which begins, "Once upon a day" (p. 5). It is as if the passage of time had been erased by placing the entire

[5]Ibid., p. 191.
[6]Henry Green, *Loving* (London: Hogarth, 1945), p. 5. All subsequent references are to this edition and in this chapter will appear in text.
[7]Stokes, p. 115.

novel in the romantic, fairy-tale past of *Caught* and *Back* where virtually anything is possible, as if it had, like the Irish house in Bowen's novel, been placed in a mythical time by its removal from the physical locale of the war.

The war does drone away in the distance in *Loving,* more like the kind of annoying household noise that can never be located or stopped than as a real threat. The servants who form most of the cast of the novel are easily worked up into a form of war hysteria, but the extravagance of their fears, the outrageousness of their fantasies, betrays their utter lack of connection with the realities of the war. The real war exists mostly in reports of "this terrible bombing" (p. 133), and it is possible that guilt over their safety from the bombing that threatens their relatives in England causes the fantasies of danger they invent for themselves. There are two conflicting fantasies, one that they are already in "enemy country" and thus in constant danger from the Irish, especially the I.R.A., and the other that the Germans are "set to cross over with drawn swords" (p. 160). The fact that no one can think of a reason for the Germans to take time off from France to invade a neutral country which is "all bog and stones" does not dispel their fears. These fears really seem to precede any facts that might justify them, as if the anxiety of the servants is a psychological given, a state that exists in the absence of an outside threat, which then must be rationalized by invented dangers. As Irving Howe says, "To symbolize and justify their unease, the servants fabricate excitement by convincing themselves they are in danger from invading Nazis and secret I.R.A. agents."[8]

One response to such fears is to keep the house as inviolate as possible, to preserve its traditions exactly as if to preserve its status as an enclave. Mrs. Tennant, English owner of Kinalty, gives her own ludicrous version of the rationale behind the great house myth when she says, "In a way I regard this as my war work, maintaining the place I mean.

---

[8]Irving Howe, "Fiction Chronicle," *Partisan Review,* 16 (Oct. 1949), 1054.

Because we're practically in enemy country here you know and I do consider it so important from the morale point of view to keep up appearances" (p. 186). Preserving her own treasures, her own privileges, and preserving the aristocratic way of life she leads become somehow in Mrs. Tennant's mind a service to civilization. Looking around the room she had decorated in an artificially rustic style, Mrs. Tennant says, "It's all French you know . . . they say it came from France which is why I try to impress it on the servants that they must be careful. There'll be so little left when this war's finished" (p. 206). Western civilization comes down in her mind to imitation pint measures in gilded wood, to Gothic imitation hammocks or French provincial milking stools, to the kind of frippery Waugh confessed he was longing for when he wrote *Brideshead Revisited*. In its portrayal of Mrs. Tennant, *Loving* is a satire on the great house myth, which is simply the identification of an insular, privileged way of life with civilization itself.

But *Loving* also analyzes the psychological dependence on place, the need for protection and isolation both in space and time which brings the great house myth into being. Bruce Bassoff says that Green accomplishes his characterizations by "stationing," a term Keats applies to Milton's tendency to give his characters a significant physical position. In Bassoff's analysis, stationing hardly seems to differ from any other kind of imagery, but it is true that each of the characters of *Loving* is "stationed" in a particular place within the castle and in a particular social station that seem fundamental to his or her identity. Kinalty Castle is, in Stokes's words, "a loose confederation of independent states ruled over by butler, housekeeper, cook and nurse."[9] The rule of each individual is absolute in his or her own place, the boundaries of which are defined by the individual's ability to exclude outsiders. The kitchen, for example, is referred to as "Mrs. Welch's kingdom" (p. 180), from which she pointedly excludes Raunce and Miss Swift. "On guard I am," she says to her nephew.

[9]Bassoff, p. 158; Stokes, p. 16.

"I daresn't abandon this kitchen day or night" (p. 167). A similar kingdom is Miss Swift's nursery, from which Raunce is also excluded. That Miss Swift is queen on her own ground is shown by the resentment of the other servants, whose judgment is that "Miss Swift is a difficult woman whilst she's up in her nursery" (p. 34). What Miss Burch, the housekeeper, envies in these two women is precisely their ability to exclude Raunce: "But then you've both of you a place you call your own. Not like me with no more than a door opening into the sink and a bit of a cupboard in all this mansion" (p. 121). Burch is ignoring her own bedroom here because the question is one of professional space, of a place identified with one's work that validates one's position in the castle by allowing the exclusion of outsiders. Even Raunce, who seems at times to exist only to give others the pleasure of excluding him, looks at his room as if it were a guardpost. He rationalizes his seizure of the butler's empty room by saying, "I'm sure Mrs. T would not wish the strongroom left unguarded of a night time" (p. 18), implicitly casting himself in the role of a policeman over all the other servants. Even Paddy, low man in the house as lampman and peacock tender, has his lamproom in which he spends the later part of the novel "locked up with them birds" (p. 208). To Michel Vinaver, the French translator of *Loving,* space in the novel "is not a static collection of material objects, it is a system of possibilities of action."[10] The castle is broken up into zones, each of which offers its freedoms only to the one person who dominates it and which is taboo to everyone else. Each room is a microcosm of the castle as a whole, doubly remote, doubly protected from all possible invaders.

Since these places are defined by profession within the household, they come to be associated with all the social usages which determine that position. Terry Eagleton exposes the double meaning of the word *place* in this context when he says of *Brideshead Revisited,* "The novel maintains that

---

[10]Anthony Quinton's article "A French View of *Loving,*" *London Magazine,* 6 (Apr. 1959), 25–35, is largely a translation of Vinaver's "Essai sur un roman," *Les Lettres Nouvelles* (June–July, 1953), 417. See Quinton, p. 29.

characteristic English upper-class commitment to 'place' and 'family' which can seem curiously independent of the precise qualities of particular people."[11] In *Loving* physical place denotes one's social place in the sense Eagleton intends of a social role independent of individuals, and Green tries to show how protection of that social place can fulfill the same function as protection of one's room. When Mrs. Tennant says, "We simply must keep things up" because "we're really in enemy country here" (p. 11), the "things" she is speaking of are social usages, such as the attitude of Raunce, who has just been named butler. Preservation of social roles is as important to her as preservation of the building, and for similar defensive reasons. But reliance on such social rules is not, as Eagleton says, confined to the upper class, at least not in *Loving*. For the servants are more punctilious in routine, more observant of small social gradations, than Mrs. Tennant, and maintenance of their own social niche has the same kind of defensive purpose that maintaining the whole social organization has for her. To fill a role completely is not, as might be expected, self-effacement in *Loving,* nor is it servility. To insist on the parameters of one's role is in this novel to achieve a free space for the self analogous to the free physical space of the kitchen, nursery, or lamproom.

The tremendous importance given to names and titles by the servants at Kinalty is an indication of the connection between social usages and self-esteem. "Don't call her cook she don't like the name" (p. 16) is a proverbial expression that crops up whenever Mrs. Welch is mentioned, obviously reflecting a long war between her and the rest of the staff over the establishment of her title. What Mrs. Welch is laying claim to is simply the standard reference due to her station: "She's only called Mrs. like all cooks" (p. 39). That some of the servants come to think of themselves as identical to their titles is made evident in Nanny Swift's habitual reference to herself as "Poor nanny" (pp. 86, 119, 123). Therefore, to trifle with a title is to trifle with the identity of the person involved,

---

[11]Terry Eagleton, *Exiles and Emigres* (New York: Schocken, 1970), p. 59.

and to insist on one's own title is to defend a prerogative linguistically as it is defended spatially.

Thus one of the main subplots of the novel is, as James Hall says, "Charley's establishing himself as Raunce, the butler, rather than Charley the footman, or 'Arthur,' the generic name Mrs. Tennant uses for all unimportant male servants."[12] Hall is not quite correct in saying that *Arthur* is a term for all lower males in the household. It is never applied, for example, to Albert, who serves under Raunce. *Arthur* is, like everything else at Kinalty, place-specific, all footmen being called Arthur after the first, "whose name really had been Arthur" (p. 8). But Mrs. Tennant does not preserve the name simply out of forgetfulness. It is a sort of assertion that one's own name is granted only at a certain social level. Her way of giving Raunce the promotion from footman to butler is to admit, "I suppose we shall have to call you Raunce" (p. 10). The real battle, however, is in the servants' quarters over the question of whether to grant Raunce the tribute of a "Mr." The reactions of Miss Burch are the most revealing, since she exclaims, actually irate, "And now I make no doubt you are counting on her addressing you as Raunce . . . with Mr. Eldon not yet in the ground" (p. 17). Burch speaks as if Raunce had appropriated something of Eldon's by taking his own surname, and in a way he has, since a surname, no matter what it might happen to be, is the prerogative of the butler. Burch exposes the fact that Raunce has not really emerged as an individual even by acquiring his own name but has simply moved to a new social place.

Though the first half of the novel follows Raunce's rise in the household from a footman to its butler and dominant figure, he does not take charge by putting his own stamp on things. Raunce's way of asserting his importance and using his power is to imitate Eldon, his predecessor. The first big step is to take Eldon's chair, a feat Raunce nerves himself up for by repeating, "This time I'll take his old chair. I must" (p. 14). Gradually, Raunce acquires Eldon's role, even his

[12]Hall, p. 71.

mannerisms, along with the chair: "Right to the last meal Mr. Eldon had taken in this room it had been his part to speak, to wind up as it were, almost to leave the impress of a bishop on his flock" (p. 34). Raunce demands Eldon's perquisites such as tea in bed in the morning, because "in Mr. Eldon's day that's the way it used to be every morning" (p. 19). But Eldon's perquisites seem to have a momentum of their own, as if they had simply adopted a new host to replace the dead one. Raunce takes Eldon's ledgers, in which the old butler has entered his embezzlements from the house, his tips, and his petty blackmail of Captain Davenport, who is having an affair with young Mrs. Tennant. So impressed is Raunce with the system that he tries it out, repeating the little catch phrases Eldon noted next to the names of frequent visitors and stunning Captain Davenport with an entirely inappropriate reference to salmon trout. Raunce even enters his first tip, though it is a dismal, ignorable threepence. The hold these ledgers come to have over Raunce is signified in an odd scene in which Kate and Edith catch him investigating the feed bins of the peacocks, one of Eldon's sources of illicit funds. When they see Raunce through the glass of the lamproom his face has been "altered by refraction to red morocco leather" (p. 52), the kind of leather the ledgers are bound in. Even when Raunce redecorates Eldon's room, which might seem to imply a conversion of it into something more identifiable with himself, he does so by taking the pictures out of "Mr. Jack's old playroom" right down to a "plain house photograph of Etonians including Mr. Jack in tails" (p. 105). He displays these borrowed decorations proudly, as if they were his own.

Raunce has virtually no existence outside his role within the social system of the house. According to Kate, he "hasn't shoved his head into the air these three years it must be" (p. 24). Raunce seems to have an objection to the outdoors, calling it "wrong side of the window" (p. 24), a real fear of it, as if without the context of the house he were defenseless. And this seems to be true, because it is on his first jaunt outside with Edith that his illness begins, an illness Raunce blames on having left the house: "It's coming away in the air 'as done it" (p. 94). Raunce is strong where habit and custom have established a traditional strength he can lay claim to, weak where there are no precedents for action. His illness in the open air signifies his utter dependence on the house and its usages for his very existence.

As Hall says, Raunce seems to have a "script" which he follows even in the simplest actions.[13] His dependence on this script makes him seem an almost mechanical being, whose movements are "automatic" (p. 46). His automatism is related at the most basic level to the physical layout of Kinalty Castle and is, like the roles of Swift and Welch, a function of space. Very early in the book Raunce is described as taking "twenty trained paces" (p. 8) between rooms. Part of the training Raunce has put himself through obviously involves counting and standardizing his steps, at first, presumably, for the sake of efficiency. This almost suspicious efficiency of movement is one of his basic characteristics. He is always popping up unexpectedly, startling Kate or Edith by appearing where he shouldn't be or moving into rooms "like an eel into its drainpipe" (p. 12). This helps to explain why enclaves such as Swift's and Welch's are defended particularly against Raunce, as a person who makes himself unpleasantly free about the house.

But this kind of training has affected what passes for Raunce's personal life as well. Even his most private moments are standardized and repetitive. The habit of writing his letters first in pencil, then inking the letters in, signifies more than the contents of the letters the utter unspontaneity of what he has to say. Green underscores the habitual, almost ritualistic nature of these letterwriting sessions by reproducing an almost identical description each time: "Then he inked it in. . . . Lastly he laid his head down on his arms, went straight off to sleep" (p. 35); "Then he inked it in. . . . After he had stamped the envelope he laid his head down on his arms and dropped off to sleep at once" (p. 118). Even Raunce's way

[13]Ibid., p. 73.

of falling asleep has a pattern to it, as if even his relaxations from routine are trained.

Raunce is, as Stokes says, "always acting."[14] His particular kind of acting is that in which a set of predetermined, standardized expressions are used to create character. Thus Raunce has certain unchanging phrases that he applies whenever the proper situation arises. The most ludicrous of these is perhaps his advice to Albert to "clean your teeth before ever you have anything to do with a woman" (p. 5). The advice recurs throughout the novel until it seems the result of some fetish. Even putting the exact content of the advice aside, its implicit message is that behavior is the orchestration of habits and that good habits are the key to a happy, successful life. Raunce's speech is a collection of such habits, and he has a tendency to see others in terms of their habitual expressions. He is the one who keeps repeating Mrs. Welch's command that she not be called cook and who uses a "high falsetto he put on whenever he referred to Nanny Swift" (p. 33). The repetition of vocal tricks signifies not only Raunce's own method of acting but his implicit assumption that the other servants can be summed up by their own proverbial expressions or patterns of speech, that habit is the key to character.

The automatic, mechanical air this gives to Raunce's behavior is at least partially calculated on his part. Walter Allen has commented that Raunce is seen "wholly from the outside."[15] But this is certainly because Raunce sees himself from the outside. His habit of referring to himself in the third person signifies this. Even more revealing is the way he alters the third-person reference according to his situation. He is "uncle" with Albert when he wants to appear avuncular (p. 70), "little Charley" with Edith when he wants to be endearing (p. 165), "Clever Charley" when he wants to be assuring (p. 189), and "Lucky Charley" (p. 224), "Busy Charley" (p. 63), or "Broadminded Charley" (p. 69) when he wants to assume other attributes. The names indicate that

[14]Stokes, p. 56.
[15]Walter Allen, *The Modern Novel* (New York: Dutton, 1964), p. 218.

Raunce plays a series of roles, each with its appropriate gestures and expressions, each with a definitive title. His habit of talking to himself before a decisive move such as his appropriation of Eldon's chair shows that Raunce assumes these roles willfully, like the kind of discipline he recommends to Albert, a way of purposely ordering his experience by way of repetition.

Such habits bring Raunce the suspicion and mistrust of most of the other servants, but not because they themselves are any more genuine. The same kind of repetition, mimicry, and self-casting appear when the lower servants deal with one another. The habit of quotation, for example, is a general one at Kinalty. Sometimes a quotation signifies that one of the lower servants has fallen into a pattern determined by a superior, as when Edith says, quoting Miss Burch, "How's the work goin' to be finished? I'll ask you that" (p. 87). Patterns of speech like this one go with particular places in the household hierarchy. When Miss Burch is too ill to take her place at table, Edith sits there and talks "quite natural in Agatha's manner" (p. 208) while there. At other times, the servants quote one another as a way of assuming well-known, stock attitudes that are appropriate to a new situation, such as the time Kate quotes Burch's "I feel faint . . . in Agatha's voice" (p. 164) to suggest that she has been abandoned to do all the work. At times the servants engage in group quotation, as when they work themselves into fits of laughter by mimicking the lisp of the insurance investigator who has come to find Mrs. Tennant's ring. This scene is the only one in the novel in which the entire group of servants lays aside its suspicions and envies in order to become something like a family. They achieve their only real warmth, not by unmasking and exchanging home truths, but by mocking an outsider. As so often in Green, the approach to intimacy is by way of some convenient fiction, and the servants become close when they begin momentarily to act in the same play.

Successful social life at Kinalty is therefore a ritual, hackneyed and automatic at least partially because the servants feel that important sentiments are those that are repeatable.

Green's own narrative style reflects the opinion of the servants in this expectation that experience will always run in certain predetermined patterns. Stokes mentions "very frequent use of 'this' or 'that' instead of the article" as the primary idiosyncrasy of the style of *Loving*. The same overuse of demonstrative adjectives is mentioned by Tindall, who concludes that they remove the noun in question to a "suitable distance."[16] But the function of the demonstrative in *Loving* seems more to be to single out a noun and to call attention to it more completely than the article does. Often in *Loving* the demonstrative presumes a prior familiarity, as when the path to the pseudo-Greek temple behind Kinalty is called "that walk to the temple" (p. 112). Here the demonstrative seems based on a prior knowledge of habits as well as of things. At times demonstrative adjectives are used to pointedly overrefer to things. An example of this is a reference to Violet Tennant, who is called "this man's wife" when she greets her husband, as if to nudge the reader slightly over her remembered adultery. The assumption of prior familiarity is also a feature of the talk of the servants, who often use pronouns with an understood antecedent even when the immediate conversation has established no antecedent. Miss Burch, for example, announces the loss of Mrs. Tennant's ring with a simple, "She's mislaid her big sapphire cluster" (p. 64), and Kate, without prelude, refers to " 'Er peacock" (p. 132), meaning the peacock that has haunted Mrs. Welch's kitchen. Green, taking the hint perhaps from Henry James, uses this habit in a number of comic scenes, in which two characters stubbornly insist on different antecedents for the pronouns they both use. Burch and Mrs. Welch, for example, speak at cross purposes for long periods of time, both refusing to clarify just which " 'e" is the subject of their conversation. This habit, like the use of demonstratives in the narration, presumes a world so small and so circumscribed that everything in it is familiar, everything seen or done before.

---

[16]Stokes, p. 222; William York Tindall, *The Literary Symbol* (Bloomington: Indiana Univ. Press, 1955), p. 97.

Loving AND *Concluding*

The servants insist on such fictions because they need to, because familiarity is part of the system of enclosure that sustains life. Some of the more poignant scenes in *Loving* illustrate the effort it takes to maintain enclosure, at times against the most glaring physical evidence. Nanny Swift, for example, must defend her nursery from unseemly thoughts as well as from physical intrusion. Swift is supposedly deaf, but within her nursery at least this deafness seems managed, and for the same reasons that she often closes her eyes when outside. When Burch attempts to introduce the subject of the cook's drinking, Swift objects, "Oh dear oh no I wouldn't wish to listen" (p. 121). When this objection fails, Swift makes an extra effort, and says, "There now I've forgotten every bit of it poor nanny" (p. 121). A more difficult test comes with the news of Violet Tennant's adultery. Since Violet was her first charge, Swift wants particularly to protect an original image of her as a blameless little girl. Therefore, when Burch enters the nursery with ominous yet secretly delighted sighs of "Ah Mrs. Jack," Swift speaks more and more quickly, using her own words to prevent others from filling the space. Finally, however, the worst comes out, but Swift seems not to hear, and lies back, "eyes closed or rather screwed shut in a wild look of alarm" (p. 125). She is never forced to acknowledge the unpleasant fact, but the solitude of her nursery has been fatally breached, and her illness, which has been mounting as things deteriorate in the castle, becomes so serious that she must keep to her room. The nursery becomes a sickroom, and Swift's complete withdrawal to it is a final retreat to a place that is identified with her own personality, as if to protect what is left of the fiction she lives by.

The need to stabilize and control a corner of reality by controlling access to and behavior within a particular corner of the castle is so universal among the servants that almost all the occurrences that form the plot of *Loving* are by nature invasions like those sustained by Nanny Swift. John Russell has identified several important actions that he says compose the plot of *Loving* and has called these actions "transgressions."[17] This is accurate only if *transgress* is used in its original sense to mean stepping across a boundary, because the key controversies of the novel all involve the invasion of territory sacrosanct to someone. Paddy's lamproom, for example, is rifled first by Edith, whose theft of peacock eggs sets up reverberations within the house that never quite die down. It is also invaded by young Albert, who strangles one of Paddy's peacocks, and by Raunce, who wants to master Eldon's method of embezzling from the meal tubs. These invasions affect Paddy just as Burch's invasion affects Swift. They put him "in a terrible state" (p. 196), in which he withdraws to the lamproom, locks the door, and refuses to come out. Another central event that is essentially an invasion is Edith's discovery of Captain Davenport in Violet Tennant's bed. This might be called a multiple invasion since Davenport is where he certainly doesn't belong and is discovered only because Edith barges into the room without knocking. Mrs. Welch's young Albert, evacuated from London, is a general invader who doesn't belong anywhere in the castle and who therefore causes havoc wherever he goes. He is defined as such by Raunce, who says of evacuees, "No matter what the homes are they've come from they're like fiends straight up from hell honey after they've been a month or more down in the country districts" (pp. 173–74). To Raunce "evacuee" and "fiend" are synonyms because evacuees lack a place and must inevitably batten on someone else's.

The castle is also a haven for hypochondriacs, and as the novel progresses more and more of the characters retire to sulk behind feigned illnesses. These illnesses, significantly, always follow an unsuccessful defense against invasion. Physical space and its prerogatives become so closely identified with the well-being of the inhabitant that an invasion of the room has the effect of an invasion of the body. Miss Burch's illness, for example, dates from the unpleasant visit of the insurance inspector, who introduces himself into the drawing room before the servants are ready and who thrusts himself

---

[17]Russell, p. 120.

into their routines to find the missing ring. Raunce's illness is also partially attributable to this investigation. Raunce first feels ill when removed from the house, but he later dates his nagging dyspepsia from the investigator's visit: "Upset me too that merchant did. There's been something wrong with my interior from that day to this. I can't seem able to digest my food" (p. 210). Being removed from the house and suffering an invasion of the house come to the same thing. Raunce's dependence on a safe place patterned by his own routines amounts to a physical dependence like that of a mollusk on its shell.

Place and routine offer more than simple protection, though. The opportunity they offer to see the self objectified, solidly represented in the physical world, is even more important. Raunce says when he begins to suffer, "I can't properly see myself these days. . . . Why I'm altogether changed" (p. 163). The way Raunce sees himself from the outside has already been described, and this comment, coming as it does with his illness, shows why such a view is crucial to his well-being. Raunce's desire for a place of his own, a chair and a room of his own, his stage management of his life so that it repeats the same predetermined routines, comes from a need to see some physical evidence of himself, to see himself from a distance as though to verify his existence. Vinaver says of the characters of *Loving*, "A person *is* in his desire to be and in his terror of being nothing."[18] Raunce *is* in the external productions, the habits, routines, and rituals that he uses to objectify and therefore substantiate his existence to himself. Raunce sickens because he feels that his place is "doomed to a natural death so to say" (p. 219) and because this death will necessarily involve his own. The same is true in a lesser degree for the other servants, especially the ones like Swift, Burch, Welch, and Paddy, who suffer physical pain when their place is violated.

Similar anxieties are caused throughout *Loving* by the loss of significant objects, losses that carry the same psychological threat as invasion. So many things are stolen or mislaid in

---

[18]Quinton, p. 30.

the novel that it is obviously inappropriate to try to find an individual symbolic association for each of them. The objects become important because they are missing, not because of any intrinsic symbolic importance in themselves. Loss worries the characters for the same reason that intrusion does, because it implies a chink in the walls, a breach both of defenses and of routines. The losses that can be identified as outright thefts obviously fall into this category. Edith's theft of the peacock eggs and Albert's theft of the peacock drive Paddy back into his lamproom, where he swears he is "goin' to lock 'em up and never let the things out any more" (p. 196). Edith's theft of Mrs. Welch's water glass is a similar violation. Welch perceives this theft as a direct attack in some sort of larger campaign against herself, an attack she refers to as "the diabolical stroke" (p. 67). She works this single theft up in her mind into an entire conspiracy, until Raunce and Edith appear to her like "a pair of squirrels before the winter layin' in a store" (p. 179).

Considered from the standpoint of the thief, such petty pilferage is like the squirrel's preparations of its nest against the winter. When, at the beginning of the novel, Raunce with his stolen whiskey meets Edith with her stolen eggs hidden in a stolen glove, it becomes obvious that, as Vinaver says, the thefts "are part of the traditional order of things."[19] Raunce sees thievery as one of his perquisites, as a privilege of the position that comes down to him along with Eldon's double set of ledgers. Edith, on the other hand, has no perquisites in the house and not much of a "place" in it. The peacock eggs are to be part of a "charm" she is concocting, a designation that, though it seems to refer to a magic potion, should remind the reader of Julia's "charms" in *Party Going*. A charm in either case is like a lucky rabbit's foot or the "mascots" of *Mood*, something that protects the owner, even giving the owner her weight and substance, as Julia's do in the memory in which they act as her ballast against the wind. In an odd

[19]Ibid., p. 29.

way Edith's story of finding Violet Tennant and Captain Davenport in bed functions as such a charm. Stolen just as much as the peacock eggs, her knowledge of this adultery becomes a possession from which Edith feels a reflected importance. She compares it to Raunce's stories of "openin' this door and seeing that when you were in a place in Dorset and lookin' through the bathroom window down in Wales an' suchlike . . . and now it's come to me" (p. 79). When Raunce, afraid, tries to downpedal the story, she says, "You're going to try to take that from me?" (p. 80). Edith perceives any denial of the story as a theft itself, a direct attack, in the same way that Welch perceives the loss of her water glass as a personal attack. The story gives Edith something to defend, so that she greets Nanny Swift as though she were an enemy. But it also makes Edith ecstatically happy, as if she is no one in the house until she has something of her own to protect.

A few of the missing objects are not stolen, but truly lost, and these have the effect of undermining the security of the entire house. Any loss is to Burch just a single example of the general deterioration that has set in since the death of Mr. Eldon: "No matter who couldn't happen to lay their hands on something he always imagined where to find it" (p. 66). Both Burch and Welch have an odd fetish for drains that is excited whenever there are rumors of a loss. They agree that the only way to find Mrs. Tennant's ring is "to get the plumbin' opened up that's all" (p. 67). Their unease is associated with "a terrible stench of drains" (p. 177) which nags at Welch and which seems to be quite imaginary. The whole preoccupation with drains is, as Mrs. Tennant says, quite fantastic, and it evaporates as soon as she challenges it, but the preoccupation is obviously never motivated by any conscious knowledge of a threat in the plumbing. The drains are feared as a breach in the house, an uncontrollable area, a kind of black hole into which matter can disappear beyond the control of the staff. This fear corresponds to the desire of the two women to see everything in the house fastened to its place. As Welch says, "There's just the one thing for it . . . every mortal object must be under lock and key" (p. 68), and she cleverly passes a thread through the handles of her pots and pans until a chain and padlock can be found.

Mrs. Tennant's lost sapphire ring therefore has a significance quite separate from any mythical or fairy-tale attributes of rings. There is a certain amount of critical confusion about this ring which seems based on simple ignorance of the plot of the novel. Both Bassoff and Hall believe the ring is a symbol of authority and power, and Hall believes that the ring passes to Edith by way of making her the dominant character in the novel. But Edith only has the ring for a brief time, after which it passes to Moira, Mrs. Tennant's young granddaughter, who eventually releases it, by way of Edith, to Mrs. Tennant. So the progress of the ring, which is circular, can hardly imply any permanent change in the power relationships of the house. Stokes agrees with Hall and reminds readers that the ring becomes "an 'engagement ring,' both literally and metaphorically." But the "literal" engagement that the ring solemnizes is not Edith and Raunce's but that of Edith to Raunce's Albert, a mock engagement that Edith concocts in order to coax the ring out of Moira's grasp.[20]

The ring might mean any number of things in its rightful place, but out of that place it is a source, not of power or authority, but of weakness and unease. And far from solemnizing the engagement of Raunce and Edith, the ring, simply because it has been lost, acts as a block to their plans. Raunce's immediate desire when Edith first shows him the ring is to give it back. The ring is too important to pilfer, and any question or investigation regarding it is likely to "gum up the whole works" (p. 128), destroying the beautiful routine that Raunce has so recently achieved. This is exactly what does happen, since the loss brings down on the house the insurance investigator, whose questions, though they are innocent enough, drive Raunce into a paranoid frenzy. His idea that the Irish Regina Assurance company is somehow connected to the Irish Republican Army is so absurd, so

[20]Bassoff, p. 151; Hall, p. 71; Stokes, p. 163.

utterly in contradiction to the very evidence he holds, that it betrays an anxiety of another sort. Raunce is terrified that Edith will be blamed and his whole life upset. He objectifies this fear as a threat from an invading army, as a threat to the house with which he is so closely identified. And the loss of the ring does spoil his position in the house, even though it is found and returned. Because its disappearance is never fully explained, Mrs. Tennant has a "feeling of distrust hanging over" her (p. 187). Because Mrs. Tennant feels uneasy, Raunce feels uneasy, naming "the uncertainty" (p. 172) as the chief cause of his discomfort after the ring is lost. The loss of the ring means a loss of security for everyone, almost as if it were an actual attack from the I.R.A. or a bacillus in the drains, and it poisons Raunce's life like a prolonged stay outdoors. As long as the ring is lost it destroys his freedom, so that every alternative Edith suggests is met with the same flat "not without we find that ring" (p. 163). As Raunce says, they can neither move nor stay so long as the ring is unaccounted for. And even after the ring is found, the suspicion surrounding it acts as a trap. Raunce tells Edith they must elope "on account of that ring. She's got her suspicions up you see love. She let Albert find his way but with us she'd raise holy Cain" (p. 227). There is nothing to suggest that this analysis is any sounder than Raunce's approach to the insurance man. What is clear is that once the house is fatally breached, once the security of place has been irreversibly destroyed by this loss, then place becomes a trap. The castle that once provided Raunce with a protective shell becomes a threat in itself once the shell has been cracked.

Though Raunce is brought low by these invasions and losses, he is not made contemptible by his dependence on the routines of his place. Because *Loving* is a comedy, Raunce's vulnerability is pardoned and his nearly complete dependence on minor social rituals does not destroy him. Raunce is a classically flat character: repetitive, mechanical, abstract in his conception of himself. Yet readers must feel that his humanity comes from his flatness, that without his fictions Raunce would not be a human being. In a way, then, Raunce is an indication that the essence of Green's comic vision is the pardon his characters receive, the permission to be flat. What makes Raunce both amusing and touching—and this is also true for all of Green's most successful characters—is the pathetic vigilance he puts into flat, artificial habits, the way the most inanimate materials provide him with the most human satisfactions.

The same kind of deliberate flatness in the single word of the title of the novel is evidence of Green's view of relationships *between* individuals. Loving is the great subject of the novel as a form, and marriage often seems the human ritual the genre was created to describe. In the most sophisticated examples—*Emma, Middlemarch, Portrait of a Lady*—protagonists are punished for using marriage as if it were a canvas on which to paint their own exquisite self-portrait. Emma, Dorothea, and Isabel seem to avoid some deeper responsibility by the marriages they construct. But Green's characters receive no such punishment for their trivialization of love and of themselves. Green seems closer to the eighteenth century when marriage was more a question of money than an ultimate test of sensibility. It is in line with his whole approach to character, with his notion that individuals sometimes exist best within artificial enclosures, that love is also a question of place in *Loving,* where sex is primarily a question of rooms and marriage a question of a house.

Sex in *Loving* appears most commonly as a kind of invasion, not necessarily of the body, but of the room or the role that is the outer representation of the body. This equation appears most comically in the long dinner-table discussion the servants have about the possibility of a German invasion. Since Burch assures them that "they're famished like a lion out in the desert them fighting men" (p. 96), the possibility of invasion is discussed almost purely in sexual terms. Even within the household itself, however, sex features primarily as a question of access to rooms, with unauthorized access appearing as a sexual fantasy gratifying in itself. Kate concocts for Edith a fantasy about opening their door to find a "great boy . . . waiting inside" (p. 38). She asks Edith repeatedly what she would do if either Raunce or Albert were to hide in their room, if "you was come alone up here . . . and found 'im waitin' on yer bed" (p. 38). Oddly enough, Raunce and Albert have a discussion about that exact possibility, or rather Raunce tortures Albert with the idea just as Kate does Edith: "Holy smoke if we was to creep upstairs tomorrow after dinner and find those two slaves of hers laid out on their little beds where they'll be of a Sunday afternoon. What would you do, eh?" (p. 69). Sex appears in both of these fantasies more as the invasion of someone's room than as a physical act requiring the invasion of a body, but it seems that in the atmosphere of Kinalty access to rooms and movement about the house is such a basic preoccupation that to possess the room is almost the equivalent of possessing the body. The fantasies never go past that first moment when a strange person enters the room, as if the significant threshhold has already been crossed at that point.

Therefore, the three significant scenes that comprise the courtship of Raunce and Edith all involve Raunce's invasion of an ad hoc environment that had been closed to outsiders. The first occurs when Kate and Edith are surreptitiously watching Paddy in his lamproom. This is an invasion in itself, the sexual nature of which becomes plain when Kate expresses the desire to strip Paddy "to give that pelt of his a good rub over" (p. 52). Raunce disturbs them, however, by appearing in the next room, as suddenly as in their fantasies, so suddenly they "stood transfixed as if by arrows" (p. 53).

The second example of such an invasion is the well-known scene in which Kate and Edith are found dancing in an empty ballroom beneath a row of reflective chandeliers. Green emphasizes Raunce's exit from the lamproom by describing the squeak of the door hinges; here he emphasizes Raunce's entrance by describing the "grate" of the phonograph needle as Raunce stops the music. Stopping the music in this case also breaks a spell, a mood in which Kate and Edith had practically melted into one another, so that they are described as "two girls, minute in purple, dancing multiplied to eternity in these trembling pears of glass" (p. 62). Kate and Edith have momentarily made the uninhabited ballroom entirely theirs, inhabited by reflections of themselves, and are lost in it as if transfixed by their own personalities. The relationship between Kate and Edith is sometimes considered by critics to be a sexual one, but in this scene, with its mirrors and doublings, it seems narcissistic and presexual.[21] The girls seem less to be dancing with a partner than each to be dancing with herself, as signified by the removal of proper names and the multiplication of images around the room. The remoteness of the room, the isolating qualities of the loud music, the reflections from the glass, make for a maximum concentration of self into which Raunce breaks as if by force. He has done so to make an obvious overture to Edith, singling her out "with his eyes" (p. 63). Suddenly with this intrusion the girls become individuals again, split apart, and Kate looks at Edith "like she might have been a stranger" (p. 63). Raunce's intrusion into this room marks the destruction of the relationship of Kate and Edith, which depends on their identification with one another as occupying the same room.

So in the third such scene Kate does not appear. This scene takes place in another uninhabited room, the Skullpier Gallery, in which Edith, Albert, and the Tennant girls play blindman's buff. These games in abandoned rooms recall the games in the artichoke grove in *Party Going,* where secrecy and seclusion are the spice of the occasion, just as they look forward to the dance at the climax of *Concluding,* which serves to isolate each individual dancer behind closed eyes. Blindman's buff intensifies the same feelings, based as it is on hiding and discovery. The gallery seems another presexual enclave in which sex is a game based on hide-and-seek, a game in which the real thrill is that of being caught in your hiding place, with the kiss as a kind of formal gesture to the sexual feelings being acted out. This fairly infantile game is disrupted, however, by Raunce, whose entrance is again emphasized by sound: "A door in the wall opened with a grinding

---

[21]See, for example, Odom, p. 92.

shriek of rusty hinge and Raunce entered" (p. 115). Raunce and Edith, it is plain, are playing the same kind of game, but on a different level. Raunce says, "I figured this was where you could be found," and Edith says, "I don't know how you managed those passages alone" (p. 116), amazed that Raunce has approached them through the house. Raunce's invasion interrupts the game, but the analogy between the game and his relationship with Edith is significant. In all of these instances, sex is associated with a secluded room, and both its threat and its promise come from the way seclusion is destroyed by the entrance of another. It is as if sex is a threat to the settled system of enclaves on which Kinalty is based, enclaves that are chiefly defended by spinsters. The enclave, which is a solipsistic world designed to repel outsiders, is at odds with sex and love, so that the fantasies of Kate and Edith, Raunce and Albert, take the form of invasion, an invasion of a room that signifies loss of control to another person. And Raunce's illness, which appears first when he leaves the castle walls and which intensifies when the castle is invaded by the investigator, is made nearly fatal by love: "I love you so much my stomach's all upset an' there you are" (p. 215).

But if sex requires the destruction of barriers, both physical and psychological, and if it is therefore inimical to closed rooms, marriage requires the construction of another enclave around the two people involved. So the relationship of Raunce and Edith, once it is at all settled, becomes a question of place. When Raunce first mentions his plans in a letter to his mother, it is the house rather than Edith which rates a specific mention: "Who knows but there might be a change in my situation one of these days. You've often said it was time I settled down. . . . But I've my eye on a nice little place in the park what the married butler before Mr. Eldon had" (p. 118). Raunce's mind seems to turn almost exclusively on shelter in this letter, and his proposal to Edith seems to preserve these priorities. He begins this proposal by asking her, "You ever noticed that little place this side of the East Gate?"

(p. 141). The cottage seems to have the same position of importance for Edith, whose chief regret when they decide to leave Kinalty is for "our little 'ouse" (p. 222).

The house is so important because Raunce and Edith, as a couple, have no space in the castle. They need a place, not just as Bert and Lily do, for romantic maneuvers, but as a focus for their domesticity, a place that can do for them what the enclaves do for individuals. Their lack of status in the rooms of Kinalty is emphasized by the irate outburst of Burch, when she finds "Edith and that man, the impudence, sat back in the armchairs" in the Red Library (p. 122). The Red Library becomes their ad hoc home as long as Mrs. Tennant is away, ostensibly because the fires kept going there for the paintings are good for Raunce's health, but actually so that they can enact domestic scenes around the symbol of home, the hearth. It is significant that Raunce and Edith are in the Red Library when the insurance investigator arrives. This intrusion upsets Raunce so much partly because he is himself out of place, in a room he has no right to, and this is signified by his anxiety over his incomplete livery, having put it off as if he were not in service. Edith must instantly kneel and pretend to clean in order to explain her presence there. It is also significant that for the brief time she has it Edith keeps the ring in the library, a room which, however, has no security for her, because the ring is instantly relost.

Raunce and Edith must elope because, as servants, they can never command enough physical or psychological space to feel secure. Anthony Quinton has pointed out that "a servants' hall is an exceedingly artificial community, its members have been brought together simply by the accident of common employment, yet, unlike most employees, they have to spend nearly all their time in this fortuitous social environment."[22] The ersatz nature of this social environment is compensated for by a single-minded cultivation of personal space, of enclaves within which an individual is safe from those he has been accidentally thrown against. But this system of enclaves is highly unstable. Most of the characters experience

---

[22]Quinton, p. 34.

invasions so disrupting to their self-esteem that physical illness or mania is the result. The endless shuffling of possessions and the attendant anxiety over security is an indication of how little possible it is for the servants to own anything. All pride of place is for them simply a willful fiction, because the places and prerogatives in which they take such pride are all determined from above. The social system here might be compared to that in *Party Going,* where the total weakness and insubstantiality of the partygoers is masked by the fictional persona they are granted as the guests of Max, and, in fact, Green compares the partygoers to servants dressed in the livery of a prince.

Raunce is in the plight of a person whose lack of independence has been exposed beyond any hope of being obscured again. All of the different explanations he gives for his illness have in common some damage done to his self-esteem as butler. Even his love for Edith only exposes Raunce's lack of place at Kinalty, and these forces all magnify the effect of one another until the very air of Ireland seems poison to him. When Raunce says, "It's this country gets me down" (p. 219), he is admitting the fact that he has always relied on physical context for his psychological well-being. The complaint that "it's too bloody neutral this country is" (p. 219) means that Ireland no longer offers him an aid to self-definition. What has happened is that Raunce has come to question his own existence as his position is assailed. His terrible fear of being kept at Kinalty is both a fear of being trapped in an insecure position and the fear that he doesn't have enough power over his own movements to escape. The terror of his position is signified by his confession that his dyspepsia is a "condition don't let up on you however you're placed" (p. 229). The place, once he has lost faith in it, becomes a trap, so that he mimics Eldon without knowing it, calling out "Edie" in exactly "that tone Mr. Eldon had employed at the last when calling his Ellen" (p. 229), as if Raunce had no more hope of having Edith than Eldon did of having his Ellen.

But Raunce is still relying on place when he decides to elope to England, substituting change of place for explanation or accommodation. He is simply reversing the equation

Bowen presents in *The Heat of the Day*, that Ireland is out of reality because it is physically removed from the war. England has become a mythical place for the servants of Kinalty, a place where fantasies are available that will cure the psychological problems they suffer from. Albert will solve his frustrations by becoming an air-gunner, while Raunce and Edith will establish a new fiction in the fairy tale of living "happily ever after" (p. 229). The fairy-tale ending of *Loving* is ironic, but not, as some critics have assumed, because it is a suggestion that Raunce dies in England. Green says himself in his article in *Contact*, "When writing the book I had no idea but that they were to have anything but a long and happy life thereafter."[23] The irony comes from the fact that Raunce and Edith make England, home of the war, the location of their fairy tale. It is obvious that the attributes of the place are of little importance; England is inviting to them, as it is to Albert, as a chance to change themselves by changing their place. And there should be no doubt that, as Green says, they will succeed, because, as he has shown in all the novels up to *Loving*, such fantasies are the normal constituents of reality, lived out in the face of all contrary evidence.

The flippancy with which Green tags the fairy-tale ending onto his book indicates his belief that people do live happily ever after, simply because they want to. He does not hold up love as a transcendent value that will solve all the problems of the characters. Yet the activity of loving, the games and rituals that go along with it, the fairy tale it ends in, provide in this novel the satisfactions the characters require. They will live happily in England, in a marriage most probably fraught with cliché, because to Green convention and cliché represent the human desires of individuals in the most authentic way, because the fairy tale is the fiction within which all true character is fostered.

[23]Henry Green, "The English Novel of the Future," *Contact*, 1 (Aug. 1950), 23. The height of pessimism about Raunce's future is reached perhaps by Barbara H. Brothers, who asserts in "Henry Green: Time and the Absurd," *Boundary*, 5 (1977), 865, that Raunce dies *at the end of the novel*.

II

Loving and *Concluding* belong together, not just because both novels are organized around the metaphor of physical space, but because both novels use that metaphor to illustrate the relationship between the interior life of the individual and the exterior, public world. Green's definition of this relationship differs in important ways from George Orwell's in *1984*, published in the same year as *Concluding*. Orwell's novel is the best example of popular ideas about authoritarianism, which is seen as essentially mechanical, objective, abstract, and impersonal, as an intensification of all that is inimical to the individual in everyday public life. The problem with this view of public life, and of its perversion in authoritarianism, is, as René Girard suggests, that the definition of the public as impersonal seems to suggest that there is no connection between people and their political systems. Girard criticizes *1984* because it fails to show "the connection between individual desire and the collective structure. We sometimes get the impression . . . that the 'system' has been imposed from the outside on the innocent masses."[24] As should be apparent from the careers of the writers of Green's generation, the relationship between public and private lives is much more complex. The calls for myth and for new conventions mentioned at the beginning of this chapter are all calls for orthodoxy at one level or another, and orthodoxy came to appeal more and more to this generation as time went on: Auden's Anglicanism, Isherwood's Vedanta, Waugh and Graham Greene's Anglo-Catholicism, Upward's Communism. Auden, at least, felt religion valuable because it freed him from personal falsification, made him more personally authentic. He returned to the Anglican Church, he says, because of an experience of demonic possession, in which he was "stripped of self-control and self-respect, behaving like a ham actor in a Strindberg play."[25]

---

[24] Girard, p. 226.

[25] Auden's statement, from an unpublished letter, appears in Charles Osborne, *W. H. Auden: The Life of a Poet* (New York: Harcourt Brace Jovanovich, 1979) p. 203.

Some of the complexity of this relationship between personal life and orthodoxy can be seen in the changing nature of the great house metaphor. Evelyn Waugh's futuristic novella, *Love among the Ruins,* takes place at Mountjoy Castle, "the ancestral seat of a maimed V.C. of the Second World War, who had been sent to a Home for the Handicapped when the place was converted into a gaol."[26] Modern totalitarianism has turned the great house into a coercive institution, but this transformation should not obscure the fact that the meaning of the great house is essentially the same in *Love among the Ruins* as it is in *Brideshead Revisited*: it stands for convention. In *Brideshead* convention and orthodoxy are sustaining, protective; in *Love among the Ruins* they are coercive. The significance of the metaphor is consistent, only Waugh's attitude and the nature of the convention have changed. But the sense of the metaphor should illuminate a fact obscured in both *1984* and *Love among the Ruins,* that people often long for convention, even for coercion, and that authoritarian political systems have their roots in personal desires such as those expressed with such exhaustion at the end of the war. As Girard suggests, there is a connection between authoritarianism and personal desire.

Concluding is about this connection. Conventional readings of the novel, which take it as just one more denunciation of the dehumanizing effects of authoritarianism, obscure its most distinctive and valuable qualities. *Concluding* is a natural continuation of *Loving,* as natural as Waugh's transformation of *Brideshead Revisted* into *Love among the Ruins,* yet Green does not make the assumption that someone else's authoritarianism is responsible for the ills of the world. He shows instead how authoritarianism is the creation of personal desires like those responsible for the great-house vogue. The public world is not, in *Concluding* or in any other Green novel, abstract and inhuman. It has always been, from *Living* on, a personal creation. The public world in *Concluding* is neither objectively

---

[26]Evelyn Waugh, *Love among the Ruins* (London: Chapman and Hall, 1953), p. 8.

true nor personally false, and only by observing this fact can the oddities of the fantastic setting and the personalities of the characters be understood.

Concluding is set in a State Institute for the training of young girls as future civil servants of a rather shadowy state. The institute is a former private mansion as isolated in space and time as Kinalty Castle. Characters disappear whenever they travel outside the grounds, just as Mrs. Tennant disappears when she visits England, and the larger world exists only in written form, in directives, charters, and communiqués. The characters owe their existence entirely to their roles within the workings of the institute. The girls who are being trained there have all mysteriously acquired names that begin with *M*, and a great many of them seem to be orphans, as Waugh's Miles Plastic is in *Love among the Ruins*. The atmosphere of danger, which in *Loving* was attributable to the war, has been preserved in *Concluding*. The disappearance of two of the girls, Mary and Merode, the arrival of a cryptic, suggestive note, and nasty rumors about various characters all put the institute and its inmates on the defensive.

As in *Loving,* the various characters in *Concluding* defend themselves against these obscure threats by identifying themselves with the space they occupy either in the house or on its grounds and with the position in the social system of the institute which that space signifies. Mrs. Blain, head cook at the institute, is, like all cooks in Green's novels, "a terror for her rights."[27] She insists that "I can't have my placed treated cavalier fashion" (pp. 27–28), and this means, as it does in *Loving,* having the right not "to be contradicted, or even corrected, in her own kitchen" (p. 114). Either to reflect the housing shortages of the immediate postwar period or to heighten the drama, Green makes the number of places at the institute too few, so the fears of the characters and their conflicts with one another are all expressed as competition for housing. George Adams, the institute's woodman, is on

---

[27]Henry Green, *Concluding* (London, 1948; rpt. New York: Viking, 1951), p. 26. All subsequent references are to this edition and in this chapter will appear in text.

edge about "rumours and buzzes" that he will lose his house. Old Mr. Rock, the scientist who has been granted a life tenancy on the grounds by their former owner, is envious of Adams's house and nervous about his own. He is locked in "what he termed his battle for the place, the roof here" (p. 33) with Miss Edge, one of the directresses of the institute. But Rock's anxiety predates Edge's campaign against his cottage. When he asks Adams early in the novel, "How d'you hold your house?" Adams reflects that he "had heard it so often these last ten years" (p, 9). Anxiety over housing seems to be a given, as little dependent on actual threats as the panics of the servants in *Loving,* as if it were related more to a general insecurity independent of facts. In this sense *Concluding* takes up where *Loving* ends, with the anxiety caused when Raunce's place is jeopardized.

Concluding begins to resemble a game of musical chairs, where there is always one place too few. In control of the music of this particular game is Miss Edge, whose desire for Rock's cottage keeps the whole chain of subordinates off balance. Edge and her cohort Baker are the characters in *Concluding* who are most completely identified with their own personal space. Edge's office is referred to as "the sanctum to which she had risen in the State Service" (p. 11). The physical office is equal to her personal office as head of the institute; like her desk, it is "equal to the authority" she possesses (p. 11). The fact that it is referred to repeatedly as a sanctum, that it has that designation among the girls and staff and has even acquired a capital letter, indicates that the highest privilege granted by the state is the right to exclude other people. Edge is outraged when Sebastian Birt enters her office, since as a member of the staff he "had no business unsummoned in the Sanctum" (p. 191). This jealousy extends to the grounds of the institute, which Edge often thinks of in the possessive: "The mist was rolling back, even below her third Terrace, all the way to her ring of beechwoods planted in line with the crescent of her House; although, off to the left, where beech trees and azaleas came down over water, her Lake still held its fog folded in a shroud" (p. 15). Edge repeatedly refers to the institute as "this great Place," and the double meaning of place is obvious in her usage as it is in Mrs. Blain's or in that of the servants of *Loving*. Edge has become completely identified with the physical grounds of the institute, each twig of which symbolizes her position in the hierarchy of the state. This is the key to her squeamishness about the flower cutting that is necessary to decorate the annual dance. She has given "the strictest instructions that they were not to cut the blooms where this could make itself felt" (p. 92). The feelings she protects are obviously her own, as if she sensed any trimming on the grounds with a physical discomfort.

Naturally, this intense identification of herself, her place in life, with the grounds makes Edge as protective of her space as Blain is. She laments "our old tumble down Park walls, which are a positive invitation to itinerant labour" (p. 93). This objection to intruders is not really fear of any action they might take but an objection to the sight of outsiders. When Mr. Rock innocently crosses the grounds to fetch swill for his pig, Edge cries out in disgust, "Rock flaunts himself" (p. 19). Later she sees Rock "deliberately exercising his animal. How intolerable, if she had taken her stroll, to have come upon him driving the slobbery pig" (p. 138). Edge is affronted that anyone else should blot her view of the grounds, and her disgust is not limited to messy animals like pigs. She says of Rock's Persian, "Who is there can stop a cat making free with the Grounds?" (p. 107). Here Edge resembles Nanny Swift, who chides Kate and Edith for walking out "where anyone could see." It is not fear or disgust or even bureaucratic strictness that causes Edge's objections but the affront to her senses caused by anything not her own. Edge spends so much time gazing out the windows of her sanctum onto the grounds because the institute is her mirror, the huge glass in which she sees her own personality reflected. Therefore, the presence of any other person, no matter how innocuous, is a blot, a flaw in the image she expects to see, as if someone had altered her physical features.

Like the characters in *Loving,* Edge has also acquired a role along with her place, one that is ironically similar to that of the former owner of the mansion that has become the institute. She is called the "guv'nor" throughout, by staff and students alike, and as her possessive pronouns suggest, she plays this proprietary role to the hilt. The other characters in *Concluding* have acquired roles of their own that, like the roles in *Loving,* are both functions and protections of their respective places. Rock, for example, has two roles, one layered over the other, both of which come with his cottage as part of his rightful tenure at the institute. The first and least fundamental of these roles is that of the swill man, an attitude and "a high cracked voice" he assumes as a way of getting a free breakfast and kitchen scraps for his pig in Mrs. Blain's kitchen. The role is a "joke he had plied for ten years" (p. 21), and he "usually plied the one jest until he won his meal" (p. 24). But the joke is more than a way of ingratiating himself with the cook. Acting the swill man is a way of working himself into the routine of the institute, of making an acknowledged place for himself by establishing a caricature in the minds of the staff and the girls. Rock ingratiates himself by repetition, finding, as Richard Roe does, that it is easier to achieve recognition for a falsified version of himself than it is for the real thing. When he is threatened or ill at ease, Rock tends to assume the swill-man role as protection, as the accepted, acknowledged version of his existence at the institute: "He then noticed Baker with the sergeant, and again had the unreasoned impulse that he must explain his presence. . . . So, instinctively, and with the swill man's yell, he called out 'Ted' " (p. 150).

The role of the swill man also bears certain faint marks of the more fundamental role beneath. Rock's repeated denunciations of "this filthy swine fever" seem to come more from the great Sage, formulator of the great, unidentified Theory which earned him the cottage. The theory is now fifty-five years old, and, if Sebastian Birt is to be believed, entirely exploded by later work. Nevertheless it makes Rock one of the "ornaments of the State" (p. 46), and is, in his own mind, a "monument" which "noone could steal" (p. 34). Green's lack of specificity about this theory is characteristic, as is the odd vagueness he allows to exist about all the other details of Rock's past. The form of the theory is unimportant precisely because it has become a monument, and Rock's past is left vague because it has all disappeared from his mind except the period surrounding his triumph: "The more distant past now made a sharper picture; the time at school, hard work, then six months chasing girls and finally the signal triumph" (p. 210). Everything after this triumph has faded away because Rock has become identified solely with his theory; he has become the sage. He insists on this role all the more strongly the more his cottage, visible reward and physical evidence of his triumph, is threatened. There is also a kind of symbiosis between the two roles. Rock's inner conviction that he is a genius makes possible "the servile courtesy he could assume at will" (p. 191). But the servility also protects Rock's inner personality from harm. He can assume "an idiot look of pride, in the way he could the swill man's cry" (p. 213) whenever he feels threatened. This is one of the reasons that Rock is such a touching character. His swillman's act would be mere cravenness, like the scraping of Tupe or Piper, if it did not mask an essential pride. But the pathos of his character comes from the fact that the pride is also a mask, the great theory a scrap of fiction Rock gathers to himself to cover an even more fundamental vulnerability.

In either case, Rock's roles are intimately related to his place at the edge of the institute. They are both an expression and a protection of that position. This is also the case with the roles of Sebastian Birt, one of the institute's less prepossessing instructors. Birt is "always in a part" (p. 29), but unlike Rock always in a different part, mimicking "the sort of lecturer he was not," the "character of an executive," a "State manager," using falsetto, all in the space of a few pages (pp. 30–32). As Bruce Bassoff says, these voices are "an avoidance of communication,"[28] but this avoidance has a particular purpose. Like Rock's idiot mask, Birt's voices protect him in moments of social unease. When Birt becomes nervous

---

[28]Bassoff, p. 25.

at lunch, he assumes a "close imitation of Mr. Rock's party manner" (p. 100). Birt's use of vocal disguises is so instinctive that he assumes them almost automatically in times of danger, when the discovery of Merode, for instance, produces "a close parody of Edge" (p. 56). And Rock's granddaughter, Elizabeth, with whom Birt is supposed to be in love, plays the role of invalid. Liz suffers from an illness supposedly brought on by overwork, but there is something purposeful, something convenient about it. She has a vague, disconnected way of speaking that rather significantly comes and goes. She takes "refuge in a vast quagmire of vagueness" (p. 42) whenever threatened or whenever an unprecedented situation offers no clues for her behavior. When they discover Merode, Liz "at once put on her vagueness for protection in the circumstances" (p. 56), just as Birt puts on his imitation of Edge. Liz's illness is a role directly related to her position at the institute, since her only justification for staying in Rock's cottage is this illness. She uses the illness as John Haye does his, working on the emotions of those around her, especially those of her grandfather, who dreads her loss.

The intricate relationship between individual characters and their places at the institute is responsible for the odd, dreamlike quality of the descriptions in *Concluding*. The exterior world, which is left virtually undescribed in *Loving*, is distorted here in peculiar ways and seems in its turn to distort the senses of the characters. Both sight and hearing seem at first to be inhibited by the institute building and the conditions of the grounds, as if the physics of the institute were different from that of the outside world. When Green refers to "Blind sun" (p. 137) he expresses in an oxymoron the fact that sunlight seems to obscure things at the institute instead of illuminating them. This is especially true of the way the sun enters through the institute windows, bisecting the kitchen, for example, where Rock waits to receive his breakfast, so that it "hid the line of girls beyond, fetching their own breakfasts at the other cooker" (p. 21). This kind of sunlight makes Rock "a blind man" (p. 25), and it has the same effect later on Baker, who tries to see her colleague across the sanctum but is "blinded by the sun," bewildered "before a hot dazzle of evening" (p. 167). Merode is "dazzled" by the same "full sunlight" (p. 65) in the same room, and Edge, looking out of the windows of that room, is unable to see, having "screwed her eyes up against the sun" (p. 138).

Sound seems to hamper communication at the institute just as light hampers eyesight, and Green emphasizes the similarity with a number of synesthetic expressions such as "loud" sunlight, and "disfiguring deafness" (p. 86), in which one property performs the frustration normally belonging to the other. The primary confusion of sound is the echo, which resounds throughout the book, of someone calling Mary's name. The echoes have a disorienting effect, so that the novel begins and ends with an argument as to the direction of the sound. They also seem to have a variable pitch, so that they seem a girl's voice answered "in so far deeper a note that it might have been a man calling" (pp. 10–11). In a very odd way Rock's deafness is associated with these echoes. Thinking to himself something discreditable about Liz, Rock "repented this last so violently he could not be sure he had not spoken out loud" (p. 7). But Adams immediately asks, "Did you hear summat?" and then claims to have heard an echo. This episode suggests that the normal boundaries between exterior and interior worlds are not respected in *Concluding* and that the surreal quality of the institute grounds comes from the subjective distortions of the characters.

Certainly, most of the characters purposely distort or frustrate their senses, and one of the ways *Concluding* most resembles Green's earlier work is in the way they willfully become blind and deaf. When Ma Marchbanks proposes to interrogate Moira, she takes off her spectacles, "as though, in the crisis, at a time when she had been left in charge, she wished to look inwards, to draw on hid reserves" (p. 47). Taking off her spectacles serves Marchbanks in her distress by protecting her from knowledge. To Marchbanks's "dull poached eggs of vision" (p. 48) Moira appears womanly and quite mature. But with her glasses back on Marchbanks realizes, "You could admire children when you were not in a position properly to focus them . . . because, soon as you had your glasses on, they were merely fat, or null, unless of course they were babies" (p. 50). When it develops that one of the runaway girls is an orphan, and therefore one of Miss Baker's special charges, Baker closes her eyes (p. 77), like Nanny Swift refusing to hear evil of the girl she raised. Edge has the same reaction when Baker introduces unpleasant information about Mary: "Like a spoiled child, she put her face away from Baker along the back of the chaise longue" (p. 144). This kind of willful ignorance can explain some of the odd effects of the sun, which may only be abetting the desires of the characters in blinding them. In the passage cited above, for example, in which Edge is blinded by the sun, it is significant that it is Rock she is unable to see, just as later in the novel she demands of him, "Where are you? I can't tell" (p. 238), even though they are in the same room. Edge may be suffering here from a congenital desire not to see Rock, to have her eyes accomplish what her powers as directress cannot. Her sanctum is, as René Girard says of the closed worlds of some of Proust's characters, "an eye which blinks out the particles of dust which might irritate."[29]

Even Rock's world is such an eye. At the same time that Edge is squinting at him through the sun, he is squinting back at her, across the reflective lake. He does not want to be seen, and hides, thinking as he does so of what he might look like to someone who "had not got his or her right spectacles" (p. 147). The joke seems to be on Edge, but Rock does not have his proper spectacles either, having sent Daisy, his pig, out to "be his eyes" (p. 147). Since it becomes clear that Rock cannot control Daisy, he has made no real advance over his own eyes, which are confused here by the sweat which fogs his spectacles. In fact, it often suits Rock to think of himself as half blind, letting his spectacles take on a blank look, both to ignore what he doesn't want to see and to give the impression of innocent ignorance. He does this, for example, at the institute dance, and in other cases when the proximity of the young girls could prove embarrassing, keeping

[29]Girard, p. 197.

himself behind "carefully expressionless, lensed eyes" (p. 196). Later at the same dance, Rock, having received a "dark sight" of Liz and Birt dancing, "almost smashed off his nose the spectacles that reflected reeling chandeliers" (p. 231). His anger here has the same protective effect as Marchbanks's prudence, removing the spectacles which expose him to such unpleasantly dark sights.

Rock's deafness also seems less a deficiency of sound than the proficiency of his mind in finding exterior echoes for his thoughts, and its ability to shield him from what he doesn't care to hear. Rock's frequent fear that he has spoken aloud some private reflection is significant, because what he hears from other people is often not their own words but echoes of something he might have said himself. When he transforms Mrs. Blain's statement about "peace and quiet" into "Pooled the diet" (p. 23), his mind is obviously on food. When Miss Edge's "How kind" becomes "How blind," Rock must be preoccupied with the difficulties caused by his glasses (p. 212). Rock's hearing is therefore active, not passive. Like blindness, poor memory, or any other sensory deficiency in Green, it is manipulative rather than simply destructive. C. J. Allen says that "Rock's predispositions form his conclusions," and this might also be said of his hearing.[30] This does not mean, however, that Rock hears only what he wants to hear. When Sebastian innocently mentions the weather, Rock, in "a wild voice," demands, "Did you say 'end of her tether,' " because he is thinking of Mary and the overwork she supposedly suffered from (p. 40). The reference he seems to hear also obviously bears on the condition of his granddaughter, who, he assumes, has been driven close to madness by the same kind of overwork. Rock's emotions about Liz often overflow in this way. One significant instance occurs when Sebastian joins them at the dance and Liz exclaims, "He's here." Rock replies, "Care? Of course I care" (p. 200). When he is feeling protective and tender Rock mishears in this way, but later, when he is angry, he mishears Liz's whispered "In a minute,"

---

[30]C. J. Allen, "Inferences and the Nature of Mind in Henry Green's *Concluding*," *Revue des Langues Vivantes*, 45 (Oct. 1979), 83.

having "misunderstood it for impertinence" (p. 231). Mishearing stems from the same pathetic defensiveness that creates the role of the swill man. Rock never simply cups his ear and asks for a repetition because his problem is overeagerness, not a deficiency of hearing. His mind is so full of panicky, half-paranoid suspicions that the world echoes for him with threats that have not occurred.

On the other hand, some of Rock's mishearing is willful. During an argument with Adams, Rock mishears on purpose "with intent to make the fellow ridiculous" (p. 161). Both Liz and Edge accuse Rock of this sort of purposeful misunderstanding, of mishearing "just what he does not wish to hear" (p. 218). Edge herself chooses to mishear in this way, though, "willfully" misunderstanding references to the disappearance of Mary (p. 76). Almost all the characters in *Concluding* use their senses at one time or another to abet their carefully contrived ignorance, as if the senses were protected by fine guard hairs that trigger the closing of eyes and ears whenever threatening information is present. Rock senses trouble in the tone of Mrs. Blain's voice and, "instantly apprehensive, decided in his own best interests that he would do better to ignore what was on the way, until he knew how grave it was" (p. 25). He has the same attitude toward his mail, which he has not opened in years: "What point could there be in finding out, it would not advantage him in what he termed his battle for the place, the roof here; and wouldn't it rather weaken his resolve if he knew" (p. 33). After an interview with Merode's aunt, Mrs. Manley, who insists on answers to embarrassing questions, Edge "closed her mind to Mrs. Manley" by standing "lovingly, sun in her eyes," to watch the park (p. 136). Her ability to ignore change or intrusion differs from Rock's only in that it has become a bureaucratic talent. Rules and regulations help the senses in their task of altering or destroying information. Since Merode is not questioned under strict institute procedures, "nothing you told her has any substance. Indeed you might just as well not have said a word. That is to say as far as we are concerned you did not speak" (p. 158).

Thus it becomes clear that the primary function of the senses in *Concluding* is defense. Whether they close altogether like fine filters against the unpleasant or, as in the case of Rock's mishearing, respond too eagerly and defensively overcompensate, the senses are always at the service of the closed world each character struggles to maintain. As René Girard says of similar worlds in Proust, "Eyes and ears are closed when the well-being and integrity of the personal universe are involved."[31] The situation resembles that of *Loving,* with each individual protecting a personal enclave, but in this case the physical walls of the enclave seem barely sufficient, and the major line of defense is at the boundary of the senses. No enclave is secure enough, so that the senses must make up in impermeability what the walls lack.

Therefore, whenever a character in *Concluding* praises his or her senses or lays claim to some superior insight, it is a sign that the defense mechanisms are out of control and that the senses are no longer even roughly accurate. Adams, having taken refuge from his supposed enemies inside a withy, shouts, "I've kept me eyes open this long time to what goes on around. . . . I saw through that like I look out of my windows, it was clear as day" (p. 160). But Adams's eyesight is very seriously distorted, since he tells Rock that "I seen you hold your tryst with that shiner and Edge" (p. 161), meaning presumably the police sergeant who has been called in to investigate the disappearances and Baker. The idea that these three, all of whom are suspicious and frightened of one another, might be in collusion is absurd, but Adams sees what he fears, just as he sees Edge, the more authoritarian of the two, instead of Baker. As he says to Rock, "It takes more'n spectacles to see round your kind" (p. 161). What Adams uses to see this nonexistent conspiracy is more than eyesight. It is a sense compounded of defensiveness and eyesight, a sense so far out of control that it drives Adams into a little covert in the reeds for protection.

[31]Girard, p. 196.

Adams's boast about his powers of sight is echoed by the more central characters when they assume their own paranoid fantasies. Rock claims, "He was not so blind . . . spectacles or no, he could see Birt coveted the cottage, would move heaven and earth to have him sent to the Sanatorium" (p. 175). It is a common boast of Rock's that "he'd eyes in his head" (p. 113), but these eyes act as his spectacles often do, blinding him with his own preconceptions, with his own delusion that he can see what is not obvious to others. Rock suspects Baker and Edge of using Birt to "break a poor old fellow down by simply driving his sad girl out of her wits" (p. 11). But this delusion is simply a mirror image of Edge's, who also claims repeatedly that "we have eyes in our grey heads" (p. 238). These eyes produce a paranoid fantasy that is just a reversal of Rock's: "For I have watched the situation grow, and I have held my hand, Rock, who I deeply suspect, his disastrous granddaughter, and a weak young man" (p. 167). Obviously, poor Birt cannot be in collusion both with Rock against Edge and with Edge against Rock, just as Rock cannot be plotting with Edge against Adams while she is plotting with Baker against Rock himself. All claims to superior insight, like those of John Haye in *Blindness,* are simply revelations of the fact that sight has become subject to the will and that insight is no more than the creation of a defensive fiction. Such a claim marks the point at which the character loses control of the systematic frustration of the senses he has been practicing, as if there were a momentum to this process which grows until the senses begin manufacturing the threats they have been primed to find.

The physical setting of *Concluding* is so surreal, and the actions of its characters so shadowy, because the desires of individuals have overrun their natural boundaries, as if their fictions had taken over and colonized the natural world. In this sense *Concluding* is the most extreme example of Green's belief that the exterior world is not necessarily an objective truth but can be as subject to personal desires as the interior world. Such desires govern the political form of the institute as they do the natural world in a way that can be seen most clearly in the character of Miss Edge. The intimate connection between Edge's iron rule over the institute and her private fears is presented at the beginning of the novel. When she opens her curtains to get a first view of the park in the morning, Edge discovers a bat, an animal of which she seems to have an irrational dread. The reader's first glimpse of this imposing authority is therefore of her with a wicker wastebasket on her head, "crouched down in case this new thing could flicker up her skirts" (p. 12). This action is significant in itself, but even more so is her sigh of relief when the bat escapes: "If we could as easily rid ourselves of Rock" (p. 13). Edge's most instinctive, least controllable fear seems to be of bodily invasion. The sexual nature of this fear is brought out by the anonymous note that flutters from the wastebasket bearing the word *furnicates*. But the aspect of sex that frightens her is the same aspect that causes Raunce to sicken, the loss of physical autonomy. Edge is a person who is instinctively, viscerally defensive, whose need for an enclave within the building is based on dread of the loss of control that physical violation implies. That her fear of bodily invasion is immediately related to her fears for the grounds is made evident when she naturally and easily equates the bat with Rock, the interloper she hopes to expel. As in *Loving,* the house here is an analogue for the body, and any invasion of the enclave is felt as a destruction of the final boundaries that the body keeps between the self and the outside world. Edge feels Rock's presence almost physically, with a physical repulsion as uncontrollable as a shudder, because the grounds are an extension of her body and management of them a way of protecting herself at a further remove.

In general, criticism of *Concluding* has portrayed Edge as a triumph of self-mechanization, as the principle of abstractionism.[32] But this is to take the wish for the deed, since all the crises Edge undergoes are physical, and all her authoritarian rule an attempt to protect a physical sensitivity that is at times almost hysterical. At lunch Edge notices whispering

[32]See, for example, Stokes, p. 51, and Weatherhead, p. 109.

among the girls, something which "startled and disgusted" her so much that she goes pale (p. 102). Edge comes over "deathly hot" and then suddenly "deathly cold" as the fantasy takes hold of her that everyone must be whispering about Mary's body, which must, she irrationally assumes, be hidden under the mass of flowers. This fear of something disgusting hiding itself at the very center of her Founder's Day celebration resembles her fear of the bat, and like that earlier fear is instantly related "back to Mr. Rock and his granddaughter Elizabeth" (p. 104).

The flowers become a center of physical unease for Edge and a focus of all her fears concerning herself and the institute. Later she sees the blooms "alive with bluebottles" and imagines a "distinctive, sickly" scent that brings back the idea she knows is "unhealthy, morbid, too absurd" (p. 126). This idea, absurd though it is, has such physical power over Edge that she retches. The derivation of the idea is clear. The scent she imagines must go back to the "stench" which is presented so forcibly to her imagination a few minutes earlier by the State Directive that they are to keep pigs. The fear of desecration, of "pigsties all over the wonderful Place" (p. 125), brings on her physical revulsion at the scent of the flowers. Finally, when Edge discovers the doll that some prankster has put underneath the blooms, she faints, primarily because she has just sustained another invasion, that of Merode's aunt, Mrs. Manley. Edge has just dismissed "from her mind each carking memory of the Manley creature" (p. 140), restored the inviolability that is necessary to her well-being, when the doll is discovered just where she had feared desecration all along.

Edge thinks of her task as one of standing "guard over the Essential Goodness of this great Place. And when we sense a threat, our duty is to exercise the initiative the State expects to avert a danger" (p. 165). She presents this vigilance as if it were a duty to "our girls," but the one who most needs protection is obviously Edge herself. This is exposed when she continues to say that evil must be got rid of "without fuss, as one does with swill" (p. 165). The last word is a reference both to Rock and to the latest, most offensive State Directive. Edge stands guard over her own place, over her own impressions, just as Blain, Adams, and Rock do, to protect herself. She sickens just as Raunce does whenever that place is violated.

Authoritarianism is for Edge a personal imperative before it is a political method. The key to the authoritarian personality, in Green's analysis, is that it uses a mass of other people as its fiction, controlling itself by controlling others. Thus Edge revives herself after a crisis by giving orders to those below her. After her first episode of weakness concerning the flowers she rallies by becoming assertive: " 'Marchbanks, I do not want any of the decorations touched before I am ready to supervise all that myself' . . . Miss Edge ordered, and then at once felt almost completely well again" (p. 105). She picks herself up after the second episode by criticizing Marchbanks and Birt under the guise of a joke. She finally closes her mind to Mrs. Manley by ordering the girls in final preparations for the dance, by concentrating on "Moira, in whom she had sensed almost an antagonism these last few weeks" (p. 135). Then, "after she had given directions, she stood at one of the windows and lovingly, sun in her eyes, watched the Park" (p. 136). Having directed the girls helps "close her mind to Mrs. Manley," helps her ignore the invasions and challenges of the day. It plays the same role in her life as the purposeful blinding she achieves by looking into the sun as it illuminates her park.

Deviation from the routine of the institute therefore presents a personal, psychological danger to Edge. Green's reference to the bat as "this new thing" shows the essential identity for her of innovation and invasion. She sees her primary role at the institute as one which should "preclude innovation" (p. 139), which should prevent the "odious deviations from what is usual" (p. 210). Deviations are particularly threatening to Edge because of her reliance on the rules and usages of the institute for self-protection. So strong is Edge's desire to keep things in their proper places that there really is no such thing as an exception in her universe. As she says of the regrettable lack of refreshments at the dance, "If we were to make an exception the once, then we would do no more than to give rise to a Rule, should we not, in a contrary sense?" (p. 191). The admission of a deviation into her system is the establishment of a new rule in two senses: it changes the former regulation into a new one, and it establishes a foreign command, an opposing rule to her own. A deviation in routine is not just a flaw but a loss of control, a form of submission to forces outside herself. This is why Edge resists with such pointless tenacity Marchbanks's idea for new decorations at the dance, why she puts so much effort into appearing to be in agreement with Baker. To allow exceptions would be to allow someone else to take control of the traditions and regulations that represent Edge to herself. If the institute were not so intimately personal to her, then deviations would be a great deal easier to tolerate.

Mary and Merode, the two missing girls, thus play a role in *Concluding* similar to that played in *Loving* by the lost ring. Their disappearance represents a flaw, a breach in the protective wall of the system, almost like a wound through which contagion could enter. When Edge says to Rock, "All Baker and I must do, is to watch that there are no departures" (p. 210), Rock wonders if this could be "a reference to poor Mary." Though Rock has misunderstood, his misunderstanding exposes the threat Mary's departure presents. Like innovation, her escape establishes a contrary rule, one that threatens to take control of Edge if it cannot be forced back into a system of her own. Thus Edge's anxiety over the absence causes hallucinations, chills, nausea, and fainting, or a lack of control over her own mind and body as if Mary's disappearance were an actual sickness.

Edge hopes to regain control over herself and the institute by an especially punctilious observance of the Founder's Day dance, which the girls have been preparing all day. Edge's insistence that the dance must go forward without alteration is based on her psychological need to reassert the routines of the institute. The fact that the dance commemorates their founder, that it marks a year in the life of the institute, shows its function even in normal times as a rejuvenation of institute life. But the dance does not serve this function for Edge alone. All the characters desire this ritual as a way of managing their own unease. Mary's absence has posed a kind of threat to everyone at the institute. Birt describes the condition of the institute as one of "equipoise," with "instances of disintegration or even of centrifugal action, whereby certain appear, now and again, to be flung out into the periphery of outer darkness" (p. 117). Though Birt is applying his pseudoprofundity to the question of tensions within the institute staff, his words could just as easily be describing the disappearance of Mary. The institute is, in his words, "a self-compensating mechanism" (p. 118) whose members right themselves by "spinning like tops on our own axis" (p. 118). That is, individual tensions and conflicts are managed by keeping the whole in a state of motion, by spinning the entire organization around its center, as it is spun in the Founder's Day dance. Even Birt fears "an incautious move towards the centre" (p. 118), that is, any disturbance that would unfix the pivot on which they all turn, Miss Edge. Birt himself is threatened by Mary's disappearance because of the suspicion against him which it might awaken in Edge. The girls also feel that "Mary's a curse" (p. 183). Their predominant reaction to the disappearance is one of annoyance that "we might've had the thing cancelled, thanks to those two" (p. 180). Therefore, Edge's desire to have the whole thing forgotten, subsumed in the ritual of the dance, is a general one, and she is really expressing the desire of the community as well as her own when she insists that the dance must take place.

Edge and Baker begin the dance "in one another's bony grip, on the room's exact centre" (p. 195). Edge's genius, the talent that makes her the center on which the institute is poised, is that she has created "out of a vacuum" a tradition that will meet on a mass basis the needs she feels in herself. The dance is a brief opportunity for the group to act as some of the individuals in *Concluding* do, closing their eyes and ears to what may threaten or displease them, living in a world entirely filled by their own emotions. As Winstanley, one of the teachers, says, "There's anaesthesia in a valse" (p. 201). Like Edith and Kate in *Loving,* each dancer is really dancing with herself, as the identical costumes and the room full of "short reflections" (p. 195) indicate. In fact, Edge and Baker, dancing among their own reflections both in the walls and in the flesh, can be seen as Kate and Edith grown into spinsters, never having left the presexual world in which the individual loves only herself.

When Edge and Baker sway out onto the dance floor, their eyes are "tight closed" (p. 195), and they are at "rest in movement, barely violable, alone." The spell that the dance has cast over them is the final perfection of the spell they've been trying to cast over themselves all day, Baker by closing her eyes to the bad news of her orphan, Edge by closing off all sense to news of invasion or variation. It is a spell the other dancers share in by collaboration, even Moira, who, dancing with Edge, "proudly noted the Principal had once more closed her eyes" (p. 198). When Marchbanks wonders if they aren't dancing just "to forget their miserable condition, their worries," her partner, Winstanley, responds, "Ah, they weren't fools," and "shut her eyes tight" (p. 201). Closing one's eyes is the purpose of dancing for Mrs. Blain, who "blindly danced" (p. 196), for her student partner, "given over to her shivering, glazed senses" (p. 197), for all the girls who dance with "great shut eyes" (p. 198). The rapture that comes with closed eyes is that of being drowned completely in the self. The dance is a mass ritual that offers the same kind of delicious isolation to each member of the mass. Both Mrs. Blain and her partner see "themselves from shut eyes," as if shutting the eyes were a prerequisite to seeing the self. Liz is described as thinking "from her closed eyes" (p. 202), as if these, and not the mind, were the source of meditations about herself. The effect of the dance is most evident in her condition after it is over, "struck into herself," without "eyes for what was lavished from above, nor ears" (p. 245).

The dance accomplishes for the mass what Rock's cottage accomplishes for him or Edge's sanctum for her. It is a momentary place analogous to the ad hoc environments Kate and Edith create in the ballrooms of Kinalty, an isolation within which the dancer can withdraw, a fiction based on blindness just as John Haye's is. This is the appeal of Edge's brand of authoritarianism and the explanation for the attraction her rule exercises over those below her. Just as she requires all the students and staff as the stuff of her fiction, they require her and achieve their own fictions by spinning around her as around a central axis. Her emphasis on tradition, on repetition in experience, on the undeviating character of the dance, answers a corresponding need in her students to use these rituals as she does, to block out all that is not conformable to their own wishes. The girls are often presented in the criticism as antagonistic to the two principals and as possessed by a sensuality that is inimical to authority.[33] But even Moira, most rebellious of the girls, conforms to the rituals of the dance, which has as its peculiar genius a use of sensuality, of rhythm, movement, sound, to combine all the girls into one perfectly choreographed mass. And the height of the dance brings about a surge of emotion for Edge and Baker, a surge that is itself "usual at these Dances" and takes the form of a gift for the principals (p. 199). Even Moira says to Edge at this point, "Ma'am . . . You're wonderful. So good" (p. 199). Edge becomes the center of the dance with all the girls whirling in a centripetal mass around her because she allows everyone to enjoy momentarily the bliss of isolation she achieves through her institute and its girls.

Green's analysis of authoritarianism is therefore founded on a human impulse recognizable in all of his characters and for this reason seems sounder than the more famous picture given at the same time in *1984*. It shows the connection between "individual desire and the collective structure" that Girard claims is missing from Orwell's novel. *Concluding* illustrates the analysis Auden gives in "The Prolific and the Devourer": "One of the strongest appeals of Fascism lies in

---

[33]See, for example, Stokes, pp. 19–20, and Russell, pp. 188–190.

its pretence that the State is one Big Family: its insistence on Blood and Race is an attempt to hoodwink the man-in-the-street into thinking that political relations are personal."[34] At the same time it offers a definition of authoritarianism which has a plausible connection to the longing for myth that grew up at the end of the war and to the taste for orthodoxy that Auden himself shares. What is achieved in the dance is the "fixity and enclosure" Trilling speaks of in connection with *Mansfield Park*. The dangers that it protects the dancers from, the "openness and chance" that are such a threat to Edge, are dissipated by the exact observance of a ritual. This dance grows naturally out of Green's earlier work and is in a way the culmination of his ideas about public life, as the figure of Raunce is the culmination of his ideas about the personal. This kind of public life is not personally false but gains its power from its ability to offer the self a limited freedom within the protection of ritual and routine. The dance is therefore a ritual to be seen ambivalently, as a beautiful expression, a fixity in movement as in "Among School Children," but also as the tool of a system that at bottom belongs to Miss Edge.

One of the crucial differences between Green's portrayal of authoritarianism and those of Orwell and Waugh is that Green is capable of seeing the system through the eyes of its perpetrators as well as through those of its victims. But Edge's system does have its victims, and *Concluding* ends with a duel between the system and one individual, Mr. Rock. The terms of this duel and the virtues that enable Rock to win it are, however, quite different from what might be expected. The duel begins at the dance itself, when both Rock and Edge make seeming overtures of peace to each other, but it is clear that both are simply maneuvering to consolidate the place they feel is in jeopardy. Taking on "the servile courtesy that he could assume at will" (p. 191), Rock offers to lecture to the girls and then is "literally choked by momentary rage"

---

[34]W. H. Auden, "The Prolific and the Devourer," *Antaeus*, 42 (Summer 1981), 20. This issue is completely devoted to a reprint of the Auden essay.

(p. 193) when Edge understands him to be offering lectures on the Great Theory itself. But Rock heroically swallows his pride and, assuming "an idiot look" (p. 213) as protection, offers lectures "along the lines of the joy, the reward, of achievement" (p. 214). The purpose of these offers is certainly to consolidate his place and that of his granddaughter at the institute, for the whole plan is destroyed by his rage when the girls ask about Liz's impending engagement to Birt. This infuriates Rock, who thunders, "We live in an ungrateful world" (p. 230), and he tells Liz, "We are not wanted. . . . We need never have demeaned ourselves" (pp. 231–32). Obviously, Rock is demeaning himself to secure Liz, to keep his small world unchanged. The girls have presented the possibility of change and even show pleasure in it, and Rock is so enraged he proclaims, "Too much freedom here. Lack of control. All they have to do is chatter" (p. 232). Rock resembles Edge very much here, stung when the organization of his private world is questioned and determined to protect it by the persecution of others if necessary.

Edge's overtures to Rock follow a similar pattern. Her annoyance at Rock's original offer to lecture mirrors his annoyance at the way she receives it. Edge "wondered at his effrontery, that he should claim kinship with their Work" (p. 214). What appears to Rock as a tremendous concession is to her offensive presumption because Edge jealously protects her work as Rock does his theory. Sharing their work is the last thing on the mind of either. Thus Edge suffers a feeling of violation similar to Rock's and now sees his presence at the dance as a "preposterous persecution" (p. 216). She even convinces herself that Rock has been drinking, claiming with the characteristic poor sight of the persecuted, "He had a flask, Hermione. I saw the bulge myself, in his pocket" (p. 217).

A tremendous change has therefore taken place when, only a few minutes later, Edge invites Rock into the sanctum, not even noticing when he sits at "the great desk of office" (p. 239). The vigilance excited to such a peak at the dance has been relaxed by tobacco. Edge thinks of cigarettes as "a special, exceptional indulgence" (p. 234), and as a self-indulgence the cigarette acts as Rock's poses do, isolating Edge behind a kind of screen, giving her the security she obviously lacks when affronted by his presence. This screen is signified by the way she speaks from a great distance, "as though from another existence" (p. 235), and by the difficulty she has in seeing even across the room. Edge is relaxed here because she has achieved complete self-absorption, a saturation of herself so thorough that it leads not to paranoia but to a kind of lofty indifference to opposition.

This mood leads to the most astonishing occurrence in *Concluding,* Edge's proposal of marriage to Rock, given with a "simper which allowed of no misinterpretation" (p. 242). The proposal is, as Edge reflects, "a desperate expedient to gain possession of a cottage" (p. 241). Like Rock's offers, it is simply a stratagem to further consolidate her own position, to finally gain the cottage by whatever means are necessary. But Edge almost laughs as she thinks this, and she certainly doesn't seem desperate as she drawls out her proposal. For Edge finally feels secure enough to proceed by assimilation rather than expulsion. She is in a mood left over from the dance, where every dancer seemed an extension of herself, and now she simply wants to extend herself further, to take care of Rock by absorbing him, letting herself languidly enlarge like an amoeba until the irritating intruder no longer exists. Her offer is not a concession at all but the final expression of a solipsism more complete even than John Haye's. She cannot see Rock or understand any of his self-pitying complaints, and persists in speaking of Moira while he speaks of Liz, confusing her pronouns as characters in *Loving* do when locked behind the sensory filters of their enclaves.

Oddly enough, Rock and Edge do achieve a kind of intimacy through their mutual self-absorption. Rock becomes Edge-like in his rage at the girls, actually complaining to her that they have too much freedom, that "they can go too far, can't they?" (p. 237) as if in cryptic, unconscious reference to Mary's escape. The two old people agree that the girls are "so terribly full of themselves, terribly" (p. 240), which seems

Loving AND *Concluding*

to be Green's joke at their expense, the two characters most choked with themselves. The two swap stories of their enemies, Rock bringing up Adams and his cottage while Edge languidly mentions, "There was a Mrs. Manley" (p. 240). Rock and Edge are alike in their fear of invasion, their mistrust of outsiders, their insistence that other people not act with the effrontery of separate wills. Their misunderstanding is total, yet they are for a moment almost intimate, with the kind of intimacy usual in Green, where two people have so little sense of the separate existence of one another that they talk almost as if speaking each to himself.

But this moment of intimacy doesn't last, and the character who emerges the winner is Rock, paradoxically, because he is the smaller, the more querulous of the two. He is completely "given over to self pity" (p. 236) but is "secure in self pity" (p. 238), proof against Edge because he feels so sorry for himself that he can hardly understand her. Instead of listening to Edge's proposal, he is "contemplating his own death with disinterest" (p. 241), so that he hears her from "the vast distance of his final, cold preoccupation, not having taken in the drift" (p. 242). If Edge's cigarettes put her at a distance, Rock's self-pity removes him even further, into an egotism so complete he can barely sense her meaning. Instead of responding to her hints, he changes the subject to his health, his age, and then simply closes the door behind him with the "one short, sharp laugh" that marks his triumph. This is the old age of John Haye, the self-pity of Green's first hero developed to such a state that preoccupation with death works like blindness. That Rock's preoccupation with his health is a form of the protective blindness that first appears with John Haye is signified on the walk home: "The trouble Mr. Rock had with his eyes, under a moon, brought him back to where he left off with Miss Edge, to health" (p. 246). It is a mark of Rock's total self-absorption at this point that he believes that health had been the real subject of their discussion. But "had he tried, he would have been unable at this precise moment to remember more of his latest talk with the Principal."

As several pieces of mysterious evidence suggest, Rock is more the master of the institute than Edge is. When Edge is in the act of denouncing Rock to Baker at the dance, the music suddenly drops, forcing her to alter her statement to "this Rock . . . upon which our Institute is Built" (p. 222). This seems merely a clever recovery until Rock's walk home after the dance, when "he turned round to view the hated mansion which the moon, plumb on it, made so tremendous that he spoke out loud the name, 'Petra' " (p. 245). What sort of odd relationship is being suggested when Green gives Rock and the mansion the same name? Furthermore, the institute is in the process of becoming more like Rock's cottage, beginning with the mysterious directive that inaugurates pig farming there. Is this the work of the powerful Mr. Swaythling, Rock's particular friend?

It is true, in a way, that as long as Rock holds out against Edge, the entire institute and not just his cottage constitutes his place. Edge and Baker may be able to ignore the absence of Mary, or cover it up, but Rock is an active presence, a piece of grit in the machinery, a rival whose egotism surpasses their own. As long as all of Edge's thoughts are turned toward his expulsion, it is with her as Girard says it is with Mme Verdurin's salon in Proust: "The hated outsiders are the true gods."[35] Rock truly is the rock on which the institute is built as long as Edge focuses all her energies on keeping him out. He becomes the master of Petra by becoming the idée fixe in the mind of its principal, until he becomes the very theme of her life, an irritation so intimate she thinks of resolving it by marriage.

Rock prevails because he is so parochial, so selfish, because he becomes a monolith with its own gravity and its own place. As Orwell abundantly shows in *1984*, the liberal virtues have little chance against organized brutality. Openness, sympathy, honesty, sincerity, all are crushed by the simple visceral fear of pain. But as Orwell also suggests, certain vices are uncrushable. Thus Winston Smith is overjoyed by the

---

[35]Girard, p. 202.

sense of sin. And Green intimates that Edge's system is insufficient primarily because people are finally too selfish for it. Like John Haye, Rock holds himself free by his own self-absorption, his self-pity. Rock rejects the public world of Miss Edge, not because it is more abstract than his own or somehow false, but because his own fictions are incomparably more complete. The individual is stronger than the system because he is smaller and therefore able to achieve a fictive completeness that Edge, with her girls leaping over the walls, can never rival. Therefore the novel ends with all of Rock's animals, once thought lost like Mary and Merode, magically returned to their places, and with Rock falling asleep "well satisfied . . . almost at once" (p. 254), just as Raunce does when everything runs according to plan.

Critics have been apt to comment that *Concluding* is misnamed because little in it is concluded.[36] But the end of the novel is conclusive in the same way the end of *Loving* is. Nothing is settled, neither the question of Mary's disappearance nor that of Liz's engagement. But Rock's satisfied sleep suggests that nothing need be settled as long as the characters are free to form conclusions of their own. Edge shows with her masterful handling of Merode's reappearance that her bureaucratic talents are equal to any variation, and her proposal to Rock shows that she is willing to make any sacrifice to keep her system intact. Rock says of his own troubles, "Everything comes if one can bide one's time" (p. 232), and this faith seems validated by the magical return of his animals. *Concluding,* like *Loving,* ends with a kind of fairy-tale promise, but one which individuals tender to themselves. It is an assurance that comes from their lifelong habit of putting things in their places, of making conclusions, of forming enclosures for themselves within which to fall asleep, as Rock does, well satisfied with himself.

---

[36]See, for example Odom, p. 111, Stokes, p. 19, and Russell, p. 182.

Conclusion
NOTHING, DOTING, and the Fictive Life

Lucky the man who can say "when," "before," and "after"! Misfortunes may have befallen him, or he may have writhed in agony: but as soon as he is capable of recounting the events in their chronological order he feels as well content as if the sun were shining straight on his diaphragm.

Robert Musil
The Man without Qualities

Loving and *Concluding* bring to a culmination ideas about private and public life that are present in all of Green's works, and it should now be possible to describe these works by defining the intimate interrelationships they construct between these commonly separated categories. When H. P. Lazarus says that Green's later work destroys "the whole fiction of self-knowledge," he is correct, but the terminology should be slightly rearranged.[1] Green shows that self-knowledge *is* fiction, that an individual achieves self-creation,

---

[1] H. P. Lazarus, "The Symbolic Apple," *The Nation,* May 24, 1952, p. 506.

not in the existential sense A. Kingsley Weatherhead intends when he adopts that term as the centerpiece of his study of Green, not by stripping off influence to emerge as a truly autonomous being, but by concocting, from whatever trash is available, a narrative to inhabit. The character of this fiction changes from John Haye's sentimental self-casting to the greeting-card clichés of Dupret and Bridges. It is characterized by symbolic objects in *Party Going,* by memories in *Caught* and *Back,* and by places in *Loving* and *Concluding.* But the consistent feature unifying all Green's characters and all his novels is that the self is invented, most often by the adoption of some exterior fact, in the way that the partygoers become Max, or Nancy becomes Rose, or Raunce becomes the butler. The sheer number of identity changes in Green's novels suggests his lack of interest in the uniqueness of individuals. Joan is transformed into June, Dy into Roe's wife, Nancy into Rose, Raunce into Eldon, the mystery man of *Party Going* into a dozen different characters. The prevalence of indistinctive, interchangeable names signifies the same thing: the application of Richard Roe to the one character who most resembles Green himself; the generic names in the fire station; the identification of names and titles in *Loving*; the persistent toying with initials, as when all the girls in *Concluding* receive names that begin with *M* or half the characters in *Party Going* names that begin with *A.* Only Roe, of all Green's characters, feels alienated in the sense that his situation in society prevents him from achieving an authentic self, and his anomalous place in Green's work is shown by the unhappy ending, unique to this novel. Only Pye experiences the classic Marxist alienation of self from work, and he is significantly the only major character to die in a novel by Green.

The fact that every Green novel is concerned as much with a group, and with the personality of the group, as with individuals also suggests that social roles have for him an import different from that of many modern writers. Trilling quotes the statement "Hell is other people" from Sartre's *Huis Clos* as a quintessentially modern sentiment,[2] but if this were applied to Green, every character would be in Hell. Even Roe, so concerned about the truth of his memories, accepts the interim personality assigned him at the fire station, and most of Green's characters positively revel in their socially determined selves. Sickness occurs when those roles are removed, when Craigan is fired, when the party is put off, when the lost ring threatens the stability of the social life at Kinalty. This sickness does not lead, as it might in Sartre, to a new autonomy and authenticity. Rather, it leads deeper into fantasy, sometimes into complete dependence as it does for Craigan. What Rosenberg asserts as a general principle is certainly true for Green, that "the opposition between self and social mask seems abstract and illusory."[3] More and more often as Green's work advances, his characters come into their own by assuming a social mask, as Raunce "arrives" by acquiring Eldon's life.

At the same time, public life appears as a rather different thing in these novels from what it is often accounted to be. The public world of Green's novels is not a place of impersonality and abstraction but a battleground of personal fictions. The groups with which Green is so largely concerned have corporate fictions like the personal ones, and public life is often more creative than private life. Gossip in *Living* and *Caught*, backbiting in *Party Going*, nostalgia in *Back*, group paranoia in *Loving*, all approach the status of literature. Group politics is not so much the balancing of impersonal social or historical forces as it is the creation of social fictions within which the members can live. The group rituals, like the cocktail-party chat in *Party Going*, the tall stories in *Caught*, the table talk in *Loving*, are all versions of the great dance at the end of *Concluding*, in which the individual is most herself when part of a huge pattern composed by a whole group. Even the attempt of one individual, such as Dupret or Edge,

---

[2]Lionel Trilling, *Sincerity and Authenticity* (Cambridge: Harvard Univ. Press, 1971), p. 102.
[3]Rosenberg, p. 202.

to become the author, to upset the collaborative nature of the fiction by imposing a fiction of his or her own, is not always harmful because, as Green shows in *Party Going* and *Concluding*, groups are often quite content to accept the fictions of individuals and to accept their identity completely from a single member.

This is not to say that Green ignores the historical and social changes that, according to Rosenberg, have made alienation one of the central concepts in modern literature. Green's characters are alienated in the sense of distance they have from powerful historical realities like the war precisely because these historical changes leave them with so little material for fiction. As Rosenberg says, "Masses who have faced death on the battlefield or in air raids, and have experienced the dissolution of accustomed forms become susceptible to moods of emptiness and detachment."[4] These moods especially afflict the characters in *Caught* and *Back,* but also those on the edges of the war as well, especially in *Party Going* and *Loving.* The real danger of the war is, as Herbert Read suggests, the way it dissolves conventions, and the response of Green's characters is to create conventions to fill the vacuum. Green's symbol for this dislocation is the interrupted train ride that appears as early as *Blindness* and is applied metaphorically to Craigan and the characters in the wartime stories as well as appearing as the basis of *Party Going*. The train is a symbol of continuity, of assured progress, almost of narrative progress, as it moves steadily from stop to stop in an orderly, directional fashion. The need for progress itself is less important than the need for an impression of progress, a sense that one experience logically follows another. The war stops this progress and destroys the illusion. Thus the danger that most afflicts Green's characters is immobility—the paralysis of Craigan, the partygoers, *Caught,* the death of Raunce's routine—and the natural antidote is narrative itself. The disjunction of experience produces a narrative desire, a need to express oneself as a fictional plot. Thus the predominance of storytelling in Green, the attempt to give experience a shape

[4]Ibid., p. 203.

Nothing, Doting, AND THE FICTIVE LIFE

by making it a story, which is shared by Craigan, Julia, Roe, and Nanny Swift, among others. Thus also the tendency for these characters to see themselves in fictional terms, to alter experience artificially within their own minds to make it conform to a myth of continuity that events have shattered. This is really the key to Green's work, that the self depends on fictions for its existence. When history withdraws the fictions on which it normally depends, by stopping the factory, or the train, or paralyzing the characters inside the fire station, or breaking the settled routine of an enclave, the characters become all the more intent on fictions as a means of achieving what Robert Musil calls "that notorious 'narrative thread' of which it then turns out the thread of life itself consists."[5]

Nothing and *Doting,* though they seem at first to be outside the main body of Green's work because of the new conversational method introduced in them, in fact summarize these ideas. The chief characteristic of the two novels is their portrayal of two different societies, represented by two generations. The older generation comes from a society reasonably rich in both economic and social terms, essentially a prewar society, while the younger feels itself growing into a poor world that is drab as much because it lacks the traditions and the conventions—in short, the fictions—of the past as because it is economically depressed. The two books portray the struggle between these two generations as a struggle between Green's own idea of the self as a conscious artificial creation and aspirations toward an identity free of the taint of social falsehood. Behind the social comedy of these two novels is Green's basic argument with this concept of authenticity, which has a particular interest here because it is expressed in generational terms. Green situates his own ideas in the experience of his generation, made suddenly clearer by the arrival of a new generation along with an entirely new age.

For these last two novels, Green exaggerated a tendency always present in his fiction to rely on conversation where other writers would have used narration or description. This

---

[5]Robert Musil, *The Man without Qualities,* tr. Eithne Wilkins and Ernst Kaiser (London: Secker and Warburg, 1967), II, 436.

method in itself illustrates both the essential ideas behind *Nothing* and *Doting* and the general epistemological assumption behind all of Green's work. Green adopts the conversational method as a kind of discipline, in acknowledgment of the fact that nothing beyond a person's words can be known. He asks in "Communication without Speech," "Do we know what other people are really like? I very much doubt it. We certainly do not know what other people are thinking and feeling. How then can the novelist be so sure?" Therefore, the novelist should not intrude narrative or description into his accounts but should present people as they present themselves, in conversation. Donald Taylor calls this the "final abdication of the determining, evaluative authorial role." But Green also abandons an even more fundamental role, that of the author as truthteller, because he proposes to present not some fundamental, intrinsic truth about characters but merely their own presentations, which are generally lies. He says, "The moment anything happens which is worthwhile . . . one goes over it verbally after, and because conversation comes into almost any experience, in going over it one adds favorable interpretations, favorable to oneself, which colour and falsify the account one gives. If the experience is particularly damning to oneself one can go to the other extreme, shame can make one exaggerate the unfavourable side." Conversation "comes into" experience; experience need not determine conversation. Experience, as in *Caught,* is fictionalized as it happens, and what Green proposes to do is to limit fiction to these fictionalizations. Thus words derive whatever meaning they have from context, as people do, and what little knowledge is accumulated in life is derived from "watching the way people around us behave, after they have spoken." Only that immediate behavior, by establishing a context, gives any meaning at all to the words that have been spoken. This skepticism determines the form of *Nothing* and *Doting,* the small, drawing-room nature of the comedy. As P. H. Newby points out, when a novelist resolves to show rather than tell, his scope must shrink, because showing has none of the summarizing powers of telling, and a large society can no longer be compressed into a small space.[6]

David Lodge maintains that modern novelists, faced with speech that is as debased as Green asserts in his articles, compensate by making "the indirect representation of consciousness" more sensitive and complicated. But Green does just the opposite. Not only does he limit himself to the words spoken but he accepts those words, debased as they are, as an operational reality. He says, in "The English Novel of the Future," "You learn more from the lies of someone who is speaking to you, if you can find these out, than you will from direct statements which generally only represent a portion of what the person you are speaking to believes. A direct lie can be infinitely revealing." The obliqueness of conversation therefore becomes almost an advantage. Because "we do not have time to define what we mean in conversation . . . we thereby arrive easier at a general conventional understanding of what is being said." This surface understanding is not to be despised, because, though it does not correspond to the essential reality, which can never be known, it does represent the lie, the fiction, by which people live. John Pomfret, asked what he means by a particular statement, responds, "Precisely the little I'm saying," and he is not really dissimulating. His statements mean no more than they appear to on the surface, and this surface is as much of an essential reality as his statements are likely to have. Granting the impossibility of absolute knowledge, Green accepts the approximations offered in everyday speech. Unlike Ivy Compton-Burnett, Green does not allow normally unspoken thoughts to intrude into conversation, nor does he stylize speech as she does, so that it often seems a compromise between revery and communication. Green's conversation novels are fundamentally unlike

---

[6]All quotations from Green in this paragraph are from "A Novelist to His Readers: Communication without Speech," *The Listener,* Nov. 9, 1950, p. 506. Donald Taylor's statement is to be found in "Catalytic Rhetoric: Henry Green's Theory of the Modern Novel," *Criticism,* 7 (1965), 82. Newby, p. 12.

Compton-Burnett's because he proposes to use conversation as a limitation, while she stretches it, distorting it to make it express all that narrative and description might have expressed.[7]

Therefore, the characters in these last two novels rarely communicate with one another in any generally accepted sense, yet they do have satisfactory conversations. No two characters come closer to one another in *Nothing* than John Pomfret and Jane Weatherby, yet they do so not by communicating but by exchanging the kind of wholly abstract noises Lily and Bert exchange: "They had been talking by fits and starts not so much in reply one to the other as to make peaceful barely related statements which had advanced very little what they presumably meant by everything they said because they now seemed in all things to agree" (p. 248). The question of "what they presumably meant" has been set aside, and though it is hard to believe that John and Jane do agree in everything, a surface agreement is sufficient for them. Their acceptance is what Green calls, in *Pack My Bag,* "the saving grace in relationships, the not speaking out, not sharing confidences, the avoidance of intimacy in important things which makes living, if you can find friends to play it that way, of so much greater interest even if it does involve a lot of lying."[8] As in *Living,* the most perfect conversation stops at the surface, accepting each person's individual conventions and achieving intimacy by accepting the fictions which, unlike the essential character of the person involved, can be least be touched.

The acceptance of lies and conventions as an operational truth becomes, in the last two novels, an acceptance of the surface facades of the characters as their ultimate personalities. Bruce Bassoff says of Green's characters in general, "We are very often not certain whether or not their substance is

---

[7]David Lodge, *Language of Fiction* (London: Routledge and Kegan Paul, 1966), p. 47; Henry Green, "The English Novel of the Future," pp. 23 and 22; idem, *Nothing* (New York: Viking Press, 1950), p. 50. Unless noted, all subsequent references are to this edition and in this chapter will appear in text.

[8]Henry Green, *Pack My Bag,* p. 126.

exhausted by their appearance." Though Green sometimes does, in other novels, use interior monologue, he achieves in *Nothing* and *Doting* the kind of literature Nathalie Sarraute predicts for the future in *The Age of Suspicion,* a literature that will deal with "only appearances." The most common stylistic trick in these two novels is the injection of *seems* or *appears* into every description involving judgment of a character. Jane speaks "with what appeared to be a false voice" (p. 38), or her eyes are "limpid with what seemed to be innocence" (p. 157). Green calls attention to this habit in "Communication without Speech," where anything stronger than *seems* is called "a too direct communication from the author." This habit, which is applied to all of the characters and not just to the more theatrical ones like Jane Weatherby, stops conjecture at the surface, warning the reader every time that everything beyond appearance is conjecture. The reader may, like Philip Weatherby, insistently demand more, but each character seems to reply, as old Arthur Morris does, "Then all you've got is the evidence of your own senses" (p. 70).[9]

The conflict between appearance and reality, between Philip's desire to know and Arthur's assurance that all beyond the surface is unknowable and therefore operationally nonexistent, is, in fact, the basic theme of Green's last two books. It is the basic question over which the two generations quarrel, lying behind all their discussions of paternity, marriage, and money. The essential difference between the two generations is illustrated in the very first scenes of *Nothing,* in the mock marriage ceremony of John Pomfret and six-year-old Penelope Weatherby. To Jane Weatherby the ceremony is a charming game, with its cigar-band wedding ring and

[9]Bassoff, p. 117; Nathalie Sarraute, *The Age of Suspicion,* tr. Maria Jolas (New York: Braziller, 1963), p. 117; Henry Green, "Communication without Speech," p. 506. It should be noted that Sarraute emphasizes the "subconversation" in Green's works. Yet her own works include this subconversation as a running commentary in a way that Green's do not. Moreover, she seems to envisage a future literature in which the surface would do all the work done in her own novels by an interplay of spoken and unspoken messages.

muslin veil, but Penelope "wed poor John in her own mind as sure as if she was actually in church" (p. 33). The social comedy of the novels, derived from the childish irresponsibility of the parents as opposed to the mature gravity of the children, rests on this more fundamental difference, that the parents see life as a set of appearances to be toyed with, while the children see it as composed of deadly realities. The various manias that Penelope acquires, her fear of losing her arm for example, are based on the same highly serious attitude toward appearance that underlies all the cautious decisions of her brother Philip.

For her mother, on the other hand, Penelope is herself a game, a fiction Jane interposes between the world and herself. John realizes this, asking, "But don't you think Pen's often a blind, Richard? Doesn't Jane use the child as a shield?" (p. 139). Penelope's anxieties, her need to be protected, which seem to be real enough for the child, serve her mother by keeping unpleasant facts out of the conversation, as John realizes. But even John is not perspicacious enough to see that the mock marriage is a fictional version of the real one Jane desires with him. Jane's characteristic way of approaching reality is at the level of play, so that the sweet, mock marriage of her daughter is gradually replaced by the bustle of the impending marriage of her son Philip to John's daughter Mary, which, it gradually appears, is to be no more than another fictional approach to Jane's ultimate goal. Jane differs from simple daydreamers in that she imposes her fiction on reality, as Dick Dupret and Miss Edge do, making the surface count for the substance.

The vice of the older generation is its superficiality, its attention to creature comforts, to convention and old habits. But Jane elevates this vice with the talent of a great actress. Her feel for the proper role is simple deceit at times, as when she assumes "a mantle of tragic calm and decision" (p. 59) when challenged about her old adultery with John. The ability to assume such a mantle, however, is necessary to certain social occasions, when acting provokes and releases true sentiment. Thus when Philip and Mary suddenly announce their engagement at Philip's "twenty-firster" Jane rises "majestically from her place" and takes "a look of infinite humility on her proud features." Jane's genius here is a feel for occasion, the way her face glows, not with actual emotion, but with "a magnificent effulgence of what all felt she must feel." There is no indication in this scene that Jane is really happy, and the engagement turns out to be a positive threat to her plans, but she is so perfect in her role that "it seemed to most the finest thing they had ever seen, the epitome of how such moments should be, perfection in other words, the acme of manners, and memorable as being the flower, the blossoming of grace and their generation's ultimate instinct of how one should ideally behave" (p. 111).

Jane is the perfect example of her generation's approach to life, the finest actress in a pageant of acted emotions. She is so adept at shaping the surface of things because she has adopted an epistemology like Green's: "Oh but we shall never get at the whole truth. I often think we're not here below to find that out ever, till I believe the truth's even stopped having any importance for me in the least" (p. 232). This disbelief in the possibility of truth is both convenient for Jane and heartening for those around her, allowing her to invent those moments of pure artifice that are the acme of good manners. She is both the most deceitful character in these two novels and the most engaging, epitomizing both the faults of her generation, its utter superficiality, and its virtues, its inventive, imaginative artificiality.

But the ignorance of ultimate truth that Jane has come to accept is precisely what tortures the younger generation. As Annabel Paynton says in *Doting,* "What do we ever learn about other people? . . . Not to trust the way they look, and that's about all."[10] This inability to trust appearance is what lies at the bottom of the anxiety of Jane and John's children. Philip and Mary are to some extent imprisoned by their parents' frivolity, since the old adultery of John and Jane presents

---

[10]Henry Green, *Doting* (New York: Viking, 1952), p. 182. Unless noted, all subsequent references are to this edition and in this chapter will appear in text.

the possibility that Philip and Mary might be siblings and thus unable to marry. The rather excessive neatness of the plot does illuminate this essential conflict, that the false marriage of the parents may make a true marriage of the children impossible, the very willingness of the parents to rest on appearance putting substance beyond the reach of the children. But most readers must also feel that Philip's insistence on substance betrays a dull mind, that his rather colorless personality comes from an ambition simply to be solid. Philip, like Richard, who occupies a kind of median position between the generations, has what Jane calls the failing "of the absolutely true . . . of being almost completely unimaginative poor dear" (p. 128).

Philip's mania for family, his belief that blood tells, is his assertion that Jane is wrong and that there is an essential reality beyond appearance. Green implicitly mocks Philip's position in several ways. His tremendous interest in heredity centers on his distant Uncle Ned, who despises the family, so that the nearest poor Philip can come to his desire of living up to his blood is to patronize his uncle's tailor. Thus even for Philip clothes represent the relationship that should appear in one's features, one's personality. Green also puts the question of Philip's paternity forever in the dark, allowing doubts to grow up around it, as if to underscore Jane's contention that the truth cannot be known. Finally, Green shows Philip grasping at straws of identity, turning his job into the determining factor that family fails to be. Liz Jennings, John's mistress, asserts that "one's evenings are a means to get right apart from what you and I have to do for a living in the daytime," but Philip insists that "how you spend your day is a part of your life" (p. 215). Philip is his work in a way that Liz and John are not, and in a way that Raunce and Edge are not. He says, "I don't know really except that our work does seriously mean something to us. Not like Mr. Pomfret with his absolutely endless complaints every time you meet him" (p. 229). It is impossible to imagine Raunce asserting that his job "means something," or even Craigan with his craftsman's pride giving his work the transcendent importance of a calling. When Green's other characters derive comfort or security or even self-definition from their jobs, it is not with this self conscious insistence that the job should supply a personality one can feel is "real." Philip uses such terms because, unlike most of Green's characters, he believes in personality as a value in itself and therefore demands a calling that will give him the sense of reality his family fails to provide.

Though Annabel Paynton in *Doting* is much more frivolous than Philip, she takes up much the same position with regard to the older generation. She tells Arthur Middleton, "I'm not like you, I really intend all I say" (p. 72). This in itself seems an act of dissimulation, because Annabel is as devious as any character in the book, but the important fact is that Annabel needs to *feel* sincere. When Arthur tells her the story of young Byass, who was pilloried at a weekend party many years before for making a rash comment about a girl's hair, Annabel decides, "Well those girls, as they were, just must have mobbed the man because they thought he wasn't genuine" (p. 49). Annabel simply ascribes her own values to the girls, but Arthur responds, "Good Lord no! . . . They were only being objectionable and hearty." He cannot imagine attacking anyone for lack of genuineness, while she cannot imagine people attacking one another out of sheer frivolity.

This difference between the generations is dramatically illustrated in *Nothing* when Philip and Mary separately travel to Brighton to ask Jane about their parentage. The question in their minds is one of ultimate identity, not just for the practical reasons associated with their engagement, but because blood is so important to a definition of their personalities. But when Mary arrives to ask Jane about her dead mother, Jane is much disconcerted and asks, "My dear . . . am I supposed to recognize you?" (p. 58). Jane is reacting to old memories of Brighton as a romantic hideaway: "No, not so very long ago one never was sure whether to go up to a friend in this wretched uncomfortable place. You see there was no knowing if they wanted to be known." Mary and Philip come for recognition, to have their essential identities established and recognized, but to Jane one is a friend or a stranger depending on social convenience. Identity is something quite different in London than it is in Brighton. The same idea is illuminated when Philip and Mary are ignored in John and Jane's favorite restaurant, plainly "not known" by the management, until John gets them a table by acknowledging them. John fumes, "They don't or won't recognize one's own children" (p. 47), but he certainly doesn't expect poor Gaspard to note a resemblance. His use of *recognize* is like Jane's, meaning a granting of attention based on social standing. Philip and Mary are poor undesirables in the restaurant until John's kiss, which transforms them into proper customers. Philip and Mary question their parents about the past, and especially about Philip's dead father and Mary's dead mother, because they want to establish some essential identity, but their only evidence for this identity comes from people for whom identity is determined largely by social ritual.

The older generation is shallow by conviction. Their happiest moments are spent in the artificial environment provided by restaurants and hotels, even though, as Jane says, "I never like to look the other side of anything in hotels" (p. 88). Yet because of this dependence on social ritual, the crucial events of *Nothing* and *Doting,* all of which are celebrations of one kind or another, mean more to the parents than to the children. The important events of *Nothing* are Philip's "twenty-firster" and the impending marriage of Philip and Mary. In *Doting* they are the two restaurant parties held in young Peter's honor, on either side of his school vacation. Giorgio Melchiori says of *Nothing,* "The external nature of this occasion is a key to the inner vacuity of feeling. What matters is the outer polish; this abolition of deeper values gives to *Nothing* a greater pungency, the peculiar nostalgia communicated by things which are so refined as to appear useless."[11] But the odd thing is that the occasions in these

[11] Melchiori, p. 208.

books fail to evoke feelings in the younger generation only, in the one that insists on "deeper values." As Philip complains, the "twenty-firster" is really for his mother, who coopts even the engagement announcement with her brilliant acting. Peter sits glum and unmoved at both of his parties, while the adults quiver with a variety of emotions. Social events are true emotional climaxes for the generation that puts its faith in the surface truth of social ritual.

The failure of these occasions to move the younger generation seems more a judgment against them, and against their expectations, than against the rituals themselves. Mary says with disgust, "One dance doesn't alter everything forever does it!" (p. 56). But in Green's other novels one dance does alter everything, as it does in *Concluding* and *Loving,* for those who allow it to. The disappointment of characters like Philip and Mary comes from unrealistic expectations, from the belief that there is an "everything" beyond the dance which is more substantial and real. All of the younger characters in these novels are unpleasantly emotionless, Philip especially, who takes the news of his broken engagement "with much composure" (p. 242). Their emotional vacuity, which far surpasses that of their parents, suggests that the social rituals may in fact *create* emotion. As with Nick Jenkins's heartfelt farewell to Mme Dubuisson, emotion sometimes seems to follow the conventional expressions, not precede them. Therefore, the children's insistence on "deeper values" prevents them from feeling the emotions excited in their parents by the stimuli provided by parties and engagements. It is for this reason that Jane Weatherby and John Pomfret take over the marriage proposed by their children, because the children simply aren't interested enough. Their ultimate lack of interest in one another is signified by their blasé attitude toward the engagement ring, which outrages their elders. John and Jane have the emotions their children should have, stimulated it seems by the preparations that mean so little to the children. For this reason they really deserve the marriage more than Philip and Mary do. The insistence of the younger generation on the real, the "genuine," deprives them of the half loaf enjoyed by their parents.

CONCLUSION

A larger significance is given this conflict by the way in which it is expressed in historical terms. The relative freedom that the adults enjoy is related to their greater economic freedom, but also to a belief that appearance can be manipulated, which has survived from an earlier era. Jane and John are true members of Green's generation. They are actors in the same way so many writers of Green's generation were. The adults of *Nothing* and *Doting* are versions of these writers with the talent removed. They locate their ability to act and to play with appearance in a specific historical period, as Jane does in *Nothing*: "But simply invented, every single word made up! I suppose people had much more time on their hands in those days which made them so dangerous" (p. 60). This old-fashioned, class-oriented sense of freedom over appearance stands them in good stead in the more constricted present because it gives them the impression of controlling events by controlling superficials, such as parties. Their bias toward fiction gives them some protection against the practical pressures of the modern world.

The children, on the other hand, have no such protection. It is not too far-fetched to assume that Mary Weatherby is the escaped student of *Concluding,* caught and brought back to work in M department, the department to which all those Moiras, Merodes, and Marions were obviously destined. In this sense *Nothing* is more futuristic than *Concluding* since it bears a greater resemblance to the Burnhamite future Orwell creates in *1984*. *Concluding* is full of ritual, and this is one of the inspirations behind the authoritarianism there. The government in *Nothing,* which employs all the young people, makes no such concessions to human desire. It offers only "a few grades" to be worked through, "year in and year out" (pp. 56–57), no celebrations, no promise of change, nothing like the dance that can be turned to fictional use. This is one of the causes of the entrepreneurial spirit Annabel Paynton brings to human relationships. As the adults say over and over in *Doting,* in the old days an accepted social mechanism existed to launch such girls toward available men. In the present, as V. S. Pritchett says, "The 'young person' on the brink of life is still eager to begin, but there is nowhere to begin"[12] The reduction of the social world to a few government grades deprives this generation of the materials for fiction. It limits their freedom both practically, by determining the path they must follow, and psychologically, by failing to present a surface that can be manipulated. It deprives them of the sense of power over their own personalities that is the great advantage of the other jobs in Green. As Mary says, "I'm no more than in a grade which I drag around with me like a ball and chain if I apply to another department" (p. 55).

Philip's passionate identification of himself with his job is a reaction to this deficiency in the present world. Philip thinks "we ought all to be in government jobs" (p. 201). He believes this because the Labour government program has become a cause with him: "We're making this country a fit place to live in at last" (p. 55). His repeated assertion is that a job is "part of your life" (pp. 215 and 239), that it "means something." This very assertion of the value of his work is Philip's fiction. It gives him the sense of personal substance that his mother so inconsiderately fails to provide. While the adults assert that there is a distance between them and their jobs, Philip insists that he and his job are identical, not because the job offers any of the protections that jobs normally do in Green, but because Philip must assert the authenticity of everything he does. Here Green is illustrating a social change described by Richard Sennett in *The Fall of Public Man*. The adults live by the social rule Sennett associates with pre-twentieth-century life, a rule that rejects "the idea that behind the convention there lay an inner, hidden reality to which the conventions referred and which was the 'real meaning.' "[13] For Philip all conventions have collapsed around the idea of "real meaning," which is the shibboleth on which he bases his life. The truthfulness of his own personality is a transcendent value for him as it is for no other character in Green, with the exception of Roe, and the pressure this need

---

[12]V. S. Pritchett, "Green on Doting," *New Yorker*, May 17, 1952, p. 121.
[13]Sennett, p. 87.

for truth puts on his life destroys all the emotions in it, making him the dull, uninvolved, dispassionate creature who finally doesn't care whether he is to be married or not.

This relationship between the generations can also be used to explain Green's anomalous position in modern British fiction, and perhaps the complicated position of his generation. In the late fifties, Kenneth Allsop attacked Green, lumping him with "the old *literati,* the candelabra-and-wine *rentier* writers" whose talent "is absorbed into the construction of elaborate, private languages, elegiac remembrances of things past, reveries that are passed like an empty parcel around an ever diminishing circle." Allsop's intention is to differentiate Green, Waugh, Spender, Lehmann, and other writers of their generation from those coming into prominence in the fifties, including Kingsley Amis, John Wain, Colin Wilson, and John Braine. He does so in terms William Van O'Connor also used several years later, defining the older generation as writers primarily concerned with interior experience, who are opposed, as O'Connor says Virginia Woolf was, to the "externality of life." O'Connor and Allsop thus announce the new generation as one which abandons the "dark places of psychology" in favor of the social examination of books like Alan Sillitoe's *Saturday Night, Sunday Morning,* or Braine's *Room at the Top.*[14]

Modern British fiction has always been divided along such lines, and it is important to remember that claims such as Allsop's were made for exactly the writers he sentences to the outer darkness of social uselessness. The argument is the old one between Virginia Woolf and Arnold Bennett, Henry James and H. G. Wells, and, as Spender points out in a review of Stansky and Abrahams's *Journey to the Frontier,* his own generation was the first to rebel against Woolf's restriction of literature to the inner psychology of the characters.[15]

---

[14] Kenneth Allsop, *The Angry Decade* (London: Peter Owen, 1958), p. 25; William Van O'Connor, *The New University Wits and the End of Modernism* (Carbondale: Southern Illinois Univ. Press, 1963), p. 147.

[15] Spender, *Thirties and After,* pp. 146–54.

Nothing, Doting, AND THE FICTIVE LIFE

But neither Green's fiction nor that of his contemporaries fits very well on either side of the boundary line that Allsop and O'Connor draw. Green's tendency as his fiction develops is to restrict himself more and more to the exterior lives of his characters, the exterior view of *Loving* becoming the conversational method of *Nothing* and *Doting*. As Green himself points out, he has never used stream of consciousness in a novel, and many of his books contain no direct representation of consciousness at all. He has, in fact, been attacked by Robert Weaver for having an obsession with "caste" that prevents him from penetrating into the lives of his characters.[16] Weaver's assumptions, which are fundamentally those of Allsop and O'Connor, prevent him from seeing the extent to which Green crosses the thick, red boundary line between exterior reality and inner psychology. All of Green's work supposes that the fulfillment that Forster, Woolf, and James supposed could come only from the sensitivities of a unique interior life can in fact be derived from any material, no matter how abstract, artificial, or shopworn. His books deny the existence of the unique self that Girard identifies as an invention of romanticism and show instead a self contrived largely from outside materials. This is a skepticism shared with other writers, with those of the same generation whose autobiographies deny the existence of a stable, genuine identity and those whose experience of the war was an experience in playacting, for example. At the same time, this belief in the fictional usefulness of conventions, clichés, and stock roles denies the solid objectivity of the exterior world, an objectivity writers like Allsop are assuming when they deprecate "psychological" writers as passé.

Thus it seems that some of the difficulty critics have had in coming to a proper estimation of Green's work arises from the way that work cuts across accepted boundaries between

---

[16]For Green's comment on stream of consciousness see Terry Southern, "The Art of Fiction XXII," *Paris Review,* 19 (Summer 1958), 73. Robert Weaver's comment appears in "The Novels of Henry Green," *Canadian Forum,* 30 (Jan. 1951), 227.

kinds of fiction, across basic assumptions upon which even Bennett and Woolf agree when they draw the line in the dust between them. Yet certain gains are made by ignoring these assumptions. Among these is the rehabilitation of convention, artifice, and therefore art. This is accomplished by expanding the definition of art as Raymond Williams does in *The Long Revolution*: "There are, essentially, no 'ordinary' activities, if by 'ordinary' we mean the absence of creative interpretation and effort. . . . We create our human world as we have thought of art being created."[17] This could be set as the motto of all of Green's novels, and belief in it transforms fiction from a specialized activity dependent on objective reality into a common human habit, a constituent of reality. The special status of the artist is sacrificed, as is the uniqueness of the individual, but what is lost in transcendent values is gained in humane ones. Literature is no longer the expression of a unique consciousness to the world nor the alteration of the world as it enters that consciousness. It is an ordinary human activity, but for that reason as fundamental and necessary as air.

Green stopped writing long before his death, and part of the reason must have been the feeling that social conditions and literary tastes were turning against his most basic ideas. Philip's insistence that his work is real is much like Allsop's insistence that the new generation of writers is finally dealing with real social issues. This change in the social and literary climate may have destroyed Green's appetite for fiction. Members of Philip's generation seem, at least in Green's work, to manage their anxiety not by inventing some protective fiction but by searching out some ultimate reality, some guarantee of authenticity such as politics or family. This urge, which is evident as well in the resurgence of documentary interest in the literature of the fifties, may have deadened Green's work just as the war had quickened it. For the effect of such an urge is to separate literature and mundane life, to set up again the old opposition between Woolf's sensibility

---

[17]Williams, *The Long Revolution*, p. 37.

and Bennett's Five Towns, and thus to destroy the world in between where Green's fiction finds its existence.

Any final evaluation of that fiction should recognize that both Green's successes as a writer and his limitations are tied to his sense of the interpenetration of public and private worlds. Green is one of the few British novelists of his time to escape the class divisions of his society, to write with the same accuracy about casual laborers and company owners. His novels manage to portray modes of social organization so basic that they can easily be transposed from the factory to the living room. This kind of breadth rests on the basic realization that ordinary life is an achievement, that even the blandest, safest routine represents a victory, and that the smooth and boring surface of normal social life is the result of a prodigious collaborative effort. This is the real work of every social organization in Green's fiction, and his most basic success is perhaps to have given some dignity to the labor.

The eminently social basis of Green's fiction prevents it, however, from satisfying some of the demands readers are used to making of modern literature. Though his interest in the fictions projected by the self may seem to bring him close to poets like Yeats, he has none of Yeats's desire for transcendence and no sense of the war between the self and its external relations that informs *A Vision*. Because so much of his fiction denies the idea of psychological depth, Green infrequently offers his readers the opportunity to enter into a central character. His novels generally lack central characters altogether, and because they so rarely contain characters who act as alter egos for the author, there is little sense in probing his work for a set of personal values, as can be done, for example, with Lawrence. Green extends his work in neither of the directions open to other moderns, neither toward the mystic reaches of Yeats nor down into the psyche, as in Joyce and Lawrence. In his fascination with social fictions Green resembles Proust, and many episodes in his work seem governed by principles also observable in *Remembrance of Things Past*. But Green's respect for the power of the everyday keeps him anchored so that pettiness and social intrigue can never

CONCLUSION

quite achieve either the grandeur or the abasement they enjoy in Proust.

Despite the social range of Green's fiction, despite its wide variety of characters, it does leave untouched many of the extremities open even to ordinary people. But these extremities have been given in a kind of trade for a wildly expanded version of the life most people lead everyday. For Green the world of the trivial is as large and convoluted as the universe of *A Vision*. To probe this world is to enlarge the space available to fiction, to enhance its power, and to change it as every important writer does. Henry Green is such a writer, and his greatest achievement is to have shown the tremendous fictional depth just where life is thought most shallow.

Index

Index

Acton, Harold, 55
Alienation, 2, 198
Allen, C. J., 177
Allen, Walter, 2, 55, 56, 88, 150
Allsop, Kenneth, 212, 213, 214
Amis, Kingsley, 212
Apocalypse, 140
"Apologia," 58
Arnold, Matthew, 3, 12
Auden, W. H., 29, 34, 40, 58, 60, 167; *Journey to a War*, 81; *Letter to Lord Byron*, 35; *The Orators*, 26–27, 30; *Paid on Both Sides*, 29, 31, 57–58; "The Prolific and the Devourer," 187; and public school, 7–8, 38; relationship to Green, 1, 51, 57; "West's disease," 97
Austen, Jane: *Emma*, 160
Authoritarianism, 167–68, 183, 187–88; see also *Concluding*; Orwell, George
Autobiography, 3–10, 13, 16, 35–43, 83

Back, 102, 123–37, 143, 196, 197, 198
Bartlett, Sir Frederick, 126–27, 132, 136
Bassoff, Bruce, 57, 60, 103, 173, 202–3; on *Loving*, 144, 158
Benjamin, Walter, 135, 136
Bennett, Arnold, 212, 214, 215
Bergonzi, Bernard, 60, 81
Blake, William, 88
Blindness, 16–24, 25, 30–31, 33–35, 137; compared to *Caught*, 135; compared to *Living*, 77, 78;

and *Concluding*, 180; train metaphor in, 102, 198
Bowen, Elizabeth, 8, 141, 142, 166
Braine, John, 212
Brogan, D. W., 19

Caught, 102, 103–23, 137, 196, 197, 198, 200; and *Back*, 123–24, 133, 134, 135; children in, 120–21; sex in, 119–20
Chappell, William, 104
"Communication without Speech," 200, 203
Communism, 4, 11, 52; see also Upward, Edward; Wood, Neal
Compton-Burnett, Ivy, 201–2
Concluding, 169–93, 195, 196, 197, 198, 209, 210; authoritarianism in, 168–69, 181; and *Loving*, 162; sensory distortions in, 174–80; see also Authoritarianism
Connolly, Cyril, 11, 32, 40, 43; *Enemies of Promise*, 4, 27, 35, 36, 42; and public school, 7, 9, 10; relationship to Green, 1, 28; on Second World War, 41, 83; *The Unquiet Grave*, 129, 140, 141

Day Lewis, Cecil, 6, 7–8, 28, 55, 82; *The Magnetic Mountain*, 80–81; *Starting Point*, 3, 35, 51–52, 53
Dickens, Charles: *Pickwick Papers*, 129; *Great Expectations*, 129

· 219 ·

INDEX

Dostoevski, Feodor, 96
Doting, 123, 205, 207, 208, 210, 213; conversational method of, 199–202; stylistic devices in, 203
Doughty, C. M., 58–60

Eagleton, Terry, 145–46
Eliot, George: *Middlemarch,* 160
Eliot, T. S., 12, 25, 40
"The English Novel of the Future," 201

First World War, 6–7, 28, 29–30, 37–38, 135; *see also* Isherwood, Christopher; Spender, Stephen
Forster, E. M., 40, 85, 213
Fuller, John, 30
Fussell, Paul, 29, 32, 117

Gascoyne, David, 81
Gathorne-Hardy, Jonathan, 7, 8
Girard, René, 2, 70, 96, 176, 179, 192, 213; on Orwell, 167, 168, 187
Goffman, Erving, 5–6, 8
Graves, Robert, 29
Green, Henry, 1–2, 32; conversational method of, 119–201; definition of fiction, 48; and Doughty, 58–60; as factory-worker, 47, 51, 54, 72; and First World War, 28, 29, 37–38; and Forster, 83–85; at Oxford, 80; position in modern British fiction, 212–15; and public school, 9, 28, 38; and Second World War, 101–3, 105, 122, 137; theory of the self, 12; *see also individual titles*
Green, Julian, 39
Green, Martin, 7, 8
Greene, Graham, 8, 9, 11, 35, 167

Hall, James, 109, 147, 149, 158
Hardy, Barbara, 62, 126, 130
Hemingway, Ernest, 135
Howard, Brian, 28
Howe, Irving, 143
Hynes, Samuel, 1, 4, 29, 35, 83

Isherwood, Christopher, 1, 5, 32, 43, 167; *All the Conspirators,* 24–26, 30; *The Berlin Stories,* 10, 11, 42, 43; on First World War, 28, 29–30; "Gems of Belgian Architecture," 29; *Journey to a War,* 81; *Lions and Shadows,* 4, 24, 27, 30, 33, 35, 37, 39, 41–42; and public school, 7–8

James, Henry, 61, 152, 212, 213; *Portrait of a Lady,* 160
Johnson, Bruce, 89
Joyce, James, 215

Kafka, Franz, 88, 104, 113
Karl, Frederick, 82
Keats, John, 144
Kermode, Frank, 85, 87, 91–92
Keynes, J. M., 9

Lane, Homer, 27
Langbaum, Robert, 3, 5–6, 10
Lawrence, D. H., 215
Lawrence, T. E., 59
Lazarus, H. P., 129, 195
Lehman, John, 1, 104, 117, 139–40, 141, 212
Living, 51, 55–79, 108, 109, 168, 202; and *Caught,* 121, 122; compared to *Party Going,* 79–80; gossip in, 67–70; as proletarian fiction, 65, 68; prose style of, 55–61
Lodge, David, 201
Loving, 123, 126, 142–66, 195, 196,

INDEX

Loving (cont.)
197, 198; compared to *Caught*, 142–43; and *Concluding*, 167, 168, 169, 170, 171, 172, 179, 181, 184, 186, 190, 193; and great house myth, 141–42, 144; Green on, 166; and *Nothing*, 209, 213; and Second World War, 102, 143–44; sex and marriage in, 160–64; style of, 152; theft and loss in, 155–59
"The Lull," 102

MacNeice, Louis, 35, 58; *Autumn Journal*, 35, 82; *The Strings Are False*, 35, 36, 40
Madge, Charles, 53
Marinetti, F. T., 81
Mass Observation, 102, 113
Melchiori, Giorgio, 57, 208
Milton, John, 144
"Mr. Jonas," 115
Montague, C. E., 29
Mood, 89–90, 156
Musil, Robert, 199

Newby, P. H., 200
Nothing, 123, 203–11, 213; conversational method of, 199–202

O'Connor, William Van, 212, 213
Odom, Keith, 20
Olney, James, 35
Orwell, George, 1, 6, 9, 10, 28, 39; on authoritarianism, 188; *Down and Out in Paris and London*, 52; on First World War, 28; "Inside the Whale," 35, 36, 40; "My Country Right or Left," 35, 37; *1984*, 167, 187, 192, 210; on proletarian fiction, 54; *The Road to Wigan Pier*, 35, 52, 54; *see also* Girard, René

Owen, Wilfred, 29, 30

Pack My Bag, 16, 35, 39, 43–49, 202; and *Caught*, 107; and Green's factorywork, 72; and *Living*, 64, 65; on memory, 112, 118; motives for writing, 52–53; and Second World War, 36, 102, 110
Party Going, 79, 83–99, 102, 156, 196, 197, 198; composition of, 80n; and *Loving*, 162, 165; symbolism in, 88–90; train metaphor in, 82–84, 87
Pound, Ezra, 5, 58
Powell, Anthony, 1, 5, 6, 28, 51, 117; *A Dance to the Music of Time*, 104; *A Question of Upbringing*, 10–11
Prévost, Jean, 7
Pritchett, V. S., 136, 210
Proletarian fiction, 53–54, 62; *see also* Day Lewis, Cecil; Orwell, George
Proust, Marcel, 70, 96, 130, 176, 179, 192, 215–16
Public schools, 7–10, 38; *see also* Auden, W. H.; Connolly, Cyril; Spender, Stephen

Quinton, Anthony, 164

Read, Herbert, 139, 198
Reed, John, 7
Rosenberg, Harold, 2, 36, 197, 198
Russell, John, 58, 93, 103, 153; on *Blindness*, 18, 23; on Green and Doughty, 59

Sansom, William, 117
Sarraute, Nathalie, 203
Sartre, Jean-Paul, 15–16, 22, 24, 32, 196–97
Sassoon, Siegfried, 31–32

INDEX

Second World War, 37, 99; literature of, 101, 104, 117, 139–40; *see also* Connolly, Cyril; Spender, Stephen
Sennett, Richard, 61, 211
Sillitoe, Alan, 212
Spender, Stephen, 5, 40, 43, 82, 212; *The Backward Son*, 35, 44; *The Burning Cactus*, 26; *The Destructive Element*, 3; "The Express," 80–81, 88; in fire service, 106–7, 117; and First World War, 29, 30, 32; on *Living*, 1, 51; "The New Realism," 41; on public school, 5, 8; on Second World War, 41; "September Journal," 35, 83; "The Soldier's Disease," 26; *World within World*, 106–7
Stein, Gertrude, 55–56, 61
Steiner, George, 45–46
Stokes, Edward: on *Caught*, 110, 112; on *Living*, 57, 63; on *Loving*, 142, 144, 150, 152, 158
Sypher, Wylie, 10

Taylor, Donald, 200
Taylor, Walt, 59
Thirkell, Angela, 141
Tindall, William York, 152
Treece, Henry, 140, 141
Trilling, Lionel, 61, 141, 142, 188, 196

Upward, Edward, 5, 11, 29, 55, 82; as communist, 167; "conversion narratives" of, 51–52; *Journey to the Border*, 3, 4, 35, 52, 53, 88; *The Railway Accident*, 29; "Sunday," 52, 53

Valéry, Paul, 45, 136
Vinaver, Michel, 145, 155, 156

Wain, John, 212
Warner, Rex: *The Aerodrome*, 104
Waugh, Evelyn, 1, 6, 51, 117, 212; *Brideshead Revisited*, 140, 141, 144, 145, 168; *Decline and Fall*, 10; on First World War, 28; *Love among the Ruins*, 168, 169, 188; *Put Out More Flags*, 104; *Unconditional Surrender*, 140, 141; *Vile Bodies*, 80
Weatherhead, A. Kingsley, 16, 88, 125, 196
Weaver, Robert, 213
Wells, H. G., 212
Welty, Eudora, 70, 89
West, Nathanael, 97–98
White, Roberta, 83, 89
Williams, Raymond, 43, 53, 214
Wilson, Colin, 212
Wilson, Edmund, 27
Wohl, Robert, 6–7
Wood, Neal, 53
Woolf, Virginia, 4, 104, 212, 213, 214

Yeats, W. B., 5, 6, 58, 88, 188, 215